GLOBAL MASCULINITIES – A NEW SERIES
FROM ZED BOOKS

Series Editor: Michael S. Kimmel

Men face common issues – the balance between work and family, fatherhood, defining masculinity in a globalizing economy, health and reproduction, sexuality, and violence. But they are experiencing these all over the world in very different contexts and are coming up with different priorities and strategies to address them. This new international series will provide a vehicle for understanding this diversity, and reflect the growing awareness that analysis of masculinity will be greatly impoverished if it remains dominated by a European/North American/Australian matrix. A number of regional and thematic cross-cultural volumes are planned.

The editor, Michael S. Kimmel, is a well-known educator specializing in gender issues. His most recent book, *Manhood in America: A Cultural History*, was published in 1996 to significant acclaim. His work has appeared in dozens of magazines, newspapers and scholarly journals, including the *New York Times Book Review*, the *Harvard Business Review*, *The Nation* and *Psychology Today*, where he was a contributing editor and columnist on male–female relationships. His teaching examines men's lives from a pro-feminist perspective. He is national spokesperson for the National Organization for Men Against Sexism (NOMAS) in the United States.

Already published

Robert Morrell (ed.), *Changing Masculinities in a Changing Society: Men and Gender in Southern Africa*

Bob Pease and Keith Pringle (eds), *A Man's World? Changing Men's Practices in a Globalized World*

Frances Cleaver (ed.), *Masculinities Matter! Men, Gender and Development*

In preparation

Lahoucine Ougzane (ed.), *Studies in Islamic Masculinities*

ABOUT THIS BOOK

Men appear to be missing from much gender and development policy. However, emerging critiques suggest the need to pay more attention to understanding men and masculinities, and to analysing the social relationships between men and women. This book considers the case for a focus on men in gender and development, including arguments based on equality and social justice, the specific gendered vulnerabilities of men, the emergence of a crisis of masculinity and the need to include men in development as partners for strategic change.

Incorporating men into gender and development requires us to reconsider some of the theories and concepts which underlie policies. This book addresses a variety of such concepts and debates including the links between modernization, development and gender, whether feminist analytical frameworks are appropriate for incorporating men and their concerns, how useful the concept of hegemonic masculinity is in understanding different cultural conceptions of manliness, and the need to find ways of combining concern with micro-level and private social relations with an analysis of macro-level trends and structures.

Chapters in this book draw on experience from a variety of geographical areas and different development projects and processes to analyse men and masculinities and to draw out implications for policy and practice. Subjects covered include working with children and in schools, impacting upon sexual health and intimate relations, and working with men in women's groups. Other chapters look at gender relations and masculinities in situations of violence and conflict, the role of the state and ideologies of nationalism in shaping masculinities, and the interlinking of gender relations with race and class. Overall they illustrate the complexity of economic and social relationships shaped by local, national and international processes, and the importance of incorporating an understanding of men and masculinities into gender and development.

MASCULINITIES MATTER!
Men, Gender and Development

EDITED BY FRANCES CLEAVER

Foreword by Michael Kimmel

Zed Books
LONDON · NEW YORK

David Philip
CAPE TOWN

Masculinities Matter! Men, Gender and Development was first published by Zed Books Ltd, 7 Cynthia Street, London N1 9JF, UK and Room 400, 175 Fifth Avenue, New York, NY 10010, USA in 2002.

www.zedbooks.demon.co.uk

Published in Southern Africa by David Philip (an imprint of New Africa Books Pty), 99 Garfield Road, Claremont 7700, South Africa

Editorial copyright © Frances Cleaver 2002
Individual chapters copyright © the individual authors 2002

Cover designed by Andrew Corbett
Set in Monotype Fournier by Ewan Smith, London
Printed and bound in Malaysia

Distributed in the USA exclusively by Palgrave, a division of St Martin's Press, LLC, 175 Fifth Avenue, New York, NY 10010

The rights of the editors and contributors to be identified as the authors of this work have been asserted by them in accordance with the Copyright, Designs and Patents Act, 1988.

A catalogue record for this book is available from the British Library

US CIP data is available from the Library of Congress

ISBN 1 84277 064 0 cased
ISBN 1 84277 065 9 limp
Southern Africa:
ISBN 0 86486 612 7 limp

Contents

About the Authors

Janet Bujra is a reader in sociology in the Department of Peace Studies, University of Bradford. She has also taught sociology and development in Dar es Salaam, Cairo and Wales. She has done thirty years of research on gender, class and development in East Africa, with her most recent work on gender and AIDS. She is the author of *Serving Class: Masculinity and the Feminisation of Domestic Service in Tanzania* (2000) and, with Carolyn Baylies, of *AIDS, Sexuality and Gender: Collective Strategies and Struggles in Tanzania and Zambia* (2000).

Frances Cleaver is a senior lecturer at the Bradford Centre for International Development. Her research, mainly in central and southern Africa, includes investigating the gendered nature of participation in local institutions and social capital. From 1998–2000 she coordinated an ESRC Seminar Series on Men, Masculinities and Gender Relations in Development.

Chris Dolan, MA, worked from 1992–96 in the Bushbuckridge area of South Africa, based at the University of the Witwatersrand Rural Facility, where he initiated the Refugee Research Programme in late 1994 as an action research programme examining the changing legal status of Mozambican refugees as a result of the UNHCR repatriation programme. From 1996–97 he coordinated a USAID-funded research project on the reintegration of ex-combatants in Mozambique for the University of Oxford Refugee Studies Programme, with particular emphasis on Manica and Zambezia provinces. He also taught 'Refugee Livelihoods' for the Refugee Studies Programme in 1997 and 1998. From 1997 to 2000 he carried out research for ACORD on the war in northern Uganda as part of a DFID-funded project on Complex Political Emergencies. He is currently writing up his work in Uganda at the London School of Economics.

Neil Doyle is a behaviour change communication consultant currently located in South East Asia. His areas of interest include the application of social marketing techniques to health interventions as well as the role of men in reproductive health.

David Forrest is a part-time tutor at the School of Oriental and African Studies and works part-time in the travel industry. He has conducted research in the Republic of Cuba on imaginings of maleness and is currently writing about the 'gendering of postmodernity' within contemporary academic and political discourse.

Helen Hambly Odame is a specialist in gender and institutions with twelve years of experience in international research and development programmes in Africa, North Africa and Latin America. She is a Research Officer with the International Service for National Agricultural Research (ISNAR), based in The Hague. Her work involves social analysis of agriculture research policy, organization and management. She has a PhD from the Faculty of Environmental Studies at York University, Toronto, Canada. She has also worked with the International Development Research Centre (IDRC) and the non-governmental sector in Canada and Kenya.

Niki Kandirikirira has been working in Africa since 1984 with VSO, the Red Cross and Crescent and ACORD. From 1984–86 she worked in Karamoja, Uganda on a weaving programme and then moved to the Red Sea Hills in Sudan, where she established a Red Crescent gender programme. After a short spell at IDS Sussex, where she studied Women, Men and Development, she returned to Uganda to coordinate a Change Agent programme. From 1992 to 2001 she headed ACORD Namibia, where she established the !Nara Participatory Development Training Institute and Total Child programme. Her work in Namibia focused on developing participatory methods and approaches to help communities and institutions to understand and address the legacies of apartheid. This work led her to develop social exclusion analysis as a tool for different actors to understand and share their perceptions of the interrelationships between racism, sexism, ethnocentrism and other forms of systemic social exclusion. Social exclusion analysis is now a core aspect of ACORD's programming strategy. In Uganda, Sudan and the Sahel this has had a significant impact on programming, which now recognizes that the construction of gender ethnic identities and their manipulation has significant impact on issues such as conflict, domestic and sexual violence, child neglect and abuse, HIV and slavery. In 2001 she returned to the UK as a consultant Methodology Adviser to ACORD and subsequently worked as the consultant Project Manager of the process to develop a pan-African implementation plan for their new strategy.

Marilyn Thomson is the gender adviser in the Policy Section of Save the Children (UK) and has a particular interest in developing work on harmful practices and gender-based violence. She lived in Latin America for many years, where she worked with a number of women's grass-roots organizations and carried out research for her PhD at the Institute of Education, University of London, on the subject of women's rights in domestic service. She is the author of *Women of El Salvador* (Zed Books, London and Institute for the Study of Human Issues, Philadelphia, 1986).

Prem Vijayan is a doctoral research fellow with the Institute of Social Studies, The Hague, and an associate professor at Hindu College, the University of Delhi. He has been working on nationalism, sexuality, masculinity and contemporary right-wing politics in India, separately and in their inter-relations, over several years.

Foreword

It has become almost axiomatic that gender is inextricably implicated in the development process. 'Human development, if not gendered, is endangered' was a central message of the 1995 Human Development Report.

The pioneering efforts of feminist scholars over the past three decades have established that development is an uneven process, not only within and between nations, but between the sexes. Women and men are differently situated culturally and economically, with unequal access to material and cultural resources, different and unequal relationships to the provision and consumption of material goods, and different and unequal access to the political process that guides economic development. Thus, we read, for example, of the global 'feminization of poverty', that women represent approximately 70 per cent of the 1.3 billion poor people in the world. Or we examine the impact of women's fertility and marital status on their access to economic and political power, the ways in which women's unpaid domestic labour remains statistically invisible in efforts to reduce or eradicate poverty.

It is still the case that when we think or read about gender, we think and read about women. In part, of course, this is as it should be. It was women scholars and policy-makers who first brought gender to our attention, through the hidden costs and statistical invisibility of women's participation. It was women who made gender visible as a category of analysis, as a variable that must be factored into any discussion of development. Today, although we understand that development is a gendered process, the impact of development on men remains relatively less well understood.

This 'invisibility' of masculinity in discussions of development has political dimensions. The processes that confer privilege on one group and not another group are often invisible to those upon whom that privilege is conferred. Thus, not having to think about race is one of the luxuries of being white, just as not having to think about gender is one of the 'patriarchal dividends' of gender inequality.

The invisibility of masculinity reproduces gender inequality, both materially and ideologically. Thus, any initiative to improve the condition of women must include efforts to involve men. In fact, we believe that any effort to further gender equality that does not include men is doomed to failure. As Anthony Sardien, representative of Gender Education and Training Network in South Africa, put it: 'Achieving committed male support in advancing women is increasingly urgent.' Of course, most initiatives towards gender equality must, and will continue to, focus on women's empowerment; but achieving the vision of gender equality is not possible without changes in men's lives as well as in women's.

Equally crucial for our understanding of the integration of masculinity into the study of development, however, is to recognize the ways in which globalization reconfigures and reshapes the arena in which these national and local masculinities are articulated, and transforms the shape of domestic and public patriarchies.

Globalization disrupts and reconfigures traditional, neocolonial, or other national, regional or local economic, political and cultural arrangements. In so doing, globalization transforms local articulations of both domestic and public patriarchy. Thus, for example, globalization includes the gradual proletarianization of local peasantries, as market criteria replace subsistence and survival.

Local small craft producers, small farmers and independent peasants traditionally stake their notions of masculinity in ownership of land and economic autonomy in their work; these are increasingly transferred upwards in the class hierarchy and outwards to transnational corporations. Proletarianization also leads to massive labour migrations – typically migrations of *male* workers – who leave their homes and populate migrant enclaves, squatter camps, labour camps.

Globalization thus presents another level at which hegemonic and local masculinities are constructed. Globalization was always a gendered process. As André Gunder Frank pointed out several decades ago in his studies of economic development, development and underdevelopment are not simply stages through which all countries pass, and there is no single continuum along which individual nations might be positioned. Rather, he argued, there is a relationship between development and underdevelopment; that, in fact, the development of some countries implies the specific and deliberate underdevelopment of others. The creation of the metropole was simultaneous and coordinated with the creation of the periphery.

As with economic development, so too with gender, with the historical constructions of the meanings of masculinity. As the hegemonic ideal was being created, it was created against a screen of 'others' whose masculinity was thus problematized and devalued. Hegemonic and subaltern emerged in mutual, but unequal, interaction in a gendered social and economic order. Thus, for example, colonial administrations often problematized the masculinity of the colonized. Thus, for example, in British India, Bengali men were perceived as weak and effeminate, though Pathans and Sikhs were perceived as hypermasculine – violent and uncontrolled. Similar distinctions were made in South Africa between Hottentots and Zulus, and in North America between Navaho or Algonquin on the one hand, Sioux, Apache and Cheyenne on the other. In many colonial situations, the colonized men were called 'boys' by the colonizers.

Today, although they appear to be gender-neutral, the institutional arrangements of global society are equally gendered. The marketplace, multinational corporations and transnational geopolitical institutions (World Court, United Nations, European Union) and their attendant ideological principles (economic rationality, liberal individualism) express a gendered logic. As sociologist R. W. Connell put it, the 'increasingly unregulated power of transnational corporations places strategic power in the hands of particular groups of men', while the language of globalization remains gender-neutral so that 'the "individual" of neoliberal theory has in general the attributes and interests of a male entrepreneur'.

As a result, the impact of global economic and political restructuring is different for women and men. At the national and global level, the world gender order privileges men in a variety of ways, such as unequal wages, unequal labour force participation, unequal structures of ownership and control of property, unequal control over one's body, as well as cultural and sexual privileges. What's more, in the economic South, for example, aid programes affect women and men differently, while in the metropole, the attack on the welfare state generally weakens the position of women, domestically and publicly. These effects, however, are less the result of bad policies or, even less, the result of bad (inept or evil) policy-makers, and more the result of the gendered logic of these institutions and processes themselves.

Happily, this volume thus begins to chart a new agenda in the literature on gender and development, focusing on the ways in which men are implicated in and affected by development processes and policies. It locates the question of men's identities, the ideology of masculinity, as a central issue in development.

To accomplish this, Frances Cleaver has deftly assembled a collection of essays that approach the question from various perspectives. Some are structural, examining the ways in which development policies operate at the level of the nation-state. Others are institutional, exploring, for example, the ways in which masculinities are implicated in the transformation of schools or when men enter women's groups. Still others examine the ways in which ideologies of masculinity, and even icons of masculinity, are transformed in the process.

Taken together, the essays in this volume urge both a conceptual transformation of development research to include both genders, and a practical transformation of development policies to incorporate masculinities, particularly in ways that can further enable women to achieve equality. Such efforts require that we engage men in the personal and political discussions about gender and development, and particularly to engage men as women's allies in their struggle for equality.

It is a project of great urgency, and with great significance for both women and men. The Human Development Report of 1995 concluded: 'One of the defining moments of the 20th century has been the relentless struggle for gender equality ... When this struggle finally succeeds – as it must – it will mark a great milestone in human progress. And along the way it will change most of today's premises for social, economic and political life.'

Let us hope that the success of that struggle will be one of the defining moments of the twenty-first century, because gender equality will enable both women *and* men to live lives of greater freedom and integrity.

Michael Kimmel
Series editor

CHAPTER I

Men and Masculinities: New Directions in Gender and Development

FRANCES CLEAVER

§ Men appear to be missing from much gender and development policy. The change of terminology from Women in Development (WID) to Gender and Development (GAD) represented a shift towards recognizing the need to analyse social relationships between men and women and to be more aware of factors such as class, age and personal agency in these. Despite this shift in emphasis, in much development policy there remains little recognition of the need to analyse and understand the lives of men as well as women.

With a few notable exceptions, men are rarely explicitly mentioned in gender policy documents. Where men are considered they are generally seen as obstacles to women's development. There is a perceived need for men to change in order to benefit women, for men to take on a greater burden of domestic work, to give up some of their control over household finances and decision-making, to cede their places on committees and public bodies to women. The assumption that a focus on men is primarily justified in terms of securing benefits to women is linked to simplified ideas about power and gender relations; women can only become empowered by men giving up power. Ideas about the mechanisms of such 'equalizing', of the incentives that will prompt men to participate in women-focused projects and the impact upon them and upon gender relations are little considered.

While a growing body of literature theorizing men and masculinities exists, encompassing the fields of gender, men's studies, social theory and social policy, much of it focuses on the experience of men in northern industrialized countries. With some notable exceptions, the studies of men in the South are predominantly exotically ethnographic or historical accounts. There is a dearth of literature illuminating how concepts of gender relations that include a focus on men and masculinities might help us in understanding the lives and livelihoods of contemporary men and women in developing countries.

This chapter reviews the case for explicitly considering men in gender analysis and planning and explores some of the key issues involved in taking this approach. In doing so, it touches briefly on some of the conceptual debates and conundrums in the masculinities field, where these relate specifically to development policy concerns.

THE CASE FOR INCLUDING MEN

A number of (sometimes contradictory) arguments have been made for the need to pay specific attention to men and masculinities in development. These are derived from ongoing GAD debates, from field research and practice and from the masculinities literature.

Gender equality and social justice Approaches to gender that argue for gender equality and social justice avoid seeing gender concerns as simply instrumental in securing the more effective delivery of development. Rather, they recognize that men as well as women may be disadvantaged by social and economic structures and that all have the right to a life free from poverty and oppression. For example, Oxfam's policy documents stress the overall objective of gender policies being to promote human dignity through overcoming pressures on both men and women (Oxfam 1993; 1998), and Sida's concern for gender mainstreaming explicitly has equality as its ultimate objective (Sida 1997a; 1997b). Such an approach implies that achieving equality can benefit all and that equalizing power relations does not necessarily involve winners and losers. Batliwala (1994) suggests that through empowerment processes both men and women can be liberated from the confines of stereotyping, resulting in beneficial outcomes for both genders.

Gendered vulnerabilities Changing gendered divisions of labour, social practices and concepts of masculinity can disadvantage as well as benefit men. While recognizing that women in general may face greater social and economic disadvantages than most men, evidence from several studies suggests that men are not always the 'winners' and that ignoring their situation risks overlooking gender-specific inequities and vulnerabilities (Jackson 1999). Examples of gendered vulnerabilities which disadvantage men are particularly notable in the area of health: in many societies young men are at greatest risk of suicide due to mental health problems; in sub-Saharan Africa the gendered positions of boys and girls may result in boys' greater risk of schistosomiasis (Michelson 1993); in South Asia gender divisions of labour mean that young men may suffer greater exposure to dangerous pesticides than women (Jackson 1998), while notions linking masculinity to virility may render men more at risk from HIV infection (Unicef 1997). Indeed, some argue that in general men may suffer more ill-health than women; Barker (1997) cites studies that show that in Latin America and the Caribbean the health burden for men is 26 per cent higher than it is for women.

Gendered social and labour practices may also generate vulnerabilities among men as illustrated in Sweetman's (1998) study of the impact of labour migrancy in Lesotho. Boys' futures as labour migrants shape adults' decisions to prioritize girls' education, resulting in higher female school attendance and literacy rates. When opportunities for migrant labour fail, young men are excluded by their lack of education from other opportunities for paid work.

The crisis of masculinity   Increasing evidence suggests that changes in the economy, in social structures and in household composition are resulting in 'crises of masculinity' in many parts of the world. Examples include: the low attainment of boys in education; economic changes resulting in the loss of men's assured role as breadwinner and provider to the family; women's increased incorporation into the labour force; the increase in proportions of female-headed households; and the absence of male role models for boys in families. Disaffected (male) 'youth' is often equated with anti-social behaviour and violence.

These issues are explored in several studies stressing the 'demasculinizing' effects of poverty and economic change (Thomson, this volume; Barker 2000). Strongly emphasized in several studies is the belief that 'being a man' involves taking on the role of provider to the family. When economic changes (for example, through structural adjustment) occur which make this difficult, men's fundamental identity is called into question. The crisis, then, is partly derived from the lack of alternative, meaningful roles for men, sometimes resulting in dysfunctional and anti-social behaviour (Bujra, this volume).

Negotiated gender roles and relations There is evidence for the highly contested nature of gender identities and the inter-relationships between private negotiations and public roles (White 1999). My research from Zimbabwe, for example, shows that while both men and women are aware of and may publicly assert 'traditional' gender roles, in private these roles may be negotiated. In various circumstances women and girls may perform 'male' tasks of clearing and fencing fields, herding and caring for cattle while men and boys may become involved in 'female' tasks such as weeding, collecting water and firewood (Cleaver 2000). The implications in respect of claims to control over the output of labour are far-reaching.

Recognition of the relational nature of gender focuses attention on the limitations of women-only projects. Women may have to negotiate their participation in such projects, to overcome or subvert men's resistance (Dikito-Wachtmeister 2000) Additionally, research suggests that men may play significant roles in women-only projects, in women's groups and in institutions designed to further the involvement of women (Hambly Odame, this volume) and that the scope and nature of men's activities should be better understood.

Strategic gender partnerships There is a strong argument that empowerment, social justice and progressive gender change can best be achieved through strategic partnerships, including gender partnerships. Men are needed to ensure that they do not become obstacles to development, because they can provide access to valuable resources and because, through solidarity and cooperation, more can be achieved for both men and women. Studies from Latin America which detail improvements in women's positions specify the strategic alliances between men and women that helped to secure such gains (Deere and Leon 1998; Macaulay 1998). Such arguments arise in a number of different ways.

Men are needed as partners to overcome the excessive labour burden of women (Sweetman 1998). While development efforts emphasize the creation of more employment and income-generation opportunities for women and their increased involvement in public life, they often do little to relieve them of domestic tasks. For example, an emphasis on women as the 'natural' managers of water reinforces their domestic responsibility in this area, makes demands on their time in terms of water management and means that it is women who are most likely to pay if water charges are introduced.

Men are needed as partners in responsibility for the family and the raising of children (Engle 1997; SCF 1999b; Unicef 1997). This includes their role in joint decision-making about family planning, child health and the education of children. Several studies emphasize the confining nature of men's traditional roles and their expressed desire to break free of these and forge more equitable partnerships (Montoya 2000).

Men are needed as partners in political movements and in development organizations to ensure that gender issues are not marginalized and underfunded. Such mainstreaming is currently fashionably advocated but recent studies show that specialist gender units and concerns in development organizations commonly remain isolated and that the perception persists that gender is about 'women's issues' (Cleaver and Kessler 1998; Farnesveden and Rondquist 1999; Roche 2000).

MASCULINITIES AND GENDER: RECURRING THEMES

In the current literature available on men and masculinities in gender and development, a number of themes occur repeatedly. Many of these relate to the difficulties of translating complex approaches to gender into practice. Others are concerned with specifically sectoral and operational issues (such as the role of men in family planning/reproductive health). Additionally, several of the issues raised relate to fundamental questions and concepts debated in the masculinities literature. The following sections outline some of the most commonly occurring themes.

Dilution of feminist gains? There is considerable anxiety among many GAD analysts that a focus on men and masculinities will distract attention from women's inequalities. Some fear that the feminist-inspired gains of the last two decades will be lost (White 2000) and that there is a risk that men will 'take over', that patterns of gender inequalities will be maintained. This fear is balanced against the perceived need to involve men in the interests of mainstreaming; to rescue gender from a 'women's issues' ghetto.

Related to the above are questions about whether feminist approaches to GAD (and the associated frameworks) are the most appropriate lens through which to view men and masculinities. The ways in which gender frameworks (such as Moser's framework) have been applied generally focus on women to the exclusion of men and much work on gender and development has been prompted by feminist political commitment (Pearson 2000b). There is debate about whether GAD frameworks can be used in a way which does not necessarily privilege women over men, or whether a specific men and development (MAD!) approach is required.

Sex or gender? The subject of masculinities reflects the difficulty of being very precise in defining just what constitutes 'gender relations', as distinct from all other forms of social interaction. Connell sees gender identity as activities, traits and values culturally and historically associated with men and women, hence 'Masculinities are configurations of practice within gender relations, a structure that includes large-scale institutions and economic relations as well as face to face relationships and sexuality' (Connell 2000: 29).

How useful is it to dichotomize men's and women's roles? One problem with conceptualizing gender is that such categorization, even if related to socially constructed roles, can easily swing into a biological essentialism positing fundamental differences between men and women (MacInnes 1998). Cornwall (2000) suggests that such an approach, which opposes 'women' and 'men' as static categories, actually creates and sustains differences, a problem, as we shall see later, for achieving gender and development goals.

Considerable debate occurs around definitions of 'gender', the differences between sex and gender as classificatory categories that are commonly elided (MacInnes 1998; el Bushra 2000). El Bushra queries the straitjacket of thinking imposed by assumptions about the importance of biological differences between men and women. She also questions the utility of the distinction used in gender and development to differentiate sex from gender; the assumption that sex is biological and gender psychological and cultural, and the normative cast of gender ideology. She asks how we might move towards more complex and nuanced understandings of social relationships and power (including gender relationships). El Bushra's points may lead us to reconsider why gender identities are privileged in development, as opposed to other forms of social identity and difference such as class or ethnicity. Several studies document the complex interplay between such identities (Morrell 2001; Kandirikirira and Forrest, this volume).

Indeed, MacInnes suggests that there is no such thing as 'gender' or 'masculinity', except as an ideology people use to make sense of some of the contradictions of modernity, in particular those caused by the remnants of a previously patriarchal order in nominally egalitarian societies. He sees capitalism as instrumental in causing the collapse of patriarchy and in overturning gender roles based on the idea of fundamental differences between men and women (MacInnes 1998).

Hegemonic masculinities   Further questioning of dichotomous thinking arises when trying to understand power relations and hierarchies based on gender identities, both between men and women and between men and other men. Stereotyping men as the oppressors and women as the oppressed is considered unhelpful by many writers in the search to understand the differences between men or the vulnerabilities that men experience in particular. The concept of hegemonic masculinity is an attempt to deal with relational issues in masculinity. Connell suggests that not all men benefit equally from the institutions of patriarchy and that some forms of masculinity are culturally elevated above others in certain times and places. The idea of hegemonic and subordinate or marginal masculinities is used to reflect the power dimensions of gender relations (Connell 1987).

Recently, writers have pointed to the need to understand different cultural concepts of manliness and to be aware of the variety and complexity of ways of 'being a man', also the dynamic creation of masculinity through gendered practices (Connell 2000). Additionally, there is a need to consider class, race and age when understanding men's and women's lives, and the ways in which they relate to each other (Cornwall 1997; White 1999). How far are dominant masculinities and gender relations in general bound up with historical relations of economic and political domination, particularly with the workings of imperialism and capitalism?

Gender analysis and development practice   Several writers note the difficulty gender analysis poses to development practice when it strays into the 'private' realm. Indeed, it is claimed that development agencies prefer to tackle the less contentious and public dimensions of gender (promoting women's involvement and so on) rather than becoming embroiled in the personal politics of intimate relationships. Investigating household allocations of resources, sexual behaviour and understandings of health all involve personal behavioural attitudes and actions. Research in this area may be difficult, policy more so.

Finally, there is a set of questions about whose voices and whose experiences are reflected in a focus on men and masculinities. The question of whether women can promote this approach mirrors previous questions along the lines of 'Can men be feminists?' Pearson suggests that it is a cause for concern that few 'mainstream' male development policy-makers seem interested in the subject, and that there is a disjuncture between the interests of southern men in challenging dominant violent masculinities and 'critical men's studies in the north', which largely focus on the changing, contradictory and fragile nature of contemporary masculinities (Pearson 2000b).

Empowerment There is general recognition of the importance of the wider social and economic structures of society and the ways in which these can oppress both men and women. This raises questions of the limitations of development projects and their ability to promote empowerment. Research on micro-credit projects for women offers contradictory evidence. Some cite the empowering effects of credit on some women (more control over household finances), the disempowering effects (men threatened by such changes resort to domestic violence), the potential of gendered partnerships achieved through household negotiation (men and women agreeing on the use of credit to the benefit of the household) and the severe limitations of such interventions (the money gained is small in quantity and does little to address structural poverty) (Osmani 1998; Goetz and Sen Gupta 1996; Schuler et al. 1998).

An example of women's empowerment often quoted is that of the women's anti-liquor campaigns in India in which direct action ensures that poor men are prevented from spending their money on alcohol. But studies of poor working men in India give us an insight into why they drink so much; the daily remorseless effort of heavy labouring jobs for low wages makes alcohol a practical escape from grim reality (Jackson 1999). This kind of example leads some analysts to question whether promoting women's empowerment at the expense of men is beneficial to all in the long term.

Personal, sexual and family issues This is perhaps the area in which the most relevant practical experience is available through projects that explicitly target men as a way of reducing domestic violence, promoting sexual and reproductive health and improving family welfare (Unicef 1997; Maxwell 1997). The importance of an awareness of changing needs and priorities over life courses is strongly emphasized here. As with much development activity there is a strong concentration on the lives of young people and adults in the reproductively and economically active age group. Older men and their concerns are notably absent from both policy and academic literature (Varley and Blasco 2000). Strong links are emphasized in the literature between 'masculinity', employment, sexual behaviour and family issues. For example, research from Latin America suggests that men's idea of what it is to 'be a man' is to be both heterosexually active and a financial provider to the family (Barker 2000; Fuller 2000). In many circumstances it is easier to achieve the former than the latter.

Projects and research show the common perception of the importance of men's roles in relation to employment and the ability to provide for families. This has become an area of crisis as the structural reform of economies results in the widespread loss of formal-sector jobs. The inability to fulfil such a role may lead to considerable insecurity and frustration, often translated into violence. Where men do fulfil such roles in conditions of extreme economic pressure, the time, effort and responsibility involved may render them vulnerable to poor health.

Economic integration is strongly linked in the literature with the ability to be a good father. Engle (1997) suggests that there are three dimensions of fatherhood: biological, economic and social. Some have illustrated a correlation between fathers' incomes and fathers living with the family and getting involved with children. Poverty is seen as a serious obstacle to being a good father; for example, poor men express anxiety about the circumstances that push them to send young children to work (Jackson 1999). Expectations of roles as husbands and fathers shape boys' developing perceptions of 'what it is to be a man', and the obligations are often experienced as heavy responsibilities (White 1999).

Sex and sexuality play a large part in discussions of men and masculinity. Greig (in White 1999) has pointed out that masculinity is deeply implicated in the harm men experience in their own lives and cause in the lives of others. This observation is particularly relevant in the area of HIV transmission. Much debate speculates about how far sexuality and relationships are the appropriate focus of development issues, and how to involve men in discussing these. Several projects and studies emphasize that it is far easier to get men involved in reflecting upon such issues when the focus is child health and well-being rather than sex and sexuality per se. Research by Doyle in Vietnam and Bujra in Tanzania

---

Box 1.1 Men as Providers: Changing Identities

As the traditional roles of men as providers in families are threatened by economic and social change, there is scope for developing new models of manliness. However, this is a difficult and slow process.

Recent studies by Save the Children UK and Oxfam UK have highlighted the link between employment opportunities for men, and their behaviour in families and relationships. Central to both studies is the decline in full-time paid employment resulting from changes in the global economy. This has given rise to uncertainty about men's roles and identities: where do men fit in what seems to be a woman's world, when they have no assured identity as the breadwinners?

Concerns emerging from Oxfam's work with disadvantaged men in three communities in Britain showed that men and women had very different attitudes towards participation in projects intended to address their problems:

- In relation to parenting, boys anticipate their main role as providers, whereas girls seem to hold a more holistic and socialized view of parental responsibility.
- Young men and young women have very different perspectives about what are everyday problems: the territorial barriers imposed by gangs, for example, are very real for boys, but not a problem for girls.
- Advertisements for 'men's projects' were counterproductive. What works for men is highlighting the recreational and technical activities that projects will involve.
- Younger men will take training if it is offered, whereas unemployed older men have their self-image in paid employment.

(both in this volume) suggests that many development initiatives to involve men in reproductive and sexual health decision-making are limited by their appeal to self-interest rather than promoting mutuality between the sexes.

Addressing male violence within families is a subject of great concern in current development activities. Studies cite widespread examples of

---

This results in older men being less likely to take up training opportunities.

- Recruiting male project workers with 'street cred' is hard as such jobs are perceived as 'women's work' and carrying a low status due to their 'care' nature.

SCF's research on perceptions by British children of changing gender roles showed that:

- Boys and girls interviewed had a wide range of views of gender roles but few reflected traditional images of men and women.
- Both boys and girls identified anatomy as the main difference between men and women, but then focused on behavioural differences.
- Children saw many jobs and roles as equally appropriate for men and women.
- When asked what the men they knew liked, most answered 'sports', 'videos', 'computer games' and 'cars'. Children believe that some men try to avoid housework, sometimes by feigning illness.
- Children's comments suggest that their fathers have more traditional roles than their mothers and that children's perceptions of roles outside the family seemed more progressive than those within the home.
- Adults' discomfort when discussing gender issues inhibits children's exploration of such issues.

The study concludes that both girls and boys need the opportunity to discuss and reflect on gender at an early age and, in particular, to see men's roles more broadly.

Sources: Smith (2000); Thomson (2000).

men being socialized through particular constructions of masculinity into violence (Kandirikirira, this volume). Violence has been linked to economic stress, low self-esteem and traditional ideas about gender roles. Emphasis is placed on the need to see boys and men as victims as well as perpetrators of violence and to involve men in discussions that deconstruct traditional perceptions of masculinity (Thomson, this volume; SCF 1999a). In overcoming 'machismo' cultures, stress is placed on the need to provide boys and young men with alternative role models, to build on 'positive deviancy' by identifying 'pathways to gender equitable manhood' and to focus on more equitable practices within the household (see Box 1.2; Poudyal 2000; Almeras 2000).

Gender and working lives The issue of the division of labour is central to gender analysis and planning in development. The concept of the excessive labour burden of women – their 'triple role' in productive, reproductive and community work – has become a mainstay of GAD approaches and has lead to oversimplified statements in policy docu-

---

Box 1.2 Alternative Models of Manliness

A study by Barker of adolescent males in a low-income settlement in Rio de Janeiro, Brazil, found a prevailing culture of 'machismo' in which heterosexual masculinity is commonly characterized by a callous attitude towards women, lack of male involvement in child-rearing and reproductive health, and frequent resort to violence. Despite this dominant form of masculinity, some men adopt different forms of behaviour:

- They are respectful in their relationships with young women.
- They participate actively in child-rearing (if they have children).
- They assume responsibility for reproductive health issues.
- They seek to stay out of violence and delinquency.

The most salient reasons for some men adopting these more gender-equitable roles were:

- They had an important relationship, or multiple relationships,

ments that 'women do all the work'. Several studies raise questions about such statements (see Box 3.1).

Firstly, the dominance of time studies showing women's greater burden of work has been questioned. While most acknowledge the usefulness of such studies in making visible domestic work, their over-simplified application has led to the assertion that men are lazy and do little work (Whitehead 1999). Time studies are shown to be problematic in their methodology and incomplete in their recording of male domestic labour and other activities, such as visiting relatives and attending social events. However, Harrison suggests that the impact of men's social reproduction work may be gendered in that it allows men to engage in particular discourses of development. While these activities may generate livelihood benefits, these cannot be assumed to be evenly felt by all members of the household (Harrison 1999).

Time studies have also been criticized for their lack of attention to other dimensions of work such as effort and intensity. Jackson suggests that when these dimensions are taken into account, gender inequities in

---

with someone who demonstrated alternative ways of being a man, or alternative gender roles.

- They belonged to an alternative peer group that reinforced a progressive version of masculinity.
- They had reflected about and found outlets to express fear related to the prevailing, gang-involved model of masculinity.

Other themes that emerged from Barker's pilot research were:

- The general lack of models of what respectful and caring male and female relationships look like.
- The lack of spaces to 'process' and deal with personal issues in a climate of trust.
- The lack of role models for what involved fatherhood looks like.
- The omnipresent pressure of finding and maintaining employment, with no social spaces where men are 'allowed' to express the stress they experience related to achieving the role of the provider.

Source: Barker (2000).

work burdens may not be so marked (Jackson 1999). Evidence for this varies considerably; place, culture, class and age are all significant variables but examples from India show that male labourers and landless workers in their reproductive years are the most nutritionally disadvantaged and vulnerable to early death (Kynch in Jackson 1999).

A common question raised is, How do gendered divisions of labour come about? Is there anything inherently 'male' about men's work, or

---

Box 1.3 Questioning Gendered Work Burdens

Labour-related vulnerabilities and risks to men Jackson suggests that it is not only women who face threats to their well-being through heavy work burdens, but that high work intensity also has adverse consequences for men. The use of time as a measurement of effort may overlook work effort intensity, which should be included in order to give a fuller understanding of the gendered experience of work and equity in labour sharing. This is because the body is the primary instrument of labour among the poor. Jackson illustrates this point by drawing mainly on research carried out in India. She found:

- Ideas of 'manliness' place the responsibility for household income on men in spite of the female contribution in poorer households.
- Strength is a widely valued male attribute among the Indian lower social group, resulting in stronger men finding work more easily and being paid higher wages.
- Manual labour is very hard; consequently, in spite of it being exalted, men seek to avoid it because of the likelihood of failure and having to live up to cultural ideals.
- Men who do not conform to cultural ideals of what 'men's work' is, are often mocked, for instance if a man cooks.
- Male adult labourers and landless workers of reproductive age are shown to be the most nutritionally challenged and vulnerable to excess mortality.

Through paying analytical attention to men's work and masculinities a better understanding of the gendered divisions of labour can be achieved.

essentially 'female' about women's work (MacInnes 1998)? The fluidity of roles and the scope for shifting these (Cleaver 2000; Unicef 1997; Engle 1997) suggest that gendered divisions of labour are far from 'natural'. There is a danger that development projects may emphasize 'natural' gendered roles (women as the natural health educators within the family, the primary managers of water and so on) and thereby reinforce gendered divisions of labour.

Time-allocation studies and the 'lazy man' Time-allocation studies can be a valuable tool in estimating unpaid work and capturing the relative work burdens of each sex. They have been instrumental in making visible women's work but it should be noted that accurate time-use data about both men and women are scarce. Critiquing research on work and labour in sub-Saharan Africa, Whitehead suggests that the use of time-allocation studies has led to distorted accounts of labour divisions between men and women. Commentators agree that many African women have heavy workloads, but in some discourses this is juxtaposed to apparently light or negligible work burdens for men. Implicitly or explicitly this construction harks back to an earlier colonial discourse of the 'lazy African'.

Time-allocation studies often fail to highlight the socioeconomic context. Men may be occupied in networking, gathering information and attempting to find work and business opportunities, all essential activities for income generation in areas where opportunities are scarce. These activities, in time-use surveys, may be classified under 'resting'.

Time-allocation studies may also fail to link men's and women's agricultural activities with other income-generating activities. While domestic production depends heavily on female labour, men tend to spend more time on off-farm activities (either casual wage work or 'business activities'). A narrow focus on labour use in farming can therefore miss on- and off-farm linkages that can ensure agricultural success. This renders the male contribution to farming and the wider economy invisible.

Sources: Jackson (1999); Whitehead (1999).

An additional question relates to the association between masculinity and hard physical labour. For example, Morrell illustrates how the celebration of physical strength in work by black miners in South Africa played a key part in asserting forms of masculinity in conditions of oppression and servitude, such masculinities being intricately linked with ethnic hierarchies (Morrell 2001).

Other questions raised about gender and work include: What constitutes equitable work-sharing in households over life courses (rather than over single working days)? What happens to men when their working lives are over? And how should 'non-work' activities involving voluntary work, collective action, building social relationships and the creation of social capital be valued?

Policy and research suggest some confusion over whether paid work is empowering or oppressing for men and women. Hard physical labour, increased time burdens, physical risks, low wages and insecurity are balanced in studies against a personal sense of worth and autonomy, increased family well-being and more gender-equitable practices. Globalization processes may have negative impacts on both poor men and poor women in terms of employment. We need to ask what kind of work is beneficial and empowering to both women and men at particular points in their life courses.

The state, masculinities and violence The role of state action in creating masculinities, or creating the conditions for changing gender relations, is emphasized in a number of studies. Particularly dominant, however, is the role for the state in generating violence and conflict, and in creating conditions which lead to distorted and anti-social expressions of masculinity. Two studies explicitly link individual behaviour to the role of the state in shaping gendered relations. Both Dolan's and Kandirikirira's chapters in this volume link state action (or inaction) to the development of damaging forms of masculinity, expressed in violence. Morrell (2001), however, draws on the South African experience to suggest how the state may be a positive agent for change.

Four overlapping strands of current debate focus attention on men, masculinities, conflict and violence (Jacobson 2000). These include:

- A concern in development with the scale and implications of men's domestic and sexual violence against women.

- A long-standing debate in feminist theory about the causality of men's violence.

- The post-Cold War global context in which development agencies may operate in situations of armed conflict where the majority of protagonists are men and where civilian populations are the principal targets of violence.

- The re-emergence of biologically-based explanations for gendered social behaviour, in particular of evolutionary perspectives which allow male aggression to be categorized, at least in part, as a 'natural' phenomenon.

Economic instability, cultural discourses, the socialization of boys and experiences of fear and weakness are seen as formative in both domestic and societal violence. Indeed, recent commentators assert the need to define conflict and violence as part of 'normal' social relations rather than a breakdown of them and to consider ways of changing or subverting the ubiquitous 'warrior discourse' through which ways of being a man are commonly defined (Large 1997; Vijayan, this volume).

Several analysts also question the common separation of conflict at societal level from domestic violence. Pankhurst and Pearce (1998) see the need to engender the study of conflict that, they claim, is usually dominated by male accounts and male experiences. They also see the need to link analyses of different levels of conflict, as post-conflict situations may involve 'gendered deals' which differentially benefit men and women. They suggest that domestic violence often increases in post-war situations and women may face the constant threat of violence from ex-combatant young men. However, several studies also show young men to be at the greatest risk of death or injury through violence, usually perpetuated by other men.

The common assumption that men are the universal aggressors in armed conflict and women the universal victims and peace-makers is a gross oversimplification that both reinforces ideas about violence being 'natural' to men and fails to explain women's roles in conflicts (Large 1997). Evolutionary and essentialist ideas about men and violence are questioned in a number of studies. In terms of war and conflict, Pankhurst and Pearce (1998) suggest that the literature shows that women are not more intrinsically peaceful than men and indeed may play key roles in supporting men in conflict.

Indeed, explanations of conflict are often oversimplified, separating out political from sociocultural factors and macro- from micro-explanations. However, the particular ways in which masculinities are shaped may critically be influenced by the role of the state and of political processes and movements such as nationalism. Several commentators trace the historical development of dominant masculinities and the role of colonial and developmental states in shaping gendered discourses. For example, in this volume, Vijayan attributes a certain form of dominant masculinity in India to a combination of Hindu nationalism and modernization, Dolan links the expression of violence by men to their fear-engendering experiences of war and state (in)action, and Kandirikirira traces distorted manifestations of masculinity and violent gender relations to the continued effects of apartheid state policies.

The challenges facing development interventions include the need to link macro-level societal and economic processes to the shaping of individual behaviour, particularly in trying to change manifestations of masculinity based on the exercise of violence. Of great interest here is the identification of personal and social factors which influence men to adopt non-violent practices and behaviours.

Gender and development organizations It has been suggested that in order to place gender concerns in the mainstream, it is necessary to involve men in development agencies more closely with the shaping of gender-related policy and practice. Indeed, some development agencies stress the need to foster an organizational culture that promotes equitable participation and distribution of power between men and women in the organization (SCF 1999a). However, this is seen to be problematic as there is a fear that men's greater involvement and a focus on men and masculinity could result in the diversion of funds and attention away from women-specific programmes (Oxfam 1993). It has also been suggested that a focus on women-only projects allows agencies to avoid becoming involved in the complicated and troublesome issue of interventions in the relationships between men and women, and in difficult issues of personal and sexual identity.

The problem of the 'patriarchal culture' of development organizations (Chant and Guttmann 2000) may result in the marginalizing of gender concerns as peripheral 'women's issues'. Oppositional constructions of gender interests may also result in a lack of men's willingness to show interest in gender issues in organizations, for fear of being cast as the oppressors. One of Oxfam's male managers interested in implementing gender policies accounts for his success as follows: 'Being a male manager may have been important too because it meant that my male colleagues were able to voice their fears without being caught out by the gender "police"' (Oxfam 1998: 5). Other men also comment on some of the issues and obstacles they face if they want to work on gender equality, ranging from the lack of family-friendly policies to opposition from both men and women (Roche 2000; Tadele 2000).

Sweetman (2000) suggests the need to understand more about the personal and professional opportunities and constraints facing both men and women working on gender issues; to understand more about identity issues; and to learn from pioneers of change of both sexes, and from parallel social movements including anti-race work.

Some development organizations do now explicitly consider men as part of their gender mainstreaming strategies (Sida 1997a). However, there may be difficulties in fully institutionalizing such policies. A study of attitudes of men in Sida suggests that many men still perceive 'gender' as low-status work, that it is considered in the organization as being primarily about women, that women themselves are sometimes hostile to men and male involvement (Farnesveden and Ronquist 2000). However, this study also shows generational differences in the attitudes of older and younger men and a willingness to change if the incentives are right.

POLICY IMPLICATIONS AND NEW DIRECTIONS

The interest in men and masculinities is a fairly new one in gender and development, and ideas about policy implications are still being formulated and debated. However, lessons drawn from a number of studies and projects suggest the need for the following directions.

Changing role models Many commentators emphasize the value of promoting self-awareness and critical reflection about gender identities both within development agencies and in beneficiary communities. Experience emphasizes the importance of improved communication, with counselling, support groups and skills development and esteem-building all instrumental in overcoming dominant male stereotypes and cultures of violence.

Self-reflection and self-awareness are intended to lead to the construction of alternative concepts of masculinity. There is a perception that current models are problematic and that boys and young men in particular need alternative role models of 'how to be a man'. Several studies show the importance of such 'alternative' role models to boys in fostering equal relationships between boys and girls and a gender-equitable balance of responsibilities within households. For example, Poudyal (2000) suggests that films, when used in association with participatory workshops, can open up space for children to question gendered roles and responsibilities. The SCF experience suggests that films can be used as a catalyst for men and boys to question patriarchal structures and to nurture respect for women and girls. Kandirikirira (this volume) claims similar potential for theatre and workshops which can open up space for critical self-reflection and dialogue. Gordon (1998) suggests the key role that schools and the education system can play in either reinforcing or challenging patriarchal relations and in manipulating gender identities.

Experience of working with men in the North and in the South leads to various suggestions about the easiest way to engage men in reconsidering gender relations. Southern studies tend to consider that it is far easier to engage men through a pragmatic focus on child survival and family welfare issues, than directly through considerations of gender identity, sexuality and violence. In particular, a focus on helping men to retain their male identities and self-esteem when economic and social roles are shifting and changing seems critical. Experience from the North suggests that a focus on recreational and technical activities is far more likely to engage men and create the opportunity for reconsidering gender roles.

The employment of men as gender-awareness trainers and facilitators (particularly young men with 'street credibility') is often seen as beneficial in promoting positive role models and overcoming stereotypes. However, recruiting men to such work is considered problematic.

New socialization processes are likely to make an impact over fairly long periods and it is important to incorporate changing roles and needs over life courses into this approach.

Advocacy, lobbying, partnerships Initiatives promoting equitable gender relations might involve using men's existing networks, influencing mass media images and using the education system to challenge cultural concepts of masculinity among boys and girls. NGOs, religious organizations and youth organizations are potential partners in furthering this process. Several of the promising projects referred to in this paper emphasize the value of the active participation of men and women, boys and girls in initiatives to overcome gender inequalities. However, there is also a perceived need to institutionalize change more broadly, and to challenge discriminatory power structures in state agencies and development organizations.

Policy reform to promote men's involvement and gender equality in the family and society might include improved labour laws (length of work day, parental leave), maintenance laws, and laws securing equal rights of boys and girls to such things as education and property (Unicef 1997). The state's role in developing family-friendly policies and employment practices that enable men to be both providers and carers are particularly strongly emphasized in studies about men in the North (see Sweetman 2000). State action to end discrimination (for example, based on a person's sexuality) could create an environment for the acceptance of more diverse ways of being a man. Some see the role of activists, development organizations and NGOs as being to hold weak or corrupt states to account in order to promote the good governance necessary to allow non-violent manifestations of masculinity to flourish and more equitable gender relations to develop (Dolan, this volume).

The need for lobbying and activism within development organizations and the increased involvement of men in gender issues are also commonly seen as critical in challenging gendered power structures and the institutional cultures which support these.

Measures of success   There is little literature on how practically to measure the success of programmes with a focus on men, partly because many such programmes are in their infancy. There is a generally perceived need to find ways of measuring changing gendered practices within relationships and in the family, although these are difficult to investigate.

Barker (2000) has suggested the need to identify and track 'pathways' to gender-equitable manhood made up of 'a constellation of development characteristics and resources that show some continuity from early childhood through adolescence'.

Various Unicef programmes have measured changes in how men spend money (more on household, less on themselves), the enrolment of girls in school, women's increased participation in public life, the decrease in domestic violence, and the increase in male participation in health initiatives (Unicef 1997).

SCF (1999a) suggest a number of ways of tracking gender policy and change that are significant to a consideration of men and masculinities, including: the detailed analysis of existing social and cultural values and attitudes, including gender analysis in basic needs assessments; baseline surveys and monitoring; the routine collection of gender and age dis-aggregated data to make men's and women's (and girls' and boys') contributions to society visible.

Research: gender, masculinities and life courses   There are several suggestions for the need for more research into men and masculinities in development; in particular in deconstructing gender identities and determining who is doing what, and why, in different cultural contexts. Related to this is the need for a life course approach to track the changing roles, needs and identities of men.

Hearn (2000), however, cautions against adopting too ethnocentric an approach to studies of men and suggests that future research should look at men in a more global context that takes seriously the implications of global political economy, structural inequalities, radical multicul-turalism and postcolonial debates.

Unicef (1997) suggests the need for more research into changing families, and changing gender roles, attitudes and practice. New exploratory studies are needed to understand the knowledge, attitudes and practices of men in child-rearing and other family responsibilities, and further to document the impact that men have on the well-being of families.

In relation to men and work, Jackson (2000) suggests the need to investigate further men's use of time (looking at regional, class, age and ethnic variations), what equity in work-sharing might look like and the changing identities of men as economic providers. In particular, there is a need to investigate relations of power and domination in working lives, and to see how gender inequities are reproduced or transformed. Other studies suggest the need further to investigate the relationship between paid work, state policies and family welfare. Harrison (2000) suggests that a more complete picture of men's and women's work must entail understanding separation and jointness within the household; decision-making; control; and ability to make choices.

Finally, in relation to men's health, Chant and Guttmann (2000) suggest that there are a number of gaps in knowledge relating to gendered vulnerabilities. In particular, they find relatively few ethnographic, epidemiological or demographic surveys with respect to male fertility.

Training   Most studies suggest the need for improved gender training within development organizations, to widen it from a concern with women alone to a concern with gender. More men are needed as gender trainers and the gender analysis frameworks currently used in development planning need review and modification.

Examples of the importance of training of and by men include those outlined by Milton Obote Joshua (2000) who shows how men's resistance to women's equality programmes can be overcome through training in Kenya. More generally, he outlines three levels of gender training: raising awareness, training in tools and frameworks, training for policy analysis and organizational change. He suggests that training activities in the first two areas predominate while only a few organizations are beginning to grapple with training related to reshaping organizational policy and practice.

Kamla Bhasin (2001) suggests that gender training with senior male policy-makers in the FAO has been useful in breaking down gendered stereotypes of men's and women's qualities and capabilities. She emphasizes the need to tread gently in organizing training with men, to avoid confrontation and provide reassurance and to recognize that men who try to break out of certain gender stereotypes may pay a price for it.

Kandirikirira (this volume) emphasizes the importance of training development staff within ministries and community work in early childhood socialization, in order to avoid the perpetuation of gender stereotypes. The need for training in gender issues in early childhood education is also strongly emphasized by Thomson (this volume).

CONCLUSION

Arguments for a focus on men originate from a number of sometimes contradictory perspectives. These range from those concerned with recognizing the complexities of the gendered exercise of power, to those citing 'male exclusion' as a backlash against gains made in favour of women. Issues currently hotly debated cover a whole range of development concerns from sexual and family health to employment, participation and empowerment. Incorporating men into gender and development necessitates a reconsideration of the theories, concepts and discourses which underlie policies.

Areas that are clearly in need of reconsideration include the links between modernization, development and gender, the appropriateness of gender analysis frameworks and the usefulness of concepts of sex, gender and hegemonic masculinity in understanding different cultural concepts of manliness. There is also a need to find ways of combining a concern with micro-level and private social relations with an analysis of macro-level trends and structures.

Experience from innovative approaches to men and masculinities in development practice echo some of the theoretical and conceptual concerns outlined above. Key issues arising from practice include defining the limits and focus of such projects, justifying an interest in men without losing ground in overcoming women's oppression, and taking account of other dimensions of social identity such as age and race. As with many other development activities, questions of how to track and evaluate changes in gender relationships prove difficult. Indeed, the whole emerging area of men and masculinities in development is a challenging one, but a focus on men as well as women can help us gain a more sophisticated understanding of gender relations and how to impact upon them.

REFERENCES

Almeras, D. (2000) 'Equitable Social Practices and Masculine Social History: A Santiago Study', *European Journal of Development Research*, 12 (2): 139–56.
Barker, G. (1997) 'Emerging Global Trends Related to the Roles of Men and Their Families', briefing notes for a brown bag discussion organized by the Chaplin Hall Centre for Children, University of Glasgow.
— (2000) 'Gender Equitable Boys in a Gender Equitable World: Reflections from

Qualitative Research and Program Development with Young Men in Rio de Janeiro, Brazil', *Sexual and Relationship Therapy*, 15 (3): 263–82.

Batliwala, S. (1994) 'The Meaning of Women's Empowerment: New Concepts from Action', in G. Sen, A. Germain and L. Chen (eds), *Population Policies Reconsidered: Health, Empowerment and Rights* (Boston, MA: Harvard University Press), pp. 127–38.

Bhasin, K. (2001) 'Gender Training with Men, Experiences and Reflections from South Asia', in C. Sweetman (ed.), *Beyond Rhetoric: Men's Involvement in Gender and Development Policy and Practice*, Oxfam Working Paper (Oxford: Oxfam).

Chant, S. and M. Gutmann (2000) *Mainstreaming Men Gender and Development: Debates, Reflections and Experiences*, Oxfam Working Paper (Oxford: Oxfam).

Cleaver, F. (2000) 'Analysing Gender Roles in Community Resources Management: Negotiation, Lifecourses and Social Inclusion', *IDS Bulletin*, 31 (2): 58–65.

Cleaver, F. and R. Kessler (1998) *Gender and Water Review*, mimeo (Global Water Partnership, University of Bradford).

Connell, R. (1995) *Masculinities* (Cambridge: Polity Press/Blackwell).

— (2000) *The Men and the Boys* (Cambridge: Polity Press).

Cornwall, A. (1997) 'Men, Masculinity and "Gender in Development"', *Gender and Development*, 5 (2): 8–13.

— (2000) 'Men, Masculinities and Development: Politics, Policies and Practice', *IDS Bulletin*, 31 (2): 1–6.

Deere, C. and M. Leon (1998) 'Gender, Land and Water: from Reform to Counter Reform in Latin America', *Agriculture and Human Values*, 15 (4): 386–95.

Dikito-Wachtmeister, M. (2000) *Women's Participation in Decision-making Processes in Rural Water Projects, Makoni District, Zimbabwe*, University of Bradford.

el Bushra, J. (2000) 'Rethinking Gender and Development Practice for the Twenty First Century', in C. Sweetman (ed.), *Gender in the Twenty First Century* (Oxford: Oxfam), pp. 55–62.

Engle, P. (1997) 'The Role of Men in Families: Achieving Gender Equity and Supporting Children', *Gender and Development* 5 (2): 31–40.

Farnesveden, U. and A. Rondquist (2000) 'Why Men? – A Pilot Study of Existing Attitudes Among Sida's Staff Towards Male Participation in the Promotion of Gender Equality in Development', *IDS Bulletin*, 31 (2): 79–85.

Fuller, N. (2000) 'Work and Masculinity Among Peruvian Men', *European Journal of Development Research*, 12 (2): 93–114.

Goetz, A. and Sen Gupta (1996) 'Who Takes the Credit? Gender, Power and Control Over Loan Use in Rural Credit Programmes in Bangladesh', *World Development*, 24 (1): 45–64.

Gordon, R. (1998) 'Girls Cannot Think as Boys Do: Socialising Children Through the Zimbabwean School System', *Gender and Development*, 6 (2): 53–8.

Harrison, E. (1999) 'Men, Women and Work in Rural Zambia', *European Journal of Development Research*, 12 (2): 53–71.

Hearn, J. (2000) 'The Naming of Men: National and Transnational Perspectives', *British Council Network Newsletter*, 21 (November).

— (2000) 'Men at Work', *European Journal of Development Research*, 12 (2): 1–22.

— (1999) 'Men's Work, Masculinities and Gender Divisions of Labour', *Journal of Development Studies*, 36(1): 89–108.

Jackson, C. (1998) 'Gender, Irrigation and Environment: Arguing for Agency', *Agriculture and Human Values*, 15 (4): 313–24.

Jacobson, R. (2000) 'Violence, Masculinities and Development: Seminar Report', Men, Masculinities and Gender Relations in Development Seminar Website: http://www.brad.ac.uk/acad/dppc/gender.html

Joshua M. O. (2000) 'Gender Training with Men: Experiences and Reflections from East Africa', in C. Sweetman (ed.), *Beyond Rhetoric: Men's Involvment in Gender and Development Policy and Practice*, Oxfam Working Paper (Oxford: Oxfam).

Large, J. (1997) 'Disintegration Conflicts and the Restructuring of Masculinity', *Gender and Development*, 5(2): 23–30.

Macaulay, F. (1998) 'Localities of Power: Gender, Parties and Democracy in Chile and Brazil', in H. Afshar (ed.), *Women and Empowerment: Illustrations from the Third World* (London: Macmillan), pp. 86–109.

MacInnes, J. (1998) 'Capitalist Development: Creator of Masculinity and Destroyer of Patriarchy?', Men, Masculinities and Gender Relations in Development Seminar Website: http://www.brad.ac.uk/acad/dppc/gender.html

Maxwell, S. (1997) 'Domestic Violence: Old Problems, New Approaches', *Links Newsletter, The Human Side of Conflict* (Oxford: Oxfam).

Michelson, E. (1993) 'Adam's Rib Awry? Women and Schistosomiasis', *Social Science and Medicine*, 37 (4): 493–501.

Montoya, O. (2000) 'Men Against Marital Violence: A Nicaraguan Campaign', *Development Research Insights*, 35 (Brighton: IDS/DfID).

Morrell, R. (ed) (2001) *Changing Men in Southern Africa* (London: Zed Books).

Osmani, L. (1998) 'The Grameen Bank Experiment: Empowerment of Women Through Credit', in H. Afshar (ed.), *Women and Empowerment: Illustrations from the Third World* (London: Macmillan), pp. 67–85.

Oxfam (1993) *Gender and Development: Oxfam's Policy for Its Programme* (Oxford: Oxfam).

— (1998) *Links: Newsletter, on Gender for Oxfam GB Staff and Partners* (Oxford: Oxfam).

Pankhurst, D. and J. Pearce (1998) 'Engendering the Analysis of Conflict: A Southern Perspective', in H. Afshar (ed.), *Women and Empowerment: Illustrations from the Third World* (London: Macmillan), pp. 155–63.

Pearson R, (2000a) 'Which Men, Why Now? Reflections on Men and Development', *IDS Bulletin*, 31 (2): 42–8.

— (2000b) 'Masculinities and Gender Analysis', *British Council Network Newsletter*, 21 (November): 2–3.

Pineda, J. (2000) 'Partners in Women Headed Households: Emerging Masculinities', *European Journal of Development Research*, 12 (2): 72–92.

Poudyal, R. (2000) 'Alternative Masculinities in South Asia: An Exploration Through Films for Schools', *IDS Bulletin*, 31 (2): 75–8.

Roche, C. (2000) 'Middle Aged Man Seeks Gender Team', in C. Sweetman (ed.), *Beyond Rhetoric: Men's Involvement in Gender and Development Policy and Practice*, Oxfam Working Paper (Oxford: Oxfam): pp. 11–15.

SCF (1999a) *Gender Equity Policy* (London: SCF).

— (1999b) *Perceptions of Men: Young Children Talking* (London: SCF and Equality Learning Centre and Working with Men).

Schuler, S. R. et al. (1998) 'Men's Violence Against Women in Bangladesh: Undermined or Exacerbated by Micro-credit Programmes?', *Development in Practice*, 8 (2): 148–58.

Sida (1997a) *Sida's Action Programme for Promoting Equality Between Women and Men in Partner Countries* (Stockholm: Sida).

— (1997b) *A Gender Perspective in the Water Resources Management Sector: A Handbook for Mainstreaming* (Stockholm: Sida).

Smith, S. (2000) 'Why Men? Why Now?', *Development Research Insights*, 35 (Brighton: IDS/DfID).

Sweetman, C. (1998) 'Sitting on a Rock: Integrating Men and Masculinities into Gender and Development', Men Masculinities and Gender Relations in Development Seminar Website: http://www.brad.ac.uk/acad/dppc/gender.html

— (2000) 'Beyond Rhetoric: Male Involvement in Gender and Development Policy and Practice, Seminar Report', Men, Masculinities and Gender Relations in Development Seminar Website: http://www.brad.ac.uk/acad/dppc/gender.html

Tadele, F. (2000) 'Men in the Kitchen, Women in the Office: Working on Gender Issues in Ethiopia', in F. Porter, I. Smyth and C. Sweetman (eds), *Gender Works: Oxfam Experience in Policy and Practice* (Oxford: Oxfam): 31–6.

Thomson, M. (2000) 'Breadwinners and Homemakers: Children Explore Gender', *Development Research Insights*, 35 (Brighton: IDS/DfiD).

Unicef (1997) *The Role of Men in the Lives of Children: A Study of How Improving Knowledge About Men in Families Helps Strengthen Programming for Women and Children* (New York: UNICEF).

Varley, A. and M. Blasco (2000) 'Exiled to the Home: Masculinity and Ageing in Urban Mexico', *European Journal of Development Research*, 12 (2): 115–38.

White, S. (1999) 'The Politics of the Personal: Seminar Report', Men, Masculinities and Gender Relations in Development Seminar Website: http://www.brad.ac.uk/acad/dppc/gender.html

— (2000) '"Did the Earth Move?" The Hazards of Bringing Men and Masculinities into Gender and Development', *IDS Bulletin*, 31 (2): 33–40.

Whitehead, A. (1999) 'Lazy Men, Time Use and Rural Development in Zambia', in C. Sweetman (ed.), *Women, Land and Agriculture* (Oxford: Oxfam).

CHAPTER 2

Nationalism, Masculinity and the Developmental State: Exploring Hindutva Masculinities

PREM VIJAYAN

§ Hindutva (Hindu nationalism) has seen a remarkable rise to political prominence over the last two decades in India. This has been accompanied by unprecedented levels of communal violence, mostly perpetrated by Hindu extremists on minority religious groups. The high-water-mark of this violence was the demolition of the Babri mosque in 1992; communal riots erupted as a consequence across the country. They were followed by frequent and intensifying incidents of violence by Hindutva forces against Christians in particular. The political transformations leading to this rise have also been accompanied by fundamental transformations in the economy of the country. Since the mid-1980s but especially since 1990, the Indian economy has undergone a process of liberalization that is still under way. In this chapter, I will set out the relations between these phenomena in the historical dovetailing of patriarchal and developmentalist agendas in the post-Independence Indian state. I will present a distinction between patriarchy as masculine hegemony, and the individual hegemonic forms of masculinity that constitute that patriarchy. I then argue that the rise of Hindutva owes a large debt to transformations within a general condition of patriarchy as masculine hegemony governing society and culture. These transformations realigned the configuration, and the social and cultural compositions, of local hegemonic masculinities negotiating for dominance in the Indian context. This will be followed by some remarks on the peculiar methodological problems of undertaking a study of this nature.

CENTRAL THEMES

There are several themes central to the idea of development that I wish to outline briefly, as preliminary and pertinent to my remarks on exploring masculinity and violence in the context of the recent rise of Hindutva in India:

- The relation of 'development' to 'modernity' and 'modernization', especially as a process of industrialization, and specifically the importance of individualism, in its many ideological forms, in the evolution of that modernity.
- The relations between modernity and the evolution of feminism(s) that remain largely unacknowledged in development literature. I draw attention here to the contradictions between various forms of individualism: those that promoted free market enterprises and liberal democracy, leading to a general division and gendering of practices into public (masculine) and private (feminine); and those that made feminism possible.
- The instrumentalist social vision that guided developmentalism, the emergence of nationalism and the consequent dominance of an almost purely masculinist understanding of modernization, especially outside the 'West'.
- The persistence, even reinforcement in many cases, of patriarchal systems in the target societies of development programmes, in and through the very processes of nationalism and 'development'.

Development and modernization   Without rehearsing the enormous debate on this concept, I should like to draw attention to its relation to the closely intertwined concept of modernity. In one well-known rendition, André Gunder Frank defines its dominant conception thus: 'development meant following step by step in our [American idealized] footsteps from tradition to modernity. The measure of it all was how fast the modern sector replaced the traditional one in each dual economy and society' (Frank n.d.). Pat Howard, in an interesting article, draws attention to the epistemic underpinnings of this ideology of development as modernization. He writes: 'the myth of the neutrality of scientific knowledge and the rationality of economic reasoning in particular disarmed the victims of progress by inculcating a conviction that their own ways of knowing ... were backward and in need of modernization'

(Howard n.d.). Howard offers no clarification of what is to be understood by this term, and seems to take it as synonymous with a 'techno-
cratization' form of development: 'Development typically involves an
attempted transfer of Western scientific knowledge and technologies
based on these scientific knowledge systems.' To examine modernization
and its sibling term, modernity, we must turn to other sources.

Benjamin Schwartz asks the question, 'What is the center or the
heart of that whole which we call modernity?' and notes the many
answers to this question as 'the scientific revolution and/or the
economic/technological rationalization'; 'the liberation of the individual
from all authority both human and supernatural'; 'the equalization of
all human conditions as the ultimate promise of modernity'; and/or
'modern secular nationalism' (Schwartz 1993: 214). He goes on to
identify 'individualism'[1] and 'collectivism' (including communism and
fascism) as some of the many ideologies that attempted to comprehend
these many different factors. Schwartz then identifies what he sees as
the core of 'modernity'. After agreeing that 'the scientific revolution
and Max Weber's notion of the unlimited "rationalization" of every
sphere of social, economic, and political life' are immediately obvious
instances of modernity, Schwartz points to 'the philosophic perspectives
[of] the radical post-Cartesian disjuncture between the human realm
conceived of as totally encapsulated within itself and a nonhuman
realm to which we relate only in theoretical, scientific and technological
terms' (Schwartz 1993: 216–17). He then proceeds to point out importantly the conceptual location and role of nationalism in this debate.
It takes the form of attempting to locate the formation of the modern
idea of the state in relation to that of the sense of nationhood or
nationalism.[2] For Schwartz:

> [The territorial states of early modern Europe], which witnessed the
> rise of many other aspects of modernity, also created the most vividly
> articulated and full-bodied image of the nation which has ever existed.
> They strongly promoted the official vernacular language, fostered the
> notion of a national high culture, affirmed the idea of the supreme
> sovereignty of the secular nation-state, and played a crucial role … in
> promoting the kind of early industrial development so much stressed by
> Ernest Gellner. (Schwartz 1993: 221)

And it is this form of the nation that proved spectacularly influential:

There can be no doubt that what attracted the eye of many in the non-Western world to the powerful nation-states of the West was the entirely unprecedented growth in the wealth and power of these states. Indeed, the fact that they were all more or less equal entities striving with each other in a battle for ascendancy as well as the more continuous fact of the inability of others to compete with them ... led to a concentrated attention on the power of nationalism as an organizing and mobilizing force. (Schwartz 1993: 223–4)

The pertinence of all this to the development debate is provided by Satish Deshpande:

At its most fundamental level, the rhetoric of development provided the former colonies with a dignified and distinctive way of obeying the imperative towards a modernity already indelibly marked as western. Thus, development acquired a powerful emotive-nationalist charge in the non-western world, because the West is 'always-already' the norm for most modern institutions and ideas, including those of the nation, development and progress. (Deshpande 1998: 149)

If we quickly recap some of the themes covered above, the main issues now appear to be the concurrency[3] of the formation of the nation-state with that of the ideas of individualism and various forms of collectivism such as nationalism, within a historical context of economic and industrial development. In fact, they appear precisely as the ideologies of governance and control of this development, whether through the state, private enterprises, or – more usually – a combination of the two. But whether through private enterprise or through the state, in Schwartz's words, '[t]he relation of individual liberty to equality remains a matter of continuous debate' (Schwartz 1993: 215). This determines both understandings of modernity and of a development oriented towards this, in postcolonial contexts.

Feminism, individualism, modernity There is little doubt that most schools of feminism may be traced back to the evolution of individualism, whether economic or otherwise, and the debates they engaged in with the state and with what we would now call civil society, in the form of the discourse of rights.[4] Wollstonecraft is only the best known of a series of original thinkers and ideologues on this issue. If we briefly return to Schwartz's earlier remarks on individualism, it seems clear that part of the contested terrain between individual and collectivity – as state, nation, or community – was the embattled space of women's rights and issues as *collective* issues, whether in economic, ethical or psychological terms. The defining of individualism as equal rights claimed by anonymous and, in principle, equal persons – as opposed to subjectively differentiated and unequal selves – had two contradictory implications. On the one hand, that these empowering rights would further sanction the power of the already empowered. On the other, its anonymous universality meant it sanctioned the extension of those rights to the weak and the disempowered. The problem of the social organization of these rights therefore proved enormous, in that their continued legitimacy depended on first equalizing social and economic discrepancies and inequalities. Fox-Genovese shows how this problem was negotiated, at least with regard to women's status and position, by resorting to a reinforcement of the ideology of motherhood, and its implicit domesticity, as the core identity for women, thereby gendering the discourse of rights as masculine, and rendering it 'innately' public.[5] That is, rights belonged to (masculine) persons, as opposed to (feminine) selves (Fox-Genovese 1991: 128). The strength of this ideology is reflected in the fact that this history remains largely unacknowledged outside feminist discussions and in the lateness with which women's issues and feminism (in the broadest, most inclusive sense) as an ideology came to be addressed in the development debate – as late as the early 1970s.

This history, then, reveals the hidden underbelly of development and its historical heritage: the transformations in the family brought about by industrial modernity, the unacknowledged and invisible contribution of women to its economy, and the consolidation of that invisibility through those very transformations in the family. Cynthia Cockburn notes how the development of a female industrial labour force

> meant [the] coming out of the enclosed sphere of the patriarchal family into the more public sphere of the patriarchal firm ... In a sense the home became a truly private sphere only once production had left it. The constitution of 'home and work', the 'private and public' as we know them was in many ways a cultural artefact of the industrial revolution. (Cockburn 1992: 206)

As Fox-Genovese notes:

> Throughout the nineteenth century, the path from the moral and intellectual responsibilities of educating children to the right to write and speak publicly on moral issues, to the property rights of married women, to the right to suffrage and through it full citizenship, led some women increasingly to protest against those limitations on their identities and roles that they perceived as legitimate. Or, more accurately, it led them to protest their exclusion from the role and identity of citizen. (Fox-Genovese 1991: 129)

This led to a gradual recognition of women's rights as individuals, and of their claim to public space, however grudgingly, precisely because the distinction between public and private, as indicated in Cockburn's statement above, was at best a tenuous one, given the overwhelming importance of female labour to the new industrial economy. Additionally, one consequence of the Lutheran Reformation was the devolution of power over women from the priest and Church to the male head of household (Nicholson 1992: 42), who was accountable more to the state than to the Church. The combination of these factors ensured that the two other most significant aspects of modernization – the idea of the liberal democratic state based on the sanctity of individual rights, and the technological transformation of life brought about by the industrial revolution – were in an intimately dynamic relationship with the growth of feminism and the (albeit incomplete) accommodation within these transformations of women's issues. All this was eventually to become part of the baggage of nationalism–development–modernity that was imported into non-western ex-colonies, in their search for development-into-modernization. Consequently, public and private spaces were reconstructed in the target societies of development, to suit the processes of industrialized modernization; but without the history of feminism that had struggled to make the new-found public spaces hospitable to women, through contesting and claiming rights as political and economic individuals.

To recap: the Indian case is thus interwoven by the complexities of, on the one hand, modernization-as-development, and the transformation in social relations demanded by this process; and, on the other, by the adoption of a political system that enshrines the rights of individuals over communities, even as it acknowledges the rights of communities to safeguard their 'Cultures'.[6] In practice then, even as the Westminster model of liberal democracy, with its ideological roots in individualism, was adopted as the form of postcolonial government by the newly independent nation, the rights of its individuals remained tangled in the issue of community rights. These are frequently vehemently and violently maintained as communities adjust, among other things, to the reconstruction of the public–private dichotomy, for instance, and the realignments in gender relations, in the carrying out of the 'national mission' of development. While gender is becoming an increasingly important consideration in planning and policy-making, as Saskia Wieringa notes rather despairingly of the concept of gender, it 'is used in such a watered down version [in present-day development literature] that women's issues have become depoliticized, that sexual oppression has been rendered invisible and that concern for women's issues has been reduced to the socio-economic component of women's lives' (Wieringa 1998: 5). There can be little doubt that this is fundamentally because the dominant understanding of development-as-modernization has been and remains instrumentalist and economistic, without taking account of the social, economic and cultural history of that model of modernization, nor of the corresponding histories of its target contexts. Yet it is this model that most newly liberated nations and their states, like India, aspire to as ideal in their developmental programmes. We continue to live with the long-term consequences of this silent privileging of the masculine. And this returns us to the question of what our understanding of masculinity is, in this immense silence on gender.

The persistence of masculinist biases through the evolution of the processes sketched above seems to suggest that they are constructed into the very processes and conditions of modernization. The emergence of feminism and the opening of the possibilities for accommodating women's issues in the public sphere – in fact, the weakening of the very construct of the public–private divide – all indicate the extent to which modernization actually proved enabling for women, and counteractive to these masculinist biases. Yet, in practice, it also meant a dispersal of masculinism into other spheres of human activity, with a concomitant gaining of masculinist control over these.[7] One thinks of the masculinization of technological and scientific knowledge, and of the social power that these represent, possess and give access to in modernity. How does one conceptualize this 'new' set of masculinist biases? It is this, often referred to in the generic term 'patriarchy', that I now wish briefly to address.

Towards understanding patriarchy as masculine hegemony   To begin with, I propose for this, albeit in a highly rudimentary and sketchy form, a renewed deployment of the idea of patriarchy[8] as a *masculine hegemony.*[9] The specifics of this may differ from context to context, and between specific hegemonic forms of masculinity. But it is in all of them indicative of a general condition of the dominance of men – essentially over women, but also over other oppressed men, the old, the very young, the infirm; and through whatever cross-sections of caste, class or race obtained. It consequently remains a dominance of the masculine, in whatever is the currently dominant, specific form of hegemonic masculinity. This apparent truism should be looked at more closely if it is to pass theoretical muster. Critiques of patriarchy theories of male dominance, while drawing attention to the inadequacies of its conceptual and analytical power, tend to ignore its primary case, that of a *general* – not *universal,* or *eternal* – condition of oppression and exploitation of women by men. To acknowledge this is seen as tantamount to accepting a transhistorically essentialist and unalterable reality, and a consequent denial of agency. In fact, it is no more than an initial insight into the bases – the conditions of possibility, the load of the dice in different situations – of gender and other relations in individual hegemonic masculinities. That is, the term ought to be understood as an analytical proposition referring to the condition of dominance that permits the hegemonic power of specific hegemonic masculinities, rather than, as is currently understood, an (inadequate) descriptive proposition with a stultifying universal applicability. In such a proposition, any given hegemonic condition may be characterized as masculine only in terms of the sustaining investment in it, as routine practice, of discourses of masculinity as a means of protecting its interests. That is, the extent to which its hegemonic power generates discourses and practices of masculinities as legitimizing, sustaining and expanding its hegemonic status. The most significant gain from such a theoretical position is the possibility of reading the *gendering of hegemonies* – economic, political, cultural, social – rather than the hegemony of individual gender-forms. It is in this sense that one may speak of patriarchy – the hegemonic system itself – not merely as if it was an impersonal objective system 'out there', but as *a set of hegemonic subjectivities*,[10] themselves inter-locked in relations that are defined economically, socially, politically and culturally, lived and practised by individual *selves*, both men and women. Without permitting the collapse of 'femininity' to 'women', and 'masculinity' to 'men', per se, it retains the strength of making them generalizable in terms of the *relations that obtain* in the material practices of individual men and women. It follows from this that different masculine hegemonies may obtain in different times and places, themselves constituted by, and constituting, different hegemonic mascu-linities within them. That such configurations need not and do not always obtain – or that, even when they do, they may be inflected differently in each case – is no refutation of the primary analytical potential of the proposition, patriarchy as masculine hegemony.[11]

Given such an understanding, it is possible to see how patriarchal systems generate masculinities. As new forms of power emerge, it produces new types of hegemonic masculinities to employ these forms, relegating the existing hegemonic types to subordinate forms of masculinity, and simultaneously producing hegemonic femininities that correspond to, and are compatible with, these different masculinities. It is possible to see how, as new discourses, forms and practices of material power emerge, and are deployed in challenging existing masculine hegemonies, they are accommodated into an already changing socius, the hegemonic equations of which are already in transformation, in the generation of new kinds and forms of masculinities to suit the new discourses and practices of power. Certainly, this helps to explain, for instance, the continued masculinization of political power on the one hand, and technological power on the other, despite the inroads made into both by women's movements internationally.

In employing this conceptual framework in the examination of the Indian case, I will begin analysis with a historical glance at the dynamics between the postcolonial state as the initial instrument of development-as-modernization in India, and the communities and identities it sought to govern. This approach permits the examination of the rise of Hin-dutva in a gendered way, not just in terms of macro-level discourses of nationhood and masculinization, but at the micro-levels of practices.

THE INDIAN CASE: HINDU NATIONALISM AND DEVELOPMENT

The historical roots of some of the elements that constitute the more 'generic' conditions of the (masculine) hegemony of Hindutva have been well rehearsed and engaged with by a host of scholars.[12] The British colonial administration carved up the legislative and judicial spheres into common-law and personal-law realms, and instituted communally quantified and proportionate representative legislation at the level of national governance. This meant that previously heterogeneous groups were realized as 'homogeneous' communities – Hindus, Muslims, Christians, Sikhs, Buddhists – with separate representative electoral bases. These groups shared the common realm, but were empowered to design their own personal codes. Besides permitting the Brahminization of Hindu personal laws this also led to frictions between religious communities developing specifically over issues of numerical strength and representation. The most significant feature of this Brahminization was the uniform relegation of women to the private realm and the family, with significant curtailment of rights and claims in relation to male members of the social order and the family. The emphasis on numerical strength as crucial to community identity became a convenient organizational and even necessary tool for those sections of the colonized elite interested in mass mobilization or even the construction of a majoritarian, distinctive 'national' identity. Proto-Hindutva formations often exploited the rhetoric and sentiments of these anti-imperial movements, but their agenda(s) remained substantially different, and were all oriented around the transformation of this convenient organizational condition into a historically (or, rather, mythologically) derivable one. The manufacture of this monolithic Hindu identity and past served mainly to consolidate the ideological hierarchies of a unitary caste system, Brahminical in conception and serving the interests of the power elites within the newly created 'homogeneous' national community. Coded in the discourses of this nationalism is what Gyan Pandey (1993) notes as the 'Western' identification of masculinity with violence and power.[13] For the proto-Hindutva nationalists of the nineteenth and early twentieth centuries, this was facilitated by the indigenous versions of a similar identification (*kshatriyaic*[14] ideals). It also permitted notions of masculinity to gravitate towards apparatuses of state power such as the legislature and the bureaucracy.[15] This mimicry of a 'western' masculinism, however, is not just a mimicry of the colonial structuring of power in gendered terms. It is also a replication of the colonial intent (perhaps inevitably) as if, postcolonially, the only way to *possess* (to claim or reclaim) an identity was through a second, 'colonizing', appropriative move. That is, for this proto-Hindutva it meant regaining a sense of power by redefining and re-enacting the imperial 'civilizing' process as the construction of the Hindu nation itself in the specific organizations of its social protocols, in the society it now addressed as its 'own'. But these protocols were embedded in a situation of rapid social change. Land reforms, for instance, were instituted by the colonial administration, and social reform movements attacked archaic and oppressive social practices, mainly to do with the status of and control over women, that had 'religious' legitimacy. As Tanika Sarkar notes, 'for the Hindu social authorities, the colonial state and liberal social reformers seemed bent on unmaking the securities and controls that the upper-caste landed *bhadralok* (respectable people) had so far been allowed to enjoy' (Sarkar 1998: 90). In the early part of the twentieth century, this insecurity extended to worries about the conversion of 'untouchables' to Islam and Buddhism leading to numerical inferiority for the Hindus.

These protocols and the changing socioeconomic field they addressed may be said to constitute the 'base' of masculine hegemony that has evolved since the nineteenth century, and that permits the designing of the nation as a conglomerate of patriarchal communities that are differently inflected in the individual agendas of their different hegemonic masculinities. Yet, to the extent to which the emerging conflicts of hegemonies were over issues of political economy, language, and perhaps most importantly, caste, there is little to indicate that they were either conceived or projected as gendered conflicts in the rhetoric employed by Hindutva. The overt gendering of conflicts is more evident in the later periods, coinciding with the large-scale investments in 'development'.

Satish Deshpande (1998), commenting on the idea that nations need to invent a past, notes that

> it is less often noticed that nations have as much if not greater need to invent a *future* – a vision of the collective destiny that its members have been elected to fulfil, a certain telos or trajectory through history. The greatest contribution of development is that it provides just such a telos,

one which allows the ethnos or people, in a sense, to grow roots into the future. (Deshpande 1998: 150)

The problem for Hindutva, though, was the perceived 'fragmentation' of the nation through the very process of development. In the period immediately after 1947 – a period dominated by Nehruvian development policies in economics and the domination of the Congress Party in politics – two small ruling elites, consisting of an urban, upper-caste, national elite, and a rural social elite of the dominant peasant castes and rural upper castes, together constituted a small middle class.[16] Pavan Varma lucidly describes the infatuation of this class, particularly its English-educated component, with the Nehruvian imagination of a socialist, industrialized and modern Indian future, even as it almost unconsciously worked to dilute this vision through its ceaseless consolidation of its own hegemonic position and character (Varma 1998). At this point in time, immediately after independence, it would be fair to say that the dominant nationalism was in fact a secular one. Not only had the Hindu Right been driven underground and lost substantial credibility because of its role in the assassination of Gandhi; but, more pertinently, this hegemonic class was still dominantly a westward-looking one, seeking the economic fruits of their 'independent' control over industrialization and technological growth promised by Nehru.

This hegemonic domination remained in place for almost three decades; yet, throughout the period, a gradual process of social change was already under way, largely due to the state's affirmative action policies which, though tardily implemented, allowed the emergence of a new, small but vocal political leadership for the lower castes. With the recommendations of the Mandal Commission (on affirmative action for lower castes) being announced in the early 1980s, and the weakening hegemony of the Congress – in its increasing inability to maintain and accommodate the diverse emergent social groups and claims within its ranks – the stage was set for a more dramatic set of changes in the social and political fields. Not only did new, locally strong political parties emerge – representing, differently, the interests of regional elites and of minorities, and indicating an increasing trend towards alliance politics at both the regional and national levels – they also represented new, economically empowered groups that clamoured for entry into the middle class in status terms that refused to acknowledge the old caste affiliations and statuses any longer. The state as chief agent of development, and therefore of resources, became the field of competitive rivalry between these various groups.

> This kind of competitive bidding for state resources leads to a situation where individually attainable demands render themselves unattainable because they call forth competing demands from rivals … The operation of an international as well as inter-class demonstration effect leads to the ironic situation where improvement in living standards … actually breeds frustrations because expectations are forever racing ahead. (Deshpande 1998: 157)

In its early years, the Indian state modelled itself as socialist in economic functioning and liberal in political functioning. This meant that the lobbies that emerged politically could dictate terms economically, with a multiplier effect. Most of these new arrivals to middle-class status were intermediate caste, land-owning peasants, like the beneficiaries of the Punjab Green Revolution. But as Yogendra Singh notes, their new status was not economically sustainable in the long term through continued dependence on agriculture, and the lack of investment in business and industry.[17] What was desired were the security, and the prestige, offered by state employment.

Economic anxiety coupled with the sense of arrival into middle-class status created conditions ripe for the emergence of right-wing nationalism in three ways. First, the new arrivals came, rather paradoxically, with a sense of the failure of the state to deliver on its promises of a developed industrialized economy; if heavy agricultural subsidies (undertaken increasingly for populist reasons) had generated wealth for them, it could not sustain the generation of this wealth. Second, this new constituency came into a public sphere that was until recently under the hegemonic control of English-educated 'westernized' industrial bourgeoisie, professionals and bureaucrats,[18] and which was dominantly upper caste. Much as they aspired to the lifestyles of these societies, there existed another legitimating discourse that they could lay claim to, in opposition to the vaunted social superiority of the existing elite, and as critique of it. The Hindu nationalist discourse had already made a renewed political impact through its participation in the broad-based anti-Emergency movements of 1975–77. It now found an extended and susceptible constituency with which to begin taking root.[19] Third, part of the process of being accepted by the existing upper-caste, middle-class elite was the indoctrination into its until now dormant religiosity – in other words, a process of Sanskritization that ensured the cultural hegemony of the caste elite. Each of these three phenomena displays the centrality of the issue of control and power to them, and the readjustments and accommodations this provoked within the Indian socius, of the existing hegemonies. What remains to be shown are the relations of these to the dominant masculine hegemony of Brahminical Hinduism.

HINDU NATIONALISM, PATRIARCHY AND MASCULINE HEGEMONY

It is to a large extent in response to these social differentiations that the recent surge to political power of Hindutva, or Hindu nationalism, has come about. Acutely aware of the numerical minority of its own (upper) class and (upper) caste constituencies, it incites and exploits anxieties, weakness and vulnerability, and displaces them on to a generalized Hindu community (Sarkar 1999: 2161).[20] In the outline of the growth of Hindu nationalism as an ideology that I have provided above, there are two processes in it that are of immediate significance: (1) The codification of personal law under colonialism. This meant, for instance, that in the crucial question of inheritance of property, even after various amendments to the original Indian Succession Act of 1865, culminating in the apparently empowering Hindu Succession Act of 1956, the strong patriarchalism of Brahminical codes of succession remained well in place (Mies 1980; Cossman and Kapur 1996); (2) The splitting of the ideals of masculinity along the lines of power-sharing that Louis Dumont (1980) described as existing in the caste system in pre-colonial India – the ascetic, Brahminical conception of power, and the warrior, *kshatriyaic* one, and their corresponding codes of masculinity. What is of specific relevance to us is the existence of these discourses of power as *types of hegemonic masculinities*, specifically in a context of state-sanctioned 'impersonal' (read genderless) individual rights. The co-incidence of views of Brahminical and Victorian codes in the process of framing Hindu personal laws – on the issue of the public–private divide and its deep gendering – though arising out of different histories and intended somewhat differently, translated into the common-law/ personal-law divide. It also translated into the differential construction of masculine hegemonies within each of these new social realms, suited to the individual demands of common-law and personal-law spaces. But these also demanded different masculinities as ideals for the sharing of power – in the personal realm, on the one hand, and in the public on the other. Personal laws, created on the deeply gendered issue of how each community could control marriage and inherited property, demanded an aggressively masculinist attitude towards their maintenance, enforcement and command, as the line that defined and came to distinguish individual communities from each other. Common law, contrarily, demanded that the power of being majoritarian be renounced in favour of an ascetic tolerance of the other communities that were thus equally defined through their personal laws.

What the emergence to power of intermediate castes did was to render frictioned the public sphere where common law applied, by their claiming the right to occupy it on equal terms with the resistant upper castes. It manifested as the emergence of regional and caste-based political constituencies that lay claim to their share of political and economic (at least in terms of employment) power. But it also was susceptible to Sanskritization, and in that to the hegemonic demand for ascetic restraint and toleration as the ideal of masculinity, in the sharing of 'public' power, particularly since their power over the personal sphere was defined in a common way, through the common (highly Brahminical) 'Hindu' law applicable to all castes. As Maria Mies writes: 'Since in the family ideology of the educated Indian middle classes Brahminic ideals were combined with puritan-Victorian ones, so through the mechanism of "Sanskritization and westernization" all groups were declared as inferior the family conception of whom did not agree with that of the dominant groups' (Mies 1980: 89).

In many senses the infamous Shah Bano case[21] catalysed this process of de-frictionalizing through Sanskritization of the Hindu community, and its currents of homogenization into a 'simple' majoritarian community. Even earlier, the aggressively masculinist definition of the community had re-emerged, almost inadvertently, and rather inversely, through the Hindu–Sikh riots of 1984. (Inversely in the sense that it was the Sikh identity that was starkly defined as different, and implicitly served to draw attention to the identity 'Hindu'.) By the late 1980s, then, the type of hegemonic masculinity that became increasingly preferred was the warrior type, demanded by the sharpening of community differences defined through increasingly different personal laws.[22] If the implementation of the Mandal Commission Report reintroduced a violent heterogeneity it was to some extent deliberately neutralized by the demolition of the Babri Masjid (mosque) in 1992, promoting thereby the hegemonic masculinity of the warrior type as the defining identity of the community. What was at stake for the Hindu nationalists in doing so was the extension of the ideology of the personal-law realm into the realm of the public – the 'Hinduization' of the world of secular relations governed by common law. What was at stake was the capture of state power itself, and the exercising of its hegemony through the instruments of that power.

In this process of the expansion of the 'national' community, several other factors are also of interest. The mother organization of Hindu nationalism, the Rashtriya Swayamsevak Sangh, promoted a careful programme of 'Swadeshi' (self-reliant) economics that argued for a controlled process of economic reform that would effectively increase the economic power of local business and industry entrepreneurs through protected privatization. Along with this, its political wing, the Bharatiya Janata Party (BJP), made political stability a major issue, suggesting that the process of economic reform required a consistent and stable government. These two campaigns served to bring large sections of the middle class, essentially the educated elite, which were earlier less attracted to the idea of a right-wing nationalist government at the centre, into the folds of the Hindu nationalists, aided to no small extent by the demonization, in deeply gendered terms of the Muslim community, that accompanied the demolition of the Babri Masjid. It permitted the coming to power of coalition governments headed by the BJP in the mid-1990s, supported mainly by regional parties which represented regional elites that more or less shared the BJP's understanding of nationalism – hawkish, aggressively patriarchal in the resistance to forms of perceived 'westernization', yet already in the process of liberalizing the economy towards the benefit of the coalition elites. It is significant that the call for liberalization of the economy came almost simultaneously with the implementation of reservations.[23] The withdrawal of the state from the production and market sectors also means that the state would, in due course, have fewer jobs to provide, since it is the market and the needs of private corporations – substantially controlled by upper-caste communities – that will determine employment.[24]

The transformations in the masculinity of the multiple hegemonies articulated by Hindutva are thus evident in the types of ideal masculinity that are called on to govern each kind of hegemonic exercise. The process of modernization that should have delegitimized personal laws served, instead, to reinforce them and sanction their gendering. Through the processes of Sanskritization that it induced and catalysed, modernization actually served to strengthen masculinist biases, even as it demanded their reorganization[25] into different but articulated masculine hegemonies, through the deployment of different hegemonic types of masculinity.

It is now possible to see Hindu nationalism as negotiating 'masculinity' in a range between (at least) two registers: the type of the virile warrior addresses the external limits of Hindutva masculinity, while the ideal of the ascetic, stressing control and reticence, addresses internal differences. But it is significant that, in either case, masculinity is always *to be* acquired since, by definition, the acquiring of one ideal inevitably threatens and negates the other; yet a masculinity, however conceived, is always to be the defining quality of the ideal to be obtained. Even if the emergent social groups of the last two decades did not necessarily project their claims to power in a strident rhetoric of masculinization, it was not because they were less 'masculinized' (in the sense of less patriarchal) in their claims to power. Rather, it was because they were laying claim to power *as a community*, as opposed to Hindutva's manoeuvrings aimed at maintaining and reinforcing its existing but threatened patriarchal hegemony.[26] The attempted erasure of the feminine in Hindutva's manoeuvrings – except as a polemical metaphor for unrealized maleness, and even in the face of an aggressive martialization of women within its more institutional orders – is carefully tailored not to encourage questioning of the existing gender divisions of labour, and to maintain, in practice, the subjection of women to male authority within the community.[27] It indicates precisely the hegemonic nature of the masculinities of Hindutva – as operating through consent as much as through force – as well as highlights the extent to which the specific conception of masculinity here is addressed to the whole community, including its women, rather than to its men alone. In fact, the martialization of its women seems to serve, if anything, to enhance the masculinity of the men they consent to subject themselves to.

Hindu nationalism's projection of the Hindu nation as Utopia (rather than as differently or partially realized with each gain in political power) at one level dovetails innocuously with the existing hegemonic discourses of development and the desire for progress. Its deeper and longer-term exertions, however, are towards the deliberate insertion of its own agendas within this developmentalist framework of discourses and policies, as the agendas of and for the nation, and *desired by* the nation. It is this that allows real and pressing issues of governance and redistribution to be compromised in favour of projecting issues such as 'political stability' and nuclearization as crying needs, and religious conversions as a pressing crisis, and therefore demanding of precedence. Welfare programmes, particularly those affecting rural development such as the subsidized public distribution system, were, and are, being rolled back with a vengeance, resulting in an already perceptible increase in overall income level disparities. There has nevertheless been a concomitant increase in the social display of wealth, and of conspicuous consumption, and not just in urban areas. This consumption becomes an index both for social power and for 'progress' and advancement. The desire for personal satisfaction through consumption is thus mapped on to the desire for the future, advanced nation, the signs of which are ceaselessly generated and displayed by the advertising industry that incites much of this desire in the first place. In such disparate conditions of access to the market, it is very easy for generated 'needs' to solicit consent to and investment in the new imaginary of the nation, and more importantly in the economic policies that promise to deliver it. This further expands the hegemonic power of Hindutva's brand of 'swadeshi', along with the idea of stability, and its effectiveness as an instrument against dissent or resistance to Hindutva's political hegemony. The masculine 'loaded dice' of this phenomenon are not so difficult to identify. It is no coincidence for instance, that it is in Bangalore (a city that perhaps more than any other is representative of the speed of the transformation to a consumer lifestyle) that there has been a sharp increase in reported 'dowry deaths' – the practice of killing wives in order to remarry for another collection of dowry – over the last two years (Menon 1999)[28]. And this is only the most visible evidence of the pressures that this process brings to bear on women.

Violence and Hindutva masculinity   I have not dealt definitively with the concept of violence here (essentially for lack of space) and have mentioned it only as an effect of developmental agendas. I am sharply aware that it cannot be reduced to this. I am aware that violence is frequently incited by, and deployed for, politically-motivated interest-groups, that most commonly use it to consolidate fragmenting political constituencies; the sense of external threat works very often to subvert internal disaffections and dissidence in any social group. The danger with this reading is that very deeply felt senses of grievance – exclusion, threat or animus – that lead to violence go largely ignored in favour of understanding them as politically motivated. The alternative seems to be to suggest that violence has a logic entirely of its own, in the dynamics between social groups or people. Tanika Sarkar incisively notes how, in some critiques of Hindutva violence,

> it is dissolved into violence as a transcendental analytical category … with innate, fixed tendencies and drives of its own that defy social, historical or political determinations of any sort … Indian men and women become mere sites and props in a theatre through whom violence moves and speaks, while the Right itself recedes from our horizon of concerns, a search for its specific history endlessly deferred. (Sarkar 1999: 2159)

Without falling into this 'transcendental' conception of violence, it is possible to think of it as *structurally inherent to any hegemonic condition*, even, or perhaps especially, if we understand hegemony in the orthodox Gramscian sense of being a mixture of force and consent.[29] Consent in hegemonies is not consensual, it is a result of at least a perception of irresistible force, understood to imply an irresistible violence if resisted. This is not to argue that all forms of violence are the same or even alike, either in form or origins. One can conceive of violence that is not necessarily innate to specific structural formations, but erupts more contingently, as for instance with mob lynchings. However, violence that erupts in conditions already defined in hegemonic terms may be said to evolve specifically out of the structural imbalances of the hege-monic condition itself. This may well appear clearer through contrast, if we look briefly at the opposite idea of non-violence. Its best-known political usage was in the Gandhian resistance to British imperialism. Gandhian non-violence was not so much a generalized practice of non-violence per se – the holocaust of the violence that preceded and ran through the partition of the country is witness to that incredible violation of Gandhian non-violence – as a very successful twist to the response to imperial hegemonic force. By turning hegemonized consent to an irresistible non-consent, Gandhi gained a powerful moral lever that broke the structure of the equation, hegemony = force + consent. But in contexts where the hegemonic force is provenly resistible in violent terms – whether as lower-caste rebellions against upper-caste oppression, or as Muslim resistance to Hindu domination – violence has to be, and is, frequently used on both sides, to (re)induce and reinforce the perception of its own irresistibility, and thereby buy consent. Where such hegemonies operate in the maintenance and reinforcement of patently patriarchal structures of the distribution of power, it goes without saying that the violence they unleash is markedly masculinist; and this is true of Hindutva.

SOME REMARKS ON METHODOLOGY

It remains now to discuss an appropriate methodology for engaging with issues that clearly require analysis both at the macro- and micro-levels. In beginning this project, I had envisioned a combination of fieldwork, involving neighbourhood studies, and discourse analysis. In the words of Fischer and Marcus:

> the point of this kind of project would be to start with some prior view of a macrosystem or institution, and to provide an ethnographic account of it, by showing the forms of local life that the system encompasses, and then proposing novel or revised views of the nature of the system itself, translating its abstract qualities in more fully human terms. (Fischer and Marcus 1986: 92)

That is, discourse analysis was intended to provide a set of 'travelling data' – an insight into the reach and spread of Hindutva's conceptual and ideological universes – while the neighbourhood studies were to provide details of how these were received and practised. For the former, I decided to generate a catalogue of the specificities of Hindutva conceptions and articulations of gender categories, involving a documentation and analysis of the various tropes, images, characterizations, marks and values invested in gender categories – specifically kinds of masculinity. In other words, a comprehensive examination of Hindutva sociopolitical programmes, manifestos, cultural prescriptions, formal ideological statements, as well as of less formal, more popularly disseminated 'grey' literatures produced by the various organs of Hindutva.

For the latter: conventionally, neighbourhood studies have meant studies of local communities, defined however loosely by geographical proximity. In the present project, however, the importance of the boundedness of the neighbourhood as a region was not so much the community that it may loosely define, as the exposure of its inhabitants to at least one common environment, and to the significant presence in this environment of Hindutva propagatory forces. The focus of study, therefore, was not the community *of* the neighbourhood so much as the individuals *in* that neighbourhood and their roles and functions in, and responses to, the propagatory forces of Hindutva that they are exposed to.

In carrying out this study, I have had to confront several problems of an essentially methodological nature. The first of these was the fact that I was working in Kerala, a state which has shown little evidence so far, at the level of state politics, of the kind of Hinduist tendency evident in most other states in the country and at the centre. The choice of Kerala was deliberate, made with the question, 'Why is Kerala apparently immune to this discourse?' in mind. The study revealed that Kerala was not, after all, immune to this phenomenon. Briefly, the difference lay in two primary facts: one, that Kerala has a demographic composition unlike any other part of the country, with a much higher proportion of Muslims and Christians. And, two, the state has a history of left-orientation politically and lower-caste movements socially, both of which resist the discursive and ideological trajectories of Hindutva. Nevertheless, I found that Hindutva had made deep inroads into the Hindu community, with a substantial number of my Hindu respondents indicating sympathy for the ideas and values of this version of nationalism. The problem lay in ascertaining the extent of political involvement this sympathy translated into, since there was clearly little reflection of it politically. The uncertain conclusion I arrived at was that the Hindutva organizations in Kerala were reconciled to the demographic factors that stood in the way of gaining state power. Consequently, they were not intent so much on local political power as on an ideological consolidation that would eventually serve as a vote bank in deciding who would form the national (or central) government.

One reason for the inability to clarify this more accurately was the mixed subjectivities I carried to the field of study, in my roles as inter-locutor, as analyst as well as 'heretic'. The last is not an unconsidered epithet: I am a Hindu by religious persuasion, officially. I am also a (relatively!) young, upper-caste, upper-middle-class, highly educated male – all of which make me an ideal candidate for the Hindu Right, as sympathizer if not activist. However, my obvious status as outsider – not just to Hindutva, but to Kerala, where I conducted my fieldwork – was compounded by the fact of my actually being a native of Kerala. (I must note here that non-resident Hindus are frequently known to be Hindutva sympathizers.) In my interactions with my respondents – primarily either members or sympathizers of Hindutva – I was therefore frequently called upon to declare my own convictions, religious and political, even to make financial contributions. Being male, my questioning of issues that should have been taken for granted or tacitly understood raised surprise if not irritation and suspicion; questions of male parental responsibilities, of the gendering of social and public spaces, of the intensity of women's participation in the movement, for instance, among others. Among my Christian respondents, too, I was viewed with a degree of suspicion, but for being Hindu. Among my Hindu respondents, I had access almost only to male respondents, and rarely was received without at least suspicion, if not hostility. The exceptions were interviews conducted under the watchful eye of a male organizational member. The members attributed this to a much smaller participation of women in the Hindutva programme, as activists; they would, I was told, therefore have nothing to say to me. Finally, the one issue that was discussed with extreme reluctance, usually only to deny or underplay it in various ways, was violence, whether communal or domestic.

In negotiating these problems, my options were to drop the neighbourhood study method in Kerala altogether; or to profess sympathy in order to gain access; or to lay my cards on the table and engage in argument and debate. I eventually settled on a mixture of the last two. I displayed sympathy where I felt I would not be ideologically compromised – in conversations on the new imperialisms for instance; avoiding what I felt were fruitless or pointless parts of the neighbourhood to explore; and entering into debate with individuals who I felt were amenable to such dialogue. The problem with this approach is almost too obvious to require stating. There is no definite selection procedure followed in determining which approach to take and when. On issues of violence I was perforce pushed into silence. Where the approach did yield results was in my showing interest in the educational agenda of the RSS (the main, parent Hindutva organization). I had the distinct impression that this was considered a safe area to expose to me, and therefore managed to learn a lot about the Balagokulam ('Children's Temple'), an RSS organization that propagates 'Hindu culture' among school children. One of my respondents, himself a product of this non-formal institution, proudly stated that its use as a strategy specifically for Kerala had made it possible to cultivate young minds at a much more impressionable age, and therefore 'sow' Hindutva much more efficiently in Kerala.

My work in the neighbourhood in Cochin suggests that there is an increasing sense of anxiety among the members of minority communities, not so much because of local Hindutva activity as the fact that, in recent months, violent incidents outside Kerala, specially against Christian communities, have been increasing. What was most striking was that there was very little articulation of any sense of unreasonableness or inappropriateness, leave alone injustice, in the Christian perception of the Hindutva demand that Hindu majoritarian India should be a Hindu country. This, for me, was the sharpest indication of the general prevalence of masculine hegemony, the rules of which govern the tensions and violence between the various communities of hegemonic masculinities.

CONCLUDING REMARKS

My work suggests that, through the adoption of different strategies of organization, discursive dissemination and through an inclusivist rather than exclusivist emphasis, the Sangh organizations in Kerala focus on minimizing internal differences (of caste, for instance) and contradictions, attempting instead to relocate the Keralite identity in a history of modernist religious reform that is 'common' to India. The focus is on the construction of a *basic* cultural identity, which may then accrete local flavours. The construction of this basic identity consists of broad understandings of the ideal Hindu, the ideal Indian, the ideal man and the ideal woman, all of which are embedded in the ideal community. The history of Kerala as different is not as important as the present of

Kerala in a modernizing India. Through its own projection of itself as superior to caste-based organizations, as reformist, as engaged nevertheless in indigenizing the processes of modernity through offering alternate yet traditional coping structures, it offers mediating mechanisms for identities to affiliate and adjust themselves to larger and disturbing social transformations. Particularly crucial in this is the sense it offers of being more modern than modernity itself, in its apparent espousal of democracy, *through* the promotion of Hinduism as already inclusively superior to all other religions. In intensifying existing role allocations – women as cultural workers, teachers, nurses, housewives and so on, men as breadwinners, protectors, decision-makers, community organizers and so on – it promotes a commonality of gender roles across communities which then forms the basis for the modern, larger, yet diverse 'Hindu' community. In my understanding, this was the strongest appeal to the younger generations: that they could lay claim to being modern, without feeling either deracinated or disenfranchised. The immediate aim and emphasis of the Sangh organizations in Kerala, therefore, seem less directly on political power and more on the construction of a community of believers – or of belief in a singular 'Hindu' community.

NOTES

1. On the evolution of individualism in the European context, and its comparative significance for the Indian one, see Louis Dumont (1980), especially pp. 237–9.

2. For a comprehensive overview of debates on nationalism see Anthony Smith (1998), though I do not share all of Smith's views.

3. I use concurrency here to suggest, not so much strict relations of causality – as if these phenomena would not have occurred without any of the others – but relations of interdependency, in which they were each influential on the forms that the other(s) took, within this specific history.

4. In the following exposition I will draw heavily on Elisabeth Fox-Genovese (1991).

5. 'The new concept of motherhood confirmed the new centrality of the individual, although not by endowing mothers with individualism. The purpose of mothers was, rather, to nurture the individual' (Fox-Genovese 1991: 125).

6. There is now a wealth of documentation of the history of how this rather peculiar political condition came to be in India. See for instance, among others, Dalmia and von Stietencron (1995); Pandey (1993); Khilnani (1997); Vanaik (1997); Peter van der Veer (1994); Chatterjee (1986).

7. There are several studies of this, but a useful sketch of the main themes of this issue is provided by Rosalind Gill and Keith Grint (1995).

8. Gill and Grint note that the use of this term in social scientific writing originated with Weber, 'who used it to refer to a particular form of household organization in which the father is dominant' (Gill and Grint 1995: 14). The significance of this as metaphor for other and different social organization lies primarily in its association of masculinity with power.

9. In the discussion that follows I use the Gramscian sense of hegemony as involving both force and consent, and as demanding the internalization of hegemonic values and principles by the oppressed or dominated groups, even if with resistance. See, for instance, his 'Americanism and Fordism' and 'State and Civil Society' (Gramsci 1996). In fact, the process of resisting hegemonies is crucial to their maintenance, as much as it may lead to the possibility of their replacement by alternative forces striving for hegemonic control.

10. As Raymond Williams notes, the concept of hegemony 'sees the relations of domination and subordination, in their forms as practical consciousness, as in effect a saturation of the whole process of living – not only of political and economic activity, nor only of manifest social activity, but of the whole substance of lived identities and relationships, to such a depth that the pressures and limits of what can ultimately be seen as a specific economic, political, and cultural system seem to most of the pressures and limits of simple experience and common sense' (Williams (1977: 110).

11. For a different, very thoughtful and useful theorizing of patriarchy, see Sylvia Walby (1990). My main point of departure from Walby's analysis is in the importance I give to changing conceptions of masculinity as changes in the *subjective engagements* with patriarchies, and the effects these have on the hegemonic operationalizing of patriarchies. For all the complexity of Walby's analysis, she tends to theorize patriarchy as an external, objective system – the weakness of most theories of patriarchy.

12. See, for instance, the particularly relevant volume of Vasudha Dalmia and Heinrich von Stietencron's (1995).

13. Gyan Pandey, in his 'Which of us are Hindus?', notes the Hindutva construction of masculinity as itself being a 'Western, colonial construction, where it is equated with military strength, violence, bourgeois rationality and a stiff upper lip' (Pandey 1993: 264).

14. Deriving from the term *kshatriya*, or warrior caste, in the classic four-fold caste system.

15. Tim Carrigan, Bob Connell and John Lee note that 'masculinities are constructed not just by power relations but by their interplay with a division of labour and with patterns of emotional attachment' (Carrigan et al. 1987: 601).

16. For a remarkably compact and incisive examination of these issues, see D. L. Sheth (1999), from which I draw heavily for the immediately following remarks.

17. 'In a generation or two even a land holding of a size within the ceiling limit permitted by the state ... gets fragmented. And without avenues for mobility to

non-agricultural employment the younger generation of peasants finds itself exposed to unavoidable downward mobility or even pauperization' (quoted by Varma 1998: 116–17).

18. Pranab Bardhan (1999) defines three categories in the middle class: the industrial bourgeoisie, the rich farmers and the professional classes. Here, I have merely opened the category of professionals to indicate the difference between state-employed bureaucrats and professionals in the public and private sectors. In this sense, with the inclusion of the rich peasantry, there would be four categories constituting the new middle class.

19. See Varma (1998: 142) for the same point.

20. Relatedly, for a good analysis of the role of communication systems as instruments of development in the creation of exclusionary conceptions of communities in India, see Sinha (1999).

21. In 1978, Mohammed Ahmed Khan divorced his wife Shah Bano Begum. Shah Bano, who was destitute, brought charges against him of vagrancy and destitution and asked for maintenance of Rs. 500/-. Her husband challenged the suit, claiming that he had fulfilled, even exceeded, his obligations under the terms of Muslim personal law. The case eventually reached the Supreme Court, where Justice Y. V. Chandrachud found in favour of Shah Bano, ruling that she was entitled to claim maintenance though the amount wasn't specified. The case generated enormous publicity. The 'Hindu community', the press and initially the Rajiv Gandhi government reacted very positively to the ruling. However, as Muslim protests against the ruling grew forceful and eventually violent, claiming that it attacked them as a minority, it became a national issue. The 'Muslim community' – the Muslim intelligentsia were in strong support of the ruling – linked this issue to issues like discriminatory employment, conversion and so on. Afraid of losing the Muslim vote, especially as some local elections were impending, the Rajiv Gandhi government introduced the Muslim Women's Bill in Parliament according to which support to divorced women would not apply to Muslim women who would instead be covered by their personal law. The Bill was passed on 6 May 1986. I am indebted to Karen Gabriel of the ISS for information on this case.

22. It may well be asked, Different to whom? For what was shared by all these communities in their personal laws was the retaining of male control over the sexuality, property and status of women, albeit in different ways. For a discussion of these issues, see Zoya Hasan (1994).

23. The quota system by which affirmative action was to be carried out.

24. Gail Omvedt makes a similar point in her article ('On Reservations') on the subject in *The Hindu*, 24 March 2000. While I disagree substantially with her perception of the current economic reforms as beneficial for the backward caste communities in the long term, I do agree with her on the issue of across-the-board reservation, irrespective of class differentials within the backward caste communities. See also Bardhan's 'Epilogue' to the revised edition of *The Political Economy of Development on India* (1998).

25. Perhaps the most striking instance of this is the gradual transformation of the matrilineal Nair community into an increasingly patrilineal one. See Mies (1980) for a succinct account of this.

26. That is, the dominant sense of the community's lack of power remained caste-defined, unlike the dominantly upper-caste Hindutva, which cast this sense of lack of power in gendered terms. For lack of space, one can account for this only very briefly here, but it is likely that the caste-defined senses of grievance, arising from genuine social oppressions and material disparities *arising out of caste status*, were sought to be redressed through organizing the community politically *in those very caste terms*; in the case of Hindutva, however, the sense of community arises from a perception of threat of loss of possessed power – identified within any patriarchy as already masculine, and hence as a depletion of masculinity.

27. See Basu, et al. (1993); Tanika Sarkar (1998); and, more directly, Sarkar (1999).

28. See also Sarkar's (1999) exploration of this issue in fieldwork among Hindutva women social workers, and their belief that women should learn to tolerate such violence.

29. I am aware that Gramsci's own use of the term is broad but largely as descriptive of the means by which the ruling *classes* in democratic states acquire and maintain what he calls 'ethical-political' control – through a combination of force and consent – over the rest of 'civil society', and thereby over the means of production. It is not possible to go into a very detailed theoretical case for its use in gender analysis, but the following points must be made. Gramsci repeatedly refers to the process of formation of hegemony, first, as a 'molecular' one, operating even in the smallest economic units (the individual, the family), irrespective of class; second, as an individual process of internalization of laws as 'principles of moral conduct', by which 'necessity has already become freedom'; and third, as a general principle evident in any society: 'in any given society, nobody is disorganised and without a party, provided that one takes organisation and party in a broad and not a formal sense' (Gramsci 1996: 56, 267–8, 264). It is clear that Gramsci himself saw the process as applicable to the relations that obtain between any given set of groups, not necessarily in class terms, even if he himself did use it mostly in the analysis of class relations.

REFERENCES

Bardhan, Pranab (1998) *The Political Economy of Development on India* (1985) (Oxford: Blackwell).

Basu, Tapan, et al. (1993) *Khaki Shorts, Saffron Flags. Tracts for the Times*, 1 (New Delhi: Orient Longman).

Carrigan, Tim, Bob Connell and John Lee (1987) 'Toward a New Sociology of Masculinity', *Theory and Society*, 14.

Chatterjee, Partha (1986) *Nationalist Thought and the Colonial World: A Derivative Discourse?* (London: Zed Books).

Cockburn, Cynthia (1992) 'Technology, Production and Power', in Gill Kirkup and Laurie Smith (eds), *Inventing Women: Science, Technology and Gender* (Milton Keynes: Polity Press).

Cossman, Brenda and Ratna Kapur (1996) *Subversive Sites: Feminist Engagements with Law in India* (New Delhi: Sage).

Dalmia, Vasudha and Heinrich von Stietencron (eds) (1995) *Representing Hinduism: The Constructions of Religious Traditions and National Identity* (New Delhi: Sage).

Deshpande, Satish (1998) 'After Culture: Renewed Agendas for the Political Economy of India', *Cultural Dynamics*, 10(2).

Dumont, Louis (1980) *HomoHierarchicus: The Caste System and Its Implications* (Chicago: University of Chicago Press).

Fischer, Michael M. J. and George E. Marcus (1986) *Anthropology as Cultural Critique: An Experimental Moment in the Human Sciences* (Chicago: University of Chicago Press).

Fox-Genovese, Elisabeth (1991) *Feminism without Illusions: A Critique of Individualism* (Chapel Hill: University of North Carolina Press).

Frank, Andre Gunder (n.d.) 'The Underdevelopment of Development', at www. underdev.html

Gill, Rosalind and Keith Grint (eds) (1995) *The Gender–Technology Relation: Contemporary Theory and Research* (London: Taylor and Francis).

Gramsci, Antonio (1996) *Selections from the Prison Notebooks*, ed. and trans. Quentin Hoare and Geoffrey Nowell Smith (Hyderabad, India: Orient Longman).

Hasan, Zoya (ed.) (1994) *Forging Identities: Gender, Communities and the State in India* (New Delhi: Kali for Women).

Khilnani, S. (1997) *The Idea of India* (Middlesex: Penguin).

Menon, Parvathi (1999) '"Dowry Deaths" in Bangalore', *Frontline*, 16(17).

Mies, Maria (1980) *Indian Women and Patriarchy: Conflicts and Dilemmas of Students and Working Women* (New Delhi: Concept Publishing House).

Nicholson, Linda J. (1992) 'Feminist Theory: The Private and the Public', in Linda McDowell and Rosemary Pringle (eds), *Defining Women: Social Institutions and Gender Division* (Milton Keynes: Polity Press).

Pandey, Gyan (ed.) (1993) *Hindus and Others: The Question of Identity in India Today* (New Delhi: Viking Penguin).

Sarkar, Tanika (1998) 'Woman, Community and Nation: A Historical Trajectory for Hindu Identity Politics', in Patricia Jeffrey and Amrita Basu (eds), *Resisting the Sacred and the Secular: Women's Activism and Politicized Religion in South Asia* (New Delhi: Kali for Women).

— (1999) 'Pragmatics of the Hindu Right: Politics of Women's Organisations', *Economic and Political Weekly*, 34(31).

Schwartz, Benjamin (1993) 'Culture, Modernity and Nationalism', *Daedalus* 122 (3).

Sheth, D. L. (1999) 'Secularisation of Caste and Making of New Middle Class', *Economic and Political Weekly*, 34(34–35).

Sinha, Dipankar (1999) 'Indian Democracy: Exclusion and Communication', *Economic and Political Weekly*, 34(32).

Smith, Anthony (1998) *Nationalism and Modernism* (London: Routledge).

Vanaik, Achin (1997) *The Furies of Indian Communalism: Religion, Modernity and Secularisation* (London: Verso).

van der Veer, Peter (1994) *Religious Nationalism: Hindus and Muslims in India* (Berkeley, CA: University of California Press).

Varma, Pavan (1998) *The Great Indian Middle Class* (New Delhi: Penguin Books).

Walby, Sylvia (1990) *Theorizing Patriarchy* (Oxford: Blackwell).

Wieringa, Saskia (1998) *Rethinking Gender Planning: A Critical Discussion of the Use of the Concept of Gender*, ISS Working Papers (The Hague: ISS).

Williams, Raymond (1997) *Marxism and Literature* (Oxford: Oxford University Press).

CHAPTER 3

Collapsing Masculinities and Weak States – a Case Study of Northern Uganda

CHRIS DOLAN

§ Much has been said about the ways in which masculinity allows men to exercise power over women. This chapter is about the ways in which masculinity, as a set of ideas, allows men to exercise power over other men. It is also about the ways in which this exercise of power is both reinforced by and contributes to a context of violence and war.[1] The chapter does not seek to pretend that men do not resort to violence; rather, it seeks to examine why they do so under some circumstances and not others, and how this is to an extent a politically manipulated process.

Drawing on material from research in northern Uganda, this chapter examines how in the face of the dynamic interaction between a model of masculinity and a context of violence, the possibility of developing alternative masculinities collapses. Unable to live up to the model, but offered no alternative, some men resort to acts of violence.

Furthermore, weak states may perceive a benefit in this collapse of alternatives: the hegemonic model creates incentives for armed forces to exercise violence on the civilian population in ways which actively undermine civilian men's sense of self. This may contribute to the state's sense of control over both civilians *and* army, both of which are necessary for national and geostrategic purposes. The role of the state in constructing and reinforcing this normative model of masculinity is therefore also examined.

CONTEXTUAL BACKGROUND

Northern Uganda, in particular Gulu and Kitgum districts, has been affected by ongoing conflict since 1986 when Museveni and the National Resistance Movement took power. There have been several phases to the conflict, each beginning with acute violence that gradually reduces – though it never disappears – until a failed peace initiative releases a renewed wave of ever-more intensive violence from those who were part of the preceding war, but not of the 'peace process'.

The first phase, beginning in late 1986 after the National Resistance Army (NRA) had taken control of northern Uganda, was marked by the formation of a number of different insurgent groups: the Uganda People's Democratic Army (UPDA), Alice Lakwena's Holy Spirit Movement (HSM), Severino Lukwoya's Lord's Army, and Joseph Kony's Lord's Resistance Army (LRA). While Lakwena's HSM was militarily defeated in October 1987, and the UPDA was brought out of the bush through political negotiation and the signing of a peace deal in May 1988, some of the remnants of both groups fed into the developing strength of the other two, the Lord's Army and the LRA.

The second phase, following the incomplete peace of first phase, began with heavy levels of violence, which then fluctuated over the following years, with a longer lull in 1991. The attempts to broker peace with the LRA by the then Minister for Pacification of the North, Mrs Betty Bigombe, raised hopes in late 1993 that peace was just around the corner. Instead, the collapse of the talks in early 1994 led to a dramatic resurgence of violence by both rebels and army.

This renewed violence continued until early 1999 when there was a noticeable lull, and some changes in the political climate again led to hopes that peace was just around the corner: an amnesty was put in place to run for six months, and the American Carter Center brokered a 'peace agreement' between the Ugandan and Sudanese governments, signed on 8 December 1999. Within two weeks of this deal, which did not appear to have involved the LRA (the 'visible actors') themselves, the LRA re-entered Uganda from Sudan. Civilians who had tentatively moved back to their home areas some six months earlier were moved back into 'protected villages' by the army, and vehicles were ambushed and burnt by the LRA on all roads out of Gulu except the Kampala highway. Phase 4 had clearly begun and is ongoing.

These dynamics cannot be understood in isolation from the web of conflicts in the region. There are clear spillovers and linkages between conflicts in neighbouring Rwanda, Sudan and DRC, and the situation in northern Uganda. In 1990 the NRA marched to invade Rwanda and overthrow its government (Prunier 1998: 130), and the Sudanese government bombed Moyo. John Garang, leader of the Sudanese People's Liberation Army, was seen staying in North View Hotel in Gulu in 1991, and the Pope prayed for peace in Gulu in 1993. People remember 1994 as the year in which 'the Rwanda Patriotic Front and the UPDF (Uganda People's Defence Force) overthrew the Rwandan Government'. Late 1999 and the whole of 2000 saw the heavy involvement of the UPDF in the fighting in the DRC, with recruitment drives being carried out in Gulu from late 1999 onwards.

Levels of insecurity have fluctuated dramatically but violence in the form of killings, rape, looting and abduction has featured heavily throughout. Hundreds of thousands of people have been internally displaced, thousands more have taken refuge outside the country. In this potentially fertile area, once one of the most productive in the country, people have lost nearly all their livestock and access to their farming land, while the availibility of health and education services has been severely reduced.

There appear to have been gradual changes in the nature of violence meted out over the course of the war, which could be characterized as an intensification of methods of violence. Phase 1 saw some appalling incidents of brutality, some of which have been explained by various academic observers as acts of revenge (NRA), or as acts of 'moral cleansing' (Alice Lakwena's HSM). Phase 2, however, saw the systematic use of maiming and mutilation, abduction and landmines, and the increasing involvement of external sponsorship. Phase 3 has seen the systematization of internal displacement through the creation of 'protected villages', and Phase 4 is likely to see more and more intense involvement of international donors and NGOs, ostensibly in the search for peace, but potentially in the spoils of war (lucrative grants for peace building, peace education, reintegration and so on).

There is thus a sense in which partial or incomplete peace-building attempts have not merely failed and thereby left the situation as it was before they collapse; they are correlated with a worsening and intensification of the situation rather than an improvement.

WHAT IS THE ROLE OF MASCULINITY IN THE WAR?

In the face of the above outline of the war in northern Uganda and its links to regional dynamics that involve a wide range of national and international actors in the stuff of international relations, it may appear odd to argue that a set of ideas about masculinity can play a role in creating and perpetuating violent conflict in northern Uganda. Nevertheless, there is a crucial connection to be made between state-level dynamics and micro-level behaviour, and the ideas which make up masculinity are a key connector between the two. To outline this connection, this chapter addresses a series of specific questions. First, does war reinforce a hegemonic model of masculinity, and does that model reinforce the war? Specifically, do notions of masculinity increase the likelihood of violence by non-combatant men, and do they make non-combatant men more vulnerable to violence by armed forces? Do notions of masculinity offer incentives to armed forces to use violence, and can this use of violence be perceived as of benefit to the state? What role does the state play in the promotion or collapse of alternative masculinities? At a more theoretical level, what do the answers to these questions mean to our understanding of the relationship between weak states and complex emergencies? and of notions such as 'crumbling social fabric' and the linked view that war offers opportunities for social change?

WHAT IS THE HEGEMONIC MODEL OF MASCULINITY IN NORTHERN UGANDA?

In analysing the role of masculinity in provoking or perpetuating violence and conflict in northern Uganda, it is necessary to distinguish between men's lived experiences of their own masculinities, which are necessarily multiple, and their lived expectations of masculinity, which are contained in a hegemonic normative model or set of ideas concerning what defines a man. The key example is probably marriage and fatherhood: not all men wish to or are able to enter into it (lived experiences), but they are *all* expected to become married at some point (lived expectations).

The model is hegemonic in that it largely precludes alternatives and is buttressed by major forms of social and political power. It is normative in that men are taught they should aspire to and judge themselves by it, and state and society in turn judge and assess them against it — before either validating, or belittling and punishing them.

In a workshop that considered various forms of discrimination in northern Uganda, and their relationship to conflict, it was apparent that a powerful admixture of pre-colonial, colonial and postcolonial messages had led to a normative model of masculinity. This model rests on polarized stereotypes and models of what women and men are like, what they should do, how they should relate to one another, and what their respective positions and roles in society should be.[2] At its simplest it can be described as based on sexist, heterosexist, ethnocentrist and adultist premises, and as entailing considerable economic responsibilities and a particular relationship with the state.[3]

Workshop participants argued that it is generally assumed that women differ from men, that they are weaker, incapable and a burden, a position legitimized by the biblical story in Genesis that man was created first, woman from his rib, and the saying that women are the 'weaker vessels'. They had been brought up to believe that women cannot perform to the level of men, and must conform to the culture of their husbands. Women are often portrayed as being like children, without knowledge or skills, or as jealous gossipers and busy-bodies who are not to be trusted and who are unable to be in solidarity with one another. There are sayings in Acholi that 'Women are always cats who seek sympathy', and that 'When there is constant drizzling it is like women quarrelling'. They are also likely to be blamed for domestic wrangles and misfortune in the family and organizations. Once a woman marries, which necessarily involves marrying into another clan, she is viewed as an outsider and therefore not to be trusted. She loses her clan identity on marriage but does not fully assume the clan identity of her husband.

These attitudes are reflected in the power which men exercise directly over women. Men pay bridewealth, women leave their homes to live in the husband's home, where they are considered the subordinates and properties/assets of men, who are richer, more educated and own other assets as well. Women do the domestic work for the family and can be beaten if they do not show respect to men. Historically, women were not allowed to eat certain foods (e.g. chicken), and they are not supposed to initiate divorce, which is seen as the prerogative of men. Their voices are often ignored and they are denied ownership of family assets. Women are regarded as there to produce children, which then belong to men; if a woman divorces she has to leave them behind.

Men are supposed to take priority in education and all other benefits.

Boys are regarded as better and brighter; indeed, traditionally a man may take another wife if the first produces only girls. Women are regarded as unfit for formal education, and it is argued that education of women is a waste of family resources because they get married and move elsewhere. Technical institutions are regarded as being for men only.

To this day, women do not participate in clan meetings or the traditional leadership; if they do, the elders will ask, 'What are women doing here in our meeting?' That women are to be put in their place if they overstep the limit is clear from an Acholi saying which translates as 'When the hen crows it must be slaughtered'.

Against this view of women, it is clear that the normative model of masculinity involves men in multiple subject positions, and is inherently relational; as Connell argues, 'masculinity' does not exist except in contrast with 'femininity' (Connell 1995: 68). Equally, while men are powerful by contrast with women, they cannot have the power without the women; the primary markers of masculinity centre round their relationship with women. To be recognized as an 'adult' and a 'man', men are expected to become husbands and fathers (preferably educated), and to exercise considerable control over wives and children. When the head of one of the major Acholi clans, Rwot Achana, died in 1999 and was to be succeeded by his unmarried son, the succession ceremony could not take place without his sister playing the role of surrogate wife.

Being able to provide the material needs of wife and children is one of the key roles contained in the model. However, satisfying the economic needs of others is not enough to define you as a 'man'. Although any young man who has a source of income will come under heavy pressure to support members of his immediate and extended family, he will continue to be seen as a youth or 'boy' until he has married and fathered children, and as such not to be taken seriously. Workshop participants noted that, 'Unmarried young people are perceived as *unable* to participate in political life' and that, whereas 'all adults are responsible (because they have children and houses and run homes)', youth are stereotyped as 'irresponsible, disrespectful, impatient, extravagant, arrogant, fun lovers who are ineffective at work' and who 'like leisure at the expense of work'. As a result, 'development is the domain of adults alone'. Adults claim their experience counts more and tell youth,

'Don't start climbing trees from the top'. Youth ideas 'are not listened to' and they are 'kept in limbo about vital information'. 'Youths' complaints and requests are ignored', and 'adults are slow to react on decisions important to the youth' (ACORD 2000). It is perhaps not surprising, therefore, that for some men having multiple wives and many children adds to their status, though here there is a conflict between Christian and non-Christian value systems in terms of polygamy.

Being able to provide physical protection is another key role for men. However, this is complicated by the fact that responsibility for provision of protection has to a large extent been taken out of the hands of individual men. They are now supposed to earn protection for themselves, their wives and children, by relating to the state as loyal citizens who put their trust in the state to protect their interests and are themselves prepared to take up arms whether as soldiers in the army, or as members of local defence units.

This contract between state and citizen is seriously undermined by a context of war, but in the northern Uganda context it is further undermined by a history of north–south opposition, and widespread perceptions of the role of ethnicity in previous periods of extreme violence and brutality. Under British divide and rule, Acholi men were singled out for service in the military and the police, and under the Obote regime prior to Museveni's takeover they dominated the armed forces and were widely blamed for the atrocities that occurred in the Luwero Triangle (one of Museveni's main areas of operation prior to 1986). This has left them with a reputation for militarism and violence that has been played upon by southerners to justify the harsh military control imposed on the area. It is also part of the portrayal of the Lord's Resistance Army which is alleged to be composed primarily of Acholi.[4]

While this national reputation for militarism sits uneasily with Acholi self-perception as being well able to effect a reconciliation with others and resolve differences through discussion, it blends almost seamlessly into wider ethnocentrist and racist discourses which equate northerners with primitivism and backwardness. It is not uncommon to meet people in Kampala who will explain how they have had to overcome their belief that northerners are 'less than human'. Among the negative messages workshop participants had heard as young children were that northern Ugandans were 'primitive', 'backward', 'poor', 'illiterate', 'swine' (ACORD 2000). This fitted into a wider racist discourse under which people could recall how as children they were told that black people were viewed as 'evil', 'animals', 'cannibals', 'monkeys, 'devils' and 'spirits' who 'don't have souls or feelings'. Furthermore, that 'they are dark and ugly', 'smell bad and dirty', and are 'jealous', 'unco-operative', 'backward', 'unintelligent' and 'associated with disease'. Some were told they were 'supposed to be servants' who were 'not entitled to anything', and 'should be puppets (to be used and thrown at will)'.

As in all such cases of widely prevalent discriminatory stereotypes, it is difficult to identify individual sources of such statements. While some are clearly linked with the colonial period, once internalized they appear to have a life independent of their original source. In a sense the source is not the issue, rather the question one must ask how this underlying and tenacious legacy of ethnocentrist racist discourses compounds the more immediate causes of suspicion and hostility at group level, destroys self-esteem and self-respect at individual level, and how these in turn feed violence and conflict.

WHAT IS THE GAP BETWEEN MODEL AND REALITY? INABILITY TO FULFIL EXTERNAL AND INTERNALIZED EXPECTATIONS

In the northern Ugandan context of ongoing war, heavy militariza-tion and internal displacement, it is very difficult, if not impossible, for the vast majority of men to fulfil the expectations of husband and father, provider and protector which are contained in the model of masculinity outlined. At least 480,000 people, or more than 50 per cent of the population of the most affected districts, have been internally displaced into 'protected villages' (IRIN, 24 July 2001), thousands more have become refugees outside the country. Within Uganda they have very little access to subsistence farming, education, employment and cash income opportunities, or legal redress, or physical protection by the state.

Subsistence farming has been drastically curtailed by the milit-ary situation and the protected village policy. Although curfews and restrictions on movement are not applied consistently in these villages, people are generally unable to return to their own lands to farm and are able to use only those lands immediately around the protected village itself.

Whereas prior to the war many families held their wealth in the form of cattle and other livestock, this source of economic security has been largely wiped out. The majority of cattle have been raided by warring parties since the mid-1980s. Often, households lost dozens of head of cattle in one raid. According to one respondent, this pushed a close family member to suicide: 'My brother drowned himself after National Resistance Army (NRA) took 100 cattle.' In the 1990s the Lord's Resistance Army at various times banned the rearing of pork, and anybody found doing so was liable to serious reprisals.

Hunting and gathering of wild foods, a further source of food and cash income, is frequently outlawed and always dangerous due to the risk of landmines, and of being captured by rebels, or treated as a rebel by the army. That people do still engage in farming, hunting and gathering activities is clear from the range of foods available in many of the village marketplaces, but the quantities are much reduced, resulting in the need for food relief. However, relief supplies from the World Food Programme are both inadequate in themselves, and very erratic due to the fluctuating security situation.

Educational opportunities are very limited, with no secondary schooling available outside district capitals, and extremely limited access to tertiary education. This contributes to the tensions between adults and youth; older people are perceived as better educated because they 'grew up when education was at its peak under the British'. Even if someone succeeds in completing secondary education, job opportunities are limited, the more so as policies of decentralization have had the effect of ethnicizing government positions at many levels. International NGOs represent perhaps one of the few growth sectors in the local economy.

For adult men with children, the economic context and the lack of schooling available has made it very difficult to pay school fees and associated costs, thus undermining one of the key responsibilities of the 'masculine' role.

While the protected villages with their high population densities may have increased sexual opportunities for some, they have also created a number of obstacles. At a most basic level accommodation in protected villages is overcrowded and does not allow the privacy which characterized pre-war settlement and accommodation patterns. For male youths who engage in sexual activity with female counterparts there is a high risk of being accused of defilement (sex with an underage female) with the risk of a six-year prison sentence if convicted, and very costly out-of-court settlements to avoid such a sentence. A further risk is in contracting HIV/AIDS. Over the course of the war, Gulu district has risen from having one of the lowest HIV rates in the country to having one of the highest. For those who wish to get married, the absence of cattle or cash as the basis for bridewealth payments resulting from over a decade of cattle rustling and raiding represents a considerable obstacle. As one youth wrote in a poem:

> Shall we marry
> Really when our animals
> Scuffled their ways
> To the so-called strongmen
> With dry woods on their shoulders
> That burnt the whole village fallowland
> Even introduced us to beg
> For the mouths from neighbours?

Where men do manage to marry and have children, their role as protector of physical security is severely compromised. Despite a military presence in many of the 'protected villages', rebels raid with impunity, seizing men, women, children and properties at will.[5] While the state still denies the individual the right to protect his own family (for example by refusing to allow people to leave the protected villages and move back to their home areas), it fails to provide a satisfactory substitute. There is often no response to civilian demands for protection. In August 1998, for example, when rebels attacked an area of Gulu town only minutes from the bank where soldiers were stationed on guard, civilians who ran to request their support were chased away. The army came to the area at around 5 a.m., some three hours after the attackers had gone, leaving a number of dead behind and having abducted several more (interviews conducted with local councillor, 9 August 1998). This pattern is repeated in many protected villages where deliveries of food relief supplies are frequently followed by rebel raids. Despite this being an oft-repeated pattern, few steps are taken to prevent it happening.

Although men can become directly involved in providing physical protection through joining the home guard or local defence units, and there are periodic recruitment drives to bolster the home guards (e.g. September 1998), there are also widespread fears that young men recruited as home guards will be forced into the army and sent far afield, for example to the DRC or Sudan.

DOES THIS SITUATION INCREASE THE LIKELIHOOD OF VIOLENT BEHAVIOUR BY NON-COMBATANTS?

It is clear that, in the context of protracted conflict, non-combatant men's ability to achieve some of the key elements in the normative model of masculinity into which they have been socialized is severely reduced. They experience a loss of domestic and political power, they cannot exercise military power, and their capacity to create a family and then provide for and protect it has been much reduced. But does this make them more liable to violence?

While it is easy to see that men who are able to conform to the model do benefit to an extent in terms of the power they can wield over women, children and youth, it is as important to see that the expectations are onerous; indeed, many men express a sense of being oppressed by them. This is particularly true for economic expectations. Not only are they almost impossible to meet in the northern Ugandan context, but the struggle to meet them at least partially leaves men with virtually no possibility of pursuing their individual aspirations.

It is also important to understand that to break out of these expectations is not really an option; men are unable to behave according to them, but they cannot afford not to try to live up to it. The social and political acceptance that comes from being seen to conform to the norm, and the access to a variety of resources which this facilitates, is critical in a conflict situation. As Kabeer has argued, access to intangible resources (solidarity, contacts, information, political clout) 'is likely to be particularly critical in situations where market or state provision of social security is missing or where access to these institutions is imperfectly distributed' (Kabeer 1994: 280).

There is much to suggest a link between feelings such as humiliation, resentment, oppression and frustration, and the use of violence. Moore uses the term 'thwarting' for this dynamic: 'Thwarting can be understood as the inability to sustain or properly take up a gendered subject position, resulting in a crisis, real or imagined, of self-representation and/or social evaluation ... thwarting can also be the result of contradictions arising from the taking up of multiple subject positions, and the pressure of multiple expectations about self-identity or social presentation' (Moore 1994: 66). Foreman makes the same argument when he argues that 'fear of ridicule, of being seen as "less than a man", lies behind much of the violence men inflict on strangers or their wives' (Foreman 1999: 20).[6] Equally, he argues that 'resentment is often manifested in anger and violence towards women and other men' (Foreman 1999: 14).

Some of the examples that follow indicate that it is also manifested in violence towards the self. In all cases the links between frustrated expectations and violence are very apparent. Example 1 describes the suicide of a young man who feared being imprisoned for 'defilement' of a young woman. Example 2 is an incident of homosexual violence which is portrayed as an act of revenge against a relative of the victim. Example 3 details an explosion of interpersonal violence by a man who was both humiliated by his wife becoming pregnant by another man and by his mother-in-law's refusal to repay the bridewealth. Example 4 outlines a man's suicide as being due to humiliation at his inability to exercise control over his wife. Examples 5 and 6 describe how people seek to reassert their right to protect themselves through resort to mob justice of a violent nature.

Example 1: Suicide   One fieldworker described the case of an eighteen-year-old male who committed suicide by hanging himself after being caught having intercourse with his niece, Miss Alice, a girl of fifteen. She was a pupil of primary six in P7 school.

> When I investigated the cause of the death of OJ, his friend Mr. Obol says that OJ said he was going to be put to prison for seven years and paying 1,000,000 shillings for the spoiling of the study of Alice.[7] Hence he thought locally to hang himself from a mango tree at 6.30 p.m. on the 8/5/99 very close to his house.
>
> According to the feeling of the people around the relatives [are] really not happy because they say OJ must not [should not have] hung himself, a sit-down discussion would [have] finished the case. The lady [Alice] on the other hand has been transferred to Kitgum to avoid shame all the time to the lady.

Example 2: Male rape

Mr. Komakech son of Oloya Andrew, who is 35 years old in the camp of A____ on the 29/08/99 at 2.00 a.m. at night was caught red-handed playing homo-sexual with a boy called Okello (12 years) the son of O Alex of LCI L____ A____. The man became caught after people hearing the cry of the boy very loudly. When people came he ran away but the boy said it was Komakech who forced him [and] played his anus which became swollen. Komakech was looked for and was arrested. When he was asked why he did it, he said he complained to be drunk. Komakech formerly was the husband of the aunt of this boy and the woman died with AIDS her name was Lucy. Immediately Komakech was taken to LCI and the LCI Chairperson transported him to police – Gulu. And at the moment he is in the prison of Gulu waiting for Court. The boy was brought to Gulu Hospital for Blood Check and I have not yet got the report from the medical personnel or the boy.

Example 3: A violent dispute over bridewealth

In one incident described by a fieldworker, and closely related to bridewealth, a non-Acholi businessman

went to his mother-in-law to demand for refund of his money since the wife had become pregnant with another man ... but the mother-in-law said there was no money for refund. He returned to the mother-in-law's house during the night and pushed his way into the house. Then, using a panga,[8] he began to cut his mother-in-law and his wife's little sister, and when he was sure that those people were in a critical condition, he vanished away. And all the attempts by Police to trace him were fruitless. The next morning those people were admitted in the hospital, and the little girl died instantly on reaching hospital. The mother-in-law died on the following day. When the woman's son arrived on the same day that his mother died he rushed to the house of his mother's attacker and immediately began to attack young children in revenge for the death of his mother and sister.

Example 4: Suicide due to humiliation at lack of control over wife

There was a man called Opio. He always drank alcohol at l____. When he came back from drinking he was completely drunk. The way which he always followed passed via his mother's door. When he was passing he asked his mother in a loud voice 'Where is my wife?' because he always liked beating his wife when he was drunk. His wife has one child only. On that day he begin to beat his wife, his wife ran away leaving him with the child. He went to his father's house looking for her ... But he found that she was not there with his father, so he picked up his child and he began to go back to his house and as he was leaving he accused his father of changing his [the son's] wife into the Queen in that home. [He threatened that] He will show to them the action. Then he laid his child on the bed to sleep. His father said, 'Opio don't shout, you go and rest in your bed freely'. But Opio's intention was to die. At around 8.00 in the evening he swallowed the battery of the watch (Cawa). In the morning his child woke up and began crying but his father had died in the house.

Example 5: Mob justice

9 January 1999: A group of thugs claiming to be rebels of the LRA went on a looting spree terrorizing the village of I___. They took advantage of the rebel raid at that village during Christmas period. Those thugs then began to move at night time pretending to be rebels to loot valuable items from the people of that village and the neighbouring village, but some people who are security conscious discovered that those people were not real rebels. Thus keen follow up was made and on the night of Friday at around 2.00 a.m. when those thugs went on with their normal routine job of looting, other courageous people followed them up from place to place and saw where they entered to sleep, and immediately went and reported to the Local Councillor of the village. So some energetic people were mobilized that night and they went and surrounded the place and in the morning they stormed it and arrested the two thugs. One of them was a well known boy of that village called Ongwech. When interrogation started going on he confessed of the offences that he had been committing in the village and he further revealed that he was in a group of about ten people, some of whom had gone to Kitgum (the neighbouring district) to sell those items they had looted from the villagers. Among the items that had just been stolen that night was a bicycle (sports bike) which was recovered from the house. Martha, the guardian of that boy Ongwech, pleaded in vain for her son to be spared (especially) when the villagers further

learnt that Ongwech had just been released from the police on the 24/12/98 on case of theft.

At around 6.00 a.m. in the morning people armed with pangas, spears and logs, stones stormed the place of Martha. All the attempts by the Local Councillors (LCs) to restrain them from beating the two captured thugs was not possible. They started beating those boys from inside the house and when they saw that the house was too squeezed they brought them outside and burnt down the hut and destroyed even the wall of the hut and by the time the mobile police came with their patrol vehicle, to rescue the boys, all the LCs had injuries and the boys were dead. They were then taken to the mortuary of Gulu hospital. When I visited the scene, the whole place was a pool of blood as if an animal had been slaughtered and the huts had burnt down into ashes. The members of that family could not be seen except those who either participated in the beating or onlookers.

At times this mob justice is directed at the military and can be seen as an expression of the lack of mutual trust between the military and civilians.

These examples suggest that the disjuncture between expectations and the ability to live up to them go hand in hand with widespread feelings of fear, intimidation, humiliation, frustration and anger, often expressed in violence against the self and others, in the forms of alcohol abuse, suicide attempts and domestic violence, and also in conflict between civilians and the military. They also demonstrate a resort to psychological violence in the form of seeking to oppress less powerful individuals, notably youths and women.

That the psychological dynamics go beyond the arena of domestic violence and into the arena of war was suggested by workshop participants who argued a link between the experience of humiliation and the perpetuation of war: 'the local population lose their human dignity; they feel unprotected by the national army and/or rebel forces and that their lives are not valued. They become aggressive in self-preservation.' Furthermore, 'people who get victimized take sides in the war with the spirit of revenging the atrocities against them or their families' (ACORD 2000).

That they also make a connection between individuals' frustrated aspirations and decisions to join armed groups is clear from the discussion about discrimination against youth: 'they defy culture by joining war in order to achieve what they have been denied', and 'since they are denied economic opportunity by elders the youth take short cuts through taking up arms' (ACORD 2000).[9]

DOES THE MODEL INCREASE MALE VULNERABILITY TO VIOLENCE?

Given a link between frustrated expectations and violence it is not unreasonable to argue that 'thwarted' masculinity has made a contribution to a climate of conflict. While much of the evidence remains hidden in the domestic sphere, occasional outbursts of mob justice or a keen response to a military recruitment drive serve as indicators of this in the public domain.

Military behaviour, by contrast, is more clearly visible to the public eye, and it is here that the links between a model of masculinity and particular forms of conflict-related violence are easier to chart. Some of the dynamics whereby this happens have already been alluded to, notably the way in which cattle rustling/raiding/theft makes bridewealth payments impossible and creates a population of youth who can never be taken seriously because they cannot marry. More direct attacks on the most fundamental bases of adult masculine identity include rape of women (wives, daughters and sisters), rape of men (themselves, brothers, fathers, sons), and abduction of their children.[10]

The wider process of militarization has further undermined civilian men's sense of their own masculinity by creating a large economic disparity which favours the soldiers over the civilians. Virtually every settlement has a military camp within it or on its outskirts. The soldiers stationed here have considerably more disposable income than their civilian counterparts, and are able to attract local women as temporary wives, though they do not pay bridewealth. Some parents encourage their children to become soldiers' wives (Dolan 2000), and some believe that youth are attracted to joining the army in order to get 'free women' (ACORD 2000).

The tensions which this causes are considerably worsened by frequent incidents of rape. While this occurs at the hands of all parties, it is particularly bitter when the rapists are the very men supposedly protecting the civilian population.

Example 6: Rape by army soldiers One fieldworker reported how on 7 February 2000 members of the Uganda People's Defence Force (UPDF) entered a village in his area

> where displaced had gone to collect foodstuff. At 8.30 p.m. one of the forces (UPDF) raped a very old mother of 70 years. She was at her home ... According to information I collected from her she complains of pain in the lower part of her stomach. She says the soldier played sex with her for many hours (2 hours). She could not make an alarm and he had a gun. According to her statement she is worried about being affected with AIDS (HIV) When I opened the cloth from her stomach, I found that it was swollen badly. This woman has got 50 grandsons and granddaughters. And she has 8 children who are now very matured. Her husband was the late Mr. O.
>
> On the 8/02/2000 at 8.00 p.m. another mother in the same village was also with another soldier raping her. She is called S. D., she is 29 years old and she has one child. The woman is now very worried about being infected with AIDS. She was [forced] to accept sex for 1 hour. Now the woman is crying all the time for fear that she has been infected with AIDS.
>
> Another woman on the 9/02/2000 was also raped, she is Mrs A. M., 43 years old and she has 3 children. This soldier took 2 hours intercoursing this old mother. At the moment she complains of the stomach pains, cervix pain and constant malaria. She is from the same village ...
>
> The case of rape became common within this area because UPDF had settled for 2 days. And at night they scatter to operate.
>
> Another case also happened to a wife of Mr. O. O. who is called A. N. She is 30 years old with 6 children. It was 7.30 p.m. that this soldier came and sent away the husband ... from his home and forced the wife to enter the house to play sex. This soldier took 10 hours to play sex with the wife of O. O. Now the woman complains of stomach pain and with a lot of worries of being infected with AIDS. She also complains of cervix pain due to over playing sex with her and might be the over size of the penis of the soldier.
>
> The husband tried to boycott the wife [i.e. not have intercourse with her] but his parents advised him not to beat the wife because it wasn't her need (wish) to meet the soldier.
>
> In conclusion, people in the camp and the few who go to collect food

are really very worried and not happy because these [soldiers] are more harmful than rebels.

In some instances the army does take disciplinary steps against soldiers who behave in this way, and at times this provokes the guilty party to extreme steps, as in the case of a home guard who, after raping a civilian woman, shot himself rather than face military discipline.

However, it is more usually the case that when soldiers who are supposed to be guarding civilians break discipline, there is no redress. As one fieldworker reported:

> The UPDF soldiers based at A__ detach are giving a lot of embarrassment to the people in the camp by beating and raping. On the 10-2-00 a UPDF soldier came to the place of Agnes at night and hid himself behind the house. When Agnes was asleep he opened the door and flashed a torch. He then landed on the neck of the woman and wanted to have sex with her forcefully but Agnes began to shout loudly for help. Then Ay – who is the cousin sister – rushed to find out what was wrong with Agnes. On hearing footsteps coming from the neighbouring houses the soldier ran away.
>
> The following morning the LCs followed the case up to the barracks and the woman identified one of the soldiers named O. But the Commanding Officer of the detach argued that the statement given by the woman was wrong because O did not go out that day. The case ended there just like that.

Another described how in February 1999 a young woman was raped and shot dead by an army soldier; her relatives (impoverished subsistence farmers) were told by the army's public relations office to obtain a signed statement from the soldier's commanding officer before they would take action. Faced with this intimidation they were unable to take action, and by August there was still no progress on the case (personal interview with the relatives).

As workshop participants noted: 'When a woman is raped, the husband feels inactive to stand up and bring change (disempowered). He was supposed to protect her, but soldiers continue raping.'

Rape of men is less common, but was prevalent in the early 1990s when respondents reported an increase in STDs, allegedly due to 'indiscriminate rape of men (*tek gungu*)[11] and women by NRA'. The level of stigma attached is even higher than that associated with female rape. While ACORD has been able to work closely with many female rape victims, it has found it almost impossible to get known victims of male rape to discuss it in any way at all. In the workshop, participants described how 'when a man is raped it takes away his manhood and he fails to act to bring change'.

The model of masculinity makes non-combatant men vulnerable to the use of violence by combatants, and the process of undermining men's sense of masculinity becomes a key channel for men to exercise power over other men. In a sense, interactions between combatants and non-combatants around masculinity are something of a zero-sum game; the civilian's loss in masculinity is the combatant's gain. In other words, it is possible for particular tactics simultaneously to reinforce the perpetrators' and undermine the victims' sense of masculinity.

In what ways does the state benefit from the hegemonic model? The interaction between individual behaviour and group intention is a complex one. It is highly unlikely that the individuals involved in acts that undermine other men's sense of masculinity do not understand the impact of their actions on the men who are their direct or indirect victims. But does this mean that the state, through military and other channels, deliberately manipulates the hegemonic model as a means to military and political ends?

There are several major elements of the state's behaviour in northern Uganda which suggest that this may be the case. At the most basic level, the state bears considerable responsibility for the social and economic conditions that make it difficult for individuals to live up to expectations of masculinity. Many acts of violence and abuse against civilians, including rape, abduction and looting, are not dealt with in any meaningful sense. Indeed, the state has itself been a frequent culprit, and has arguably used these practices as instruments of war at particular times.[12] Furthermore, the state is directly responsible for the increasing militarization of the war zone in the form of 'protected villages' – but also for failing to provide adequate protection within these.

At a more insidious level, the state has consistently promoted a militarist approach to dealing with the LRA (at least in terms of rhetoric and visible militarization) that goes hand in hand with preventing the emergence of alternative forms of masculinity based on practices of negotiation, reconciliation and non-violence. Repeated calls for negotiation from people in northern Uganda have been repeatedly ignored by the state. The president's frequent statements that he will not negotiate with Kony because he is a 'madman' also implicitly suggest that he regards those who would try to negotiate with Kony as mad. Similarly, the government's approach to developing an amnesty bill in 1999 demonstrated a singular lack of commitment to the idea, despite the overwhelming support for it expressed by people in northern Uganda themselves.

From a more strategic perspective, it can be argued that the Ugandan state may see benefits in sustaining a context of conflict which helps to justify the maintenance of a large military force for deployment in other regional theatres of war (most recently the DRC and South Sudan). From such a perspective, addressing the situation of northern Uganda is not a relevant consideration; indeed, the creation of a context that empowers military and disempowers civilians may be seen as strategically justified. The selective way in which discipline is applied to soldiers who engage in acts of violence against civilians suggests that playing on soldiers' sense of masculinity is used both to reward them and to control them.

Similarly, given a belief system that portrays the north as a threat to the south, the state may see a benefit in the creation of a disempowered male population that turns violence on itself rather than against the state, and in the maintenance of a context of violence that justifies military intervention and the strengthening of army control over the civilian population in the area.

MASCULINITY OR MASCULINITIES? DOES CONFLICT REINFORCE A HEGEMONIC/NORMATIVE MODEL?

The study of masculinities and their relationship to violence is important in a number of ways. First, it reflects a healthy concern not to reduce the equation between men and violence to simple biological determinism. Second, it aims to dispel the notion that there is only one way to be a 'real man'. The very notion that there are masculinities rather than a single masculinity acknowledges that there are potentially many ways 'to be a man'. Much of the literature has set out to prove this by demonstrating empirically the great diversity of lived experiences which cannot be described as conforming to hegemonic models of masculinity, and which suggest the reality of multiple masculinities. However, it should be clear by this point that lived experiences and lived expectations are two very different things.

The lived experiences of men in northern Uganda are very heterogeneous; whereas in a peace-time context it was possible for a majority of men to attain a reasonably close match between expectations and experiences, war sees an increasing heterogeneity of experiences and growing polarization between those who are able to attain the markers of masculinity and exercise the power which these bring, and those who are unable to fulfil expectations and are thus deeply disempowered. Some (most clearly the youth) have little power whether in the domestic or the political/public sphere; others exercise considerable power in the domestic sphere over their wives and children, but little power over other men; others (notably military) exercise power in all spheres and over both men and women.

Paradoxically, the increasing heterogeneity of experience goes hand in hand with a further homogenizing of expectations; while marriage and fatherhood, provision and protection become harder to achieve, they do not become less desirable as a result, in fact they become more desirable as they appear to provide anchors and points of leverage in the midst of the economic, social and political uncertainty created by war. The attainment of different components of the model creates a hierarchy among men – and a man's position in this hierarchy is not completely fixed. Although it has become ever more difficult to do this in a civilian context, and levels of domestic violence bear witness to this, it remains possible in principle to attain a full masculine identity, and social expectations are fully in support of this. Individuals subscribe to the model for economic and psychological survival reasons, and their family have a vested interest in ensuring that they do so for economic security reasons. Militarism provides a route for some, with full support from a state policy of increasing militarization and associated recruitment drives into both home guard and the army itself.

Under these circumstances the space for multiple masculinities largely collapses. The destruction of educational opportunities has removed one avenue for alternative forms of achievement, as has the destruction of an economic environment in which it is possible to become somebody through wealth. Attempts to promote alternative visions of how to resolve the situation are ridiculed both implicitly and at times explicitly: implicitly by policies of non-protective militarization, explicitly by the utterances of various key leadership figures. Even if people were able to pursue one or more of these alternative sources of identity, a national-level populist discourse which links key sources of identity (e.g. sexuality, nationality and being 'African') serves to restrict further the room for individual manoeuvre. For example, a Ugandan doctor who did not marry would have a difficult life, however brilliant he might be. Similarly, a politician. With this ever narrower horizon and fewer and fewer windows of opportunity, what people are left with as sources of identity and power is each other. The war has not led to the emergence of alternative masculinities, rather to the bolstering of a hegemonic model.

This model of masculinity is shown to be relational not just between men and women, but between men and men. While masculinity is articulated in terms of how it differs from femininity, between men it is lived as a zero-sum game that allows power differentials between them, notably between military and civilian men, to be established. Whereas women cannot be removed from the achievement of a masculine identity, the removal of other men is a key part of that process. The very sources of power for men contained in the prevalent model of masculinity are also the roots of their vulnerability, generating the possibility of any man being both a perpetrator and a victim of violence. It is therefore not surprising that the bundle of ideas which goes to make up masculinity exercises such a hold over men – sufficient to prompt many into acts of suicide when they find that they cannot succeed within the only sphere of influence which remains open to them, and to prompt others into acts which demonstrate their power relative to other men; rape, pillaging and so on.

This points to a critical issue in discussing the relationship between masculinity and violence. Although there appears to be a correlation between 'masculinity' and violence, the use of violence is probably better understood as a potential means to achieve an end, namely masculinity, rather than an integral component of that masculinity. While the hegemonic model of masculinity is a complex animal involving multiple roles and behaviours (and there are some paradoxes within this, such as the compatibility of beating your wife for stepping out of line and providing her with protection), there is relatively little within the model which explicitly encourages or celebrates the use of violence. Rather, there is a kind of loud silence on the issue.

Within the civilian population it is the thwarting of men's wish to achieve masculinity that appears to reduce them to acts of domestic violence; violence becomes the last resort of those who are unable to achieve 'masculinity'. Within the military on the other hand, the institutional framework and the removal of soldiers from more general social networks to an extent promotes the use of violence as an easy route to masculinity. Those in the military gain in domestic power as they are in a stronger position to provide economically and to protect militarily, and they enjoy military power and social status over other men at the same time. The resort to violence by the military can be seen as a conscious or subconscious strategy to exercise control over civilians which is effective in that it strengthens the perpetrator's masculinity through weakening that of the victim. That this vulnerability is deliberately targeted is clear from many descriptions of rape in war situations in which the husband or father is forced to watch a wife or daughter being raped. In other words, it is not merely the sexual act that is gratifying, but the capacity to humiliate another man at the same time. Furthermore, the perpetrators' individual aspirations to exercise power over others (for they, too, are by and large from deprived backgrounds) go hand in hand with the state's need for control over the population in general.

The normative model is thus shown to have considerable destructive power that can be manipulated by the state for purposes of social control and creating more space for political and military manoeuvre – and the nexus of 'masculinity', power, violence and conflict begins to come into focus. Within this nexus it is impossible to dissociate power relations between individual men from the power relationships existing between individual men and the state. The gap between individual psychology and state-level power plays is bridged.

IMPLICATIONS FOR INTERVENTIONS IN THE AREA OF MASCULINITIES

It is only in the last decade that gender 'experts' in development organizations have really attempted to view gender as a relational issue, let alone make tentative attempts to address issues of masculinity (Oxfam 1997: 2–7). For a whole raft of reasons there is resistance from both men and women to 'mainstreaming' men in gender debates (Chant and Gutmann 2000: 16–21). Despite the explicit recognition in some theories of the role of social power and authority structures in determining masculinities, the debate has been skewed towards discussion of the ways in which masculinities allow men to exercise power over women and away from the power they give men over other men – not surprisingly, given that both feminists and sexists stand to lose from an awareness of differentiation among men. This rather two-dimensional vision of masculinity as an inter-sex rather than intra-sex issue has hindered awareness of the many ways in which normative models of masculinity can be manipulated for political ends, particularly for sustaining contexts of conflict.

To the limited extent that present-day peace-building and peace education initiatives address the relationship between masculinities and violence, they reflect this lack of theoretical and empirical scrutiny, and fail to situate the link between masculinities and violence within a more complex nexus of masculinity, power, violence and conflict. The findings of this chapter suggest a number of key issues which need to be taken into account if that nexus is to be undone.

First, men's lived experiences are heterogeneous. Even if in a particular context they share a model of masculinity, there is a need to differentiate their personal positions by age, marital/social status, class and so on.

Second, the dominance of a single model of masculinity at the expense of multiple masculinities makes men more vulnerable to acts of violence against themselves and their families. As a UNESCO report suggests: 'Humiliation might not happen so easily if it were not for exaggerated ideas of masculine honour' (UNESCO 1997: 9). Promoting multiple models of masculinity along less sexist, heterosexist and adultist lines, would reduce the incentives for the use of violence by armed forces.

Third, this dominance can be taken as an indicator of a 'weak state', in several senses: a weak state lacks the political will and/or capacity to provide a context of security and protection of rights within which it would be less imperative to adhere to a normative model, and within which multiple masculinities could emerge. Also, a weak state will actively reinforce a model of masculinity as a political strategy in the absence of the mechanisms of legitimacy available to a stronger one.

Interventions to promote alternative masculinities must simultaneously address the role of the state in undermining these alternatives – in particular in failing to protect its own citizenry, failing to support non-military solutions to conflict, and linking masculinity to other questions of identity. The responsibility to protect is the basis of the political theories that inform current trends in 'democratization' and human rights; the state's right to the monopoly of violence derives from its capacity to protect all its citizens, not just in terms of immediate physical security, but also in terms of the ability to fulfil the non-violent expectations those citizens have been socialized into. Persistent state inaction in the face of assaults on its citizenry, and inability to create a climate in which people can live according to their own expectations, in principle disqualifies the state from enjoying that monopoly.

Fourth, hegemonic models of masculinity are manipulated by states, notably by linking masculinity with other key markers of identity such as ethnicity and race. Interventions to work with men to develop alternative masculinities should not only challenge sexist, adultist and heterosexist assumptions and stereotypes that underpin the model of masculinity for individuals, but also seek to break the connections with ethnicity and race that provide politicians with so much leverage over individuals and groups.

Fifth, the fact that conflict reinforces a hegemonic model of masculinity both confirms and contests the notion that war results in a 'crumbling social fabric'. It confirms it to the extent that as the possibility of alternative masculinities is reduced so the number of threads which go to make up the social fabric is also reduced. It contests it in the sense that some of the central threads of the social fabric are reinforced – at least as ideas if not in practice.

Finally, and linked to the previous point, the fact that conflict re-inforces a hegemonic model of masculinity goes a long way to explaining why the gains in women's emancipation, which some have attributed to the social space created by war situations, are largely illusory. Interventions that seek to capture this emancipation are therefore flying in the face of the overall dynamic of post-conflict reconstruction. If anything, given that the coming of peace will be associated with opportunities for civilian men to reclaim their masculinity, we should not be surprised to find ostensibly empowered women pushed back into the kitchen within a very short period. Interventions that hope to secure women's emancipation must also ensure that men have alternative sources of domestic and political power and credibility beyond a position as husband and father.

NOTES

1. Fieldwork was conducted by ACORD over the period May 1998 to January 2000 for DFID as part of COPE (Consortium for Political Emergencies). The examples given in this chapter are drawn largely from fieldworkers' written reports and my personal observations over that period, and from the proceedings of a planning workshop conducted with ACORD staff and fieldworkers in April 2000 which began with a participatory analysis of social exclusion in northern Uganda. This is 'the workshop' referred to in the text (ACORD 2000). All names have been changed.

2. The workshop itself was male dominated, with nineteen male and five female participants – so what is presented here can be said with some confidence to reflect what men have been told about women.

3. This chapter does not attempt to explore the historical development of this dominant model, though it is clear that it has been influenced heavily by Christianity, and more recently by elements drawn from the women's movement. For a discussion of how western ideals of masculinity 'have been exported through colonialism to mingle with local notions of masculinity' (Oxfam 1997: 4), see Cornwall and Lindisfarne (1994)

4. While it is the case that the majority of those forcibly abducted into the ranks of the LRA are Acholi, it is not clear that the entire leadership are Acholi, nor that they perceive themselves as an Acholi movement.

5. Abduction of children is a feature of this war that has been frequently commented on, though generally to emphasize the evil nature of the LRA rather than to highlight the state's failure to provide adequate protection from them. Unicef suggest about 50 per cent of abductions are of children; at least 8,000 children have been abducted, and only a small proportion have so far been returned to date.

6. An argument behind the frequent assertion that homophobic men are often those who are least secure in their own sexuality and fear the ridicule of being exposed as inadequate.

7. It is common practice for the parents of a girl who falls pregnant while still at school to demand compensation from the father of the child on the argument that she will have to stop or at least interrupt her schooling to have the child, thereby causing them a loss of their financial investment in her education.

8. A sharp instrument commonly used for cutting trees.

9. An argument also made by Large (1997).

10. The term 'victim' here is used in the sense adopted by the South African Truth and Reconciliation Commission, namely to include relatives and dependants of victims of direct abuse and violence (Goldblatt and Meintjes, 1998: 34). Whereas

the TRC used it to ensure that women and children were given full consideration, I am using it to ensure that men are given full consideration as psychological victims. Surely the argument that 'it is difficult to separate the psychological pain of a mother whose child has been tortured from that child's physical and psychological pain' (ibid.) holds true for men who witness atrocities being perpetrated against their wives and children?

11. It is difficult to give a literal translation, but essentially means to rape someone while they are bending over.

12. See, for example, the examples and discussions about the use of rape in Mozambique, Rwanda, Chad, Liberia and elsewhere in Turshen and Twagiramariya (1998).

REFERENCES

ACORD (2000) *Northern Uganda Planning Workshop Report*, Gulu, Uganda, 25 April–3 May 2000.

Chant, S. and M. Gutmann (2000) *Mainstreaming Men into Gender and Development: Debates, Reflections and Experiences*, Oxfam Working Paper (Oxford: Oxfam).

Connell, R. W. (1995) *Masculinities* (Cambridge; Polity Press).

Cornwall, A. and N. Lindisfarne (1994) 'Dislocating Masculinity: Gender, Power and Anthropology', in A. Cornwall and N. Lindisfarne (eds), *Dislocating Masculinities: Comparative Ethnographies* (London: Routledge).

Dolan, C. (2000) *What Do You Remember? A Rough Guide to the War in Northern Uganda, 1986 2000*, COPE Working Paper, 33.

Dolan, C. and J. Schaeffer (1997) *The Reintegration of Ex-combatants in Mozambique*, Refugee Studies Programme, Unpublished report for USAID, University of Oxford.

Foreman, M. (ed.) (1999) *Aids and Men* (London: PANOS/Zed Books).

Goldblatt, B. and S. Meintjes (1998) 'South African Women Demand the Truth', in M. Turshen and C. Twagiramariya (eds), *What Women Do in Wartime* (London: Zed Books), pp. 33–61.

IRIN (2001) Integrated Information Network, www.irinnews.org

Kabeer, N. (1994) *Reversed Realities: Gender Hierarchies in Development Thought* (London and New York: Verso).

Large, J. (1997) 'Disintegration Conflicts and the Restructuring of Masculinity', *Gender & Development*, 5(2).

Moore, H. (1994) *A Passion for Difference* (Cambridge: Polity Press).

Oxfam (1997) 'Men and Masculinity', *Gender and Development*, 5(2).

Prunier, G. (1995) *The Rwanda Crisis, 1959–1994: History of a Genocide*, London: Hurst and Company.

Turshen, M. and C. Twagiramariya (1998) *What Women Do in Wartime* (London: Zed Books).

UNESCO (1997) *Male Roles and Masculinities in the Perspective of a Culture of Peace*, Report of Expert Group Meeting, Oslo, Norway, 24–28 September 1997.

CHAPTER 4

Lenin, the *Pinguero*, and Cuban Imaginings of Maleness in Times of Scarcity

DAVID FORREST

> We must remember that while not all men are rapists, all men are
> potential rapists. (Paper given at a recent conference on men in dev-
> elopment)
>
> The emotions are stirred more quickly than man's intelligence ... it
> is much more easy to have sympathy with suffering than it is to have
> sympathy with thought. (Oscar Wilde, 'The Soul of Man under
> Socialism')

§ Within development discourse, the practitioners and theorists who
put 'Women in Development' (WID) on to the agenda later conceded
that, in effect, what had happened had been the creation of an 'add
women and stir' approach. Its successor – 'Gender and Development'
(GAD) – was supposed to have created a much more holistic framework, the ingredients – relationships between women, men and children
– being more vigorously theorized, examined and inter-related. Yet,
many of the very same practitioners and theorists who buried WID and
nursed GAD to prominence are now showing signs of turning MAD –
towards 'Men and Development'. Alarmed and dismayed at the lack of
attention paid to men as a specific 'group' within development theory
and practice, 'men' or 'masculinities' are due to be dusted down and set
to become the latest recognized group on to which development practice
and theorizing will focus. In this chapter I neither seek to welcome nor
to criticize this new-found focus on men and masculinity per se. Instead,
using data collected during research undertaken in the Republic of Cuba
from September 1996 to September 1997, I wish to illustrate, in some
modest capacity, the potential difficulties in bringing *all* gendered cat-

egories to the fore in our attempts to understand the dynamics of 'social inequality' and the processes of 'empowerment', the implications of which for development practice and theory are somewhat disturbing.

The first part of this chapter looks at some of the generic practical and theoretical problems associated with concepts such as 'masculinity' and 'gender', not least the neglect in many accounts of the social structures and processes within which *all* personal and social relations take place. I then look at the positioning of Cuban men in the complex web of political, economic and social relations, from the personal level through to the national and international sphere, turning first towards the sociocultural contexts based around race, sex and sexuality, and then towards the broader material and political contexts – Cuba's 'planned' economy and the Marxist–Leninist ideology. Neglecting these broader structures and processes, I argue, can only impoverish both our understanding of what I call *imaginings of maleness* – what an individual (male or female) *considers* to be important in defining what it means to be male, and our prescriptions for social change. The rest of the chapter then looks at imaginings of maleness within the phenomenon known locally as *jineterismo* – the largely informal, sexual and non-sexual, relationships contemporary Cuban men and women forge with foreign visitors and residents.

MASCULINITIES AND MEN: PROBLEMS OR PROBLEMATIC CONCEPTS?

It seems that masculinity has become a term into which we can throw almost any form of behaviour, thought or utterance that we don't like.[1] As Cornwall and Lindisfarne point out, 'images, attributions and metaphors of masculinised power are so pervasive that they are frequently used to signify power in settings in which they have little or nothing to do with men at all' (Cornwall and Lindisfarne 1995: 148). For example, in Ian Lumsden's comprehensive account of Cuban homosexuality we are told that the Cuban leader – Fidel Castro, 'whatever his affirmations to the contrary – exalts in his unquestioned role as the *caudillo*, the *Comandante en Jefe*, [and is] in short the epitome of *machismo* [roughly translated as male chauvinism]' (Lumsden 1996: 129). We probably ought to consider this statement as simple political critique. However, on closer inspection, statements such as these raise a number of awkward questions: not whether Castro is a *machista* (male chauvinist), but about the relationship between a political or official position (commander-in-chief, president or *caudillo*) and a negative term (for the most part) like *machismo*. In many senses it runs contrary to Weber's sober assertion that under modern industrial capitalism (and we ought to include socialism here) we have the rule of offices, not men, and, crucially, it obscures the very social relations that create such offices and structures. Instead, we are asked to shift our focus onto ill-defined gendered categories.

To illustrate this tendency further, here is an extract from a 1986 Cuban educational text and Lumsden's response: the passage he quotes states that 'the principal characteristic of the new man is his great optimism and confidence in his creative possibilities, without fear of what is entailed' (Lumsden 1996: 119). He retorts by adding that this *'glorification of traditional masculine values* suggests that Cuba's leadership has remained impervious to the way in which *machismo* has been challenged by the women's movement in modern countries since Che Guevara first popularised the notion of the "new man" in the mid-1960s' (emphasis added). In juxtaposing 'glorification' and 'masculine values' alongside *machismo*, Lumsden again forces us to inquire after the supposed *nature* and *origins* of 'masculine values', clumsily periodized here as 'traditional', and ask why 'great optimism and confidence in ... creative possibilities' is necessarily bad.

In his polemical work *The End of Masculinity*, MacInnes mentions how 'aspects of modernity which have no intrinsic connection to sex, such as the logic of instrumentalism or the monopolisation of the means of violence by the state, come to appear as a product of masculinity' (MacInnes 1998: 57; see also Forrest 1999). Patricia Hill Collins, for example, talks of models of oppression that are 'firmly rooted in the either/or dichotomous thinking or Eurocentric, *masculinist* thought' (Collins 1990: 225) (emphasis added). MacInnes, however, contextualizes and problematizes this type of approach, looking instead at how supposed flaws (such as violence and hatred) are now treated as deficiencies of the masculine gender: 'What were once claimed as manly virtues (heroism, independence, courage, strength, rationality, will, backbone, virility) have now become manly vices (abuse, destructive aggression, coldness, emotional inarticulacy, detachment, isolation, an inability to be flexible, to communicate, to empathise, to be soft, supportive or life-affirming)' (MacInnes 1998: 47).

The main problem appears to lie with the sex–gender dichotomy. 'Masculinity' is a gendered concept and, as MacInnes states, gender ideology was born in an Enlightenment crisis in which the spiritual-based 'natural order of things' was fast collapsing within a none the less stubbornly inegalitarian world. Gender, he suggests, was used to defend sexual inequalities, not overcome them; in other words, gender identity 'drew upon the suppression of natural similarities' (Rubin 1975: 179). The separation of sex and gender has, he claims, perplexed us ever since:

> The concept of gender thus implied [is] ... able to hold two diametrically opposed beliefs at once: that masculinity (and its counterpart femininity) was socially constructed (and thus in theory constructible by members of either sex) and that it was naturally determined (so that there was a special connection between masculinity and being male). Without both sides of the paradox the concept of masculinity does not work. Without the first masculinity collapses back into maleness, without the second it loses all connection to sex at all. (MacInnes 1998: 25)

This paradox, he asserts, 'is routinely expressed in the way most uses of the term casually and un-self-consciously slip between discussion of "masculinity" and analysis of empirically existing men'.

There are a number of practical and theoretical problems in simply treating 'sex' as 'empirically existing', as Cornwall and Lindisfarne (1994), Butler (1990) and others have shown. Nevertheless, since my purpose is to critique existing practices, rather than to offer definitions, MacInnes's observations are useful in exposing some of the pitfalls of social constructionism. Authors such as Connell (1995) may have attempted to add dynamism to gendered categories by referring to 'layering', 'gendering', and 'doing masculinities', but ultimately they raise the same sorts of questions; they fail to clarify either the component parts of gender/masculinity or the relationship between sex and gender. The problem again seems to be that 'Notions of maleness, designations of manhood and attributions of masculinity have no essential referent, nor even a finite range of referents' (Cornwall and Lindisfarne 1994: 10).

This need not overturn more useful cultural constructionist interpretations. Indeed, many Foucauldian-inspired poststructuralist critiques have questioned the unity of a number of taken-for-granted concepts and categories, not least our tendencies to essentialize dichotomies.

These critiques have gone hand in hand with a more radical deconstruction of the very notion of a 'unitary subject', and we are asked instead to focus on 'subject positions' or 'positionality', whereby the focus shifts on to what a certain individual imagines, claims or practises (or, more accurately, on the interpretation of such thought and action) *under specific circumstances* (Forrest 1999). Hence, John MacInnes is able to assert that we can never *fix* what we are, 'but only *imagine* ourselves to inhabit any number of socially produced identities' (MacInnes 1998: 127).

It is nonsense to think that maleness can be imagined as anything other than a number of subject positions. There is a wealth of recent literature covering this complexity of the person or individual: Hollway and Moore's notion of *intersubjectivity* (Moore 1994), Marriott's notion of the *dividual* (Strathern 1988; Cornwall and Lindisfarne 1994), de Lauretis's Lacanian notion of the *I* understood as 'a complicated field of competing subjectivities and competing identities' (cited in Moore 1994), Alcoff's (1997) *positionality*, as well as MacInnes's (1998) and Butler's (1990; 1997) critiques of gender and identity. As Moore puts it, 'individuals ("dividuals") are multiply constituted subjects, and they can, and do, take up multiple subject positions within a wide range of discourses and social practices. Some of these subject positions will be contradictory and will conflict with each other' (Moore 1994: 55).

However, while we must celebrate poststructuralist accounts for their anti-essentialist shift, if this celebration of difference and complexity goes hand in hand with what Nancy Fraser (1997) calls the 'postsocialist' abandonment of the 'politics of redistribution', then we have simply thrown out the baby with the bath water. Like Gross and Levitt's (1998) withering attack on fashionable postmodern feminist critiques of the physical sciences, Fraser tries to show that if feminists wish to maintain adherence to the project of eradicating social inequalities there can be no similar fashionable elaboration of categories or differences or even complexities 'in abstraction from social relations and social structures, including political economy' (Fraser 1997: 186). If we are to take heed of Fraser's call then perhaps we ought to start any analysis of maleness by paraphrasing Marx on his analysis of the negro as slave: 'What is a man? A male of the species. The one explanation is as good as the other. A man is a man. He only becomes a worker, a husband, a soldier, a playboy, a prostitute, or a human mechanical producer in certain relations. Torn from these relationships, he is no more the oppressor of women or other men than gold in itself is money.' We can say that if one 'is' a Cuban man, then that is not all one is; 'the term fails to be exhaustive' (Butler 1997: 158). Men, and *imaginings of maleness*, therefore, must be considered within a multiplicity of social relations (class, racial, inter-national) and structures (the state, the market) within which men and women live out their everyday lives. It is to these contexts that I now turn.

CULTURE, CLASS, RACE AND THE 'MARKETING' CUBAN *FOGOSIDAD*

In a newspaper article about the (hetero) sexual habits and imaginings of young Cubans, the author noted that 'when one enquires as to how they [the Cubans questioned] characterise themselves sexually, the definitions are mainly positive ... almost half of the interviewees stated that we are included among the most passionate [*fogosos*] and sensual in the world ... only 0.4 per cent placed their country below [average] ... Thirty per cent even said that we are "beyond comparison".'[2] The article also stated that Cubans often imagine (wrongly, it asserts) that 'the colour of the skin determines the *fogosidad* [the level of passion] of people, [and that] this passion diminishes as we go from the eastern [where there are proportionately more darker-skinned people] to the western end of the island'. The article seemed to imply that Cubans often 'talked up' racial and sexual stereotypes; as one local man uttered in response to this article, 'Cubans aren't necessarily great at sex; they are just good at convincing others that they are – they are good at bullshitting.'

This racialized sexual chauvinism is in no small part integral to local imaginings of both Cubanness and maleness: of how Cubans – black, white and mixed race – imagine themselves in relation to others. I will return to this shortly. Importantly for the purposes of this argument is to look at how the 'material' and the 'socio-cultural' become manifest in imaginings of Cubanness in general, both *within* and from *outside* of Cuba. To some extent, the figure of *el bicho* is perhaps an ideal way in which to look at these imaginings. Roughly translated here as 'the cunning and devious creature', *el bicho* appeared to be imagined more as male than female in that he had characteristics traditionally associated with the male psyche, in particular a more 'scientific', 'logical' and 'rational' approach to problem-solving. He was audacious (some might say rude), cunning and willing to 'have a go', and not afraid to look silly (since to do otherwise would prevent him from being audacious). Importantly, he was often imagined by black and white Cubans as *un negro* (black), primarily for the reason that *los negros* were assumed to be poorer with fewer resources, but also due to the lower level of education attributed to, though not altogether accurately so, *los negros*. Often this would be phrased in terms of someone *de baja nivel* (of a lower level or class). Moreover, according to some, *el bicho* in this instance was as much a product of *una sistema soviética* (a Soviet system) as he was of any 'race' or imagined innate 'Cubanness'. In other words, he was a product of the lack of basic resources needed to accomplish a specific task. I will return to this later.

This intersection of race and class is perhaps best examined using Peter Wade's notion of 'blackness'. He notes, 'what makes an act typical of blackness is that it is evidence of motivation by self-interest rather than by the socially approved norms. It is an act more typical of an animal than a human, of those closer to nature than those closer to culture' (Wade 1995: 67). In Cuba people often referred to this as acting without shame – *sin vergüenza*. Moreover, as with Wade's notion of 'blackness', *las cosas de negros* (the things black people do) may be attributed to white and black alike. In the Cuban context we might be better off using a term like *orientalismo* (borrowed from Edward Said's 'Orientalism'). Drawing upon internal views of a backward eastern part of the island, traditionally referred to by its old provincial name of *Oriente, orientalismo* here might refer to *tendencies* among many Cubans, young and old, to categorize their fellow citizens in a hierarchical manner, and along flexible racial lines.

In many senses *orientalismo* is a product of the contradictions lying at the very heart of the Cuban economic and political system, and, like 'blackness', it has very little to do with race, even though it would be difficult to consider these sorts of imaginings outside a racialized context. From the very earliest days of the Revolution, anti-bourgeois discourses combining familiarity and fraternity with a deep suspicion of people who maintained or cultivated *un estilo refinido* (a refined manner) to some extent 'liberated' many poorly educated peasants and unskilled workers from rather rigid, bourgeois rules governing behaviour. However, as many older Cubans now bemoan, there is a fine line between fraternal familiarity and rudeness, lack of education or anti-social behaviour. Few, though, would also dispute the fact that the present economic crisis (see below) has created a greater level of frustration and anxiety among and between ordinary Cubans as they go about their complicated daily tasks.

Orientalismo again might be a useful concept through which we can approach Cuban sexuality, especially when looking at those Cuban–foreigner relationships falling within the sphere of *jineterismo*, which I will return to later. There is much to be said about the intricacies of local sexualities, but for the purposes of brevity it is perhaps useful to consider two specific aspects of localized imaginings of Cuban (hetero) sexuality in some depth. The first, alluded to earlier in our references to *fogosidad*, concerns notions of *virilidad* (virility). A great many *orientalista* imaginings of maleness emanating from the Havana youth told of men's innate desires and sexual 'needs', the ferocity of which forced some men in the more 'backward' *Oriente* to expand their range of sexual 'targets' to include other men and animals should there be a lack of women to hand (see Forrest 1999). The character of the *bugarrón* was one such figure of *orientalista* imaginings; a man whose sexual appetite compelled him to have penetrative sex with other men providing, in the public eye at least, he was doing the penetrating. Many younger nominally homosexual Cubans, however, saw this less as insatiable hyper-sexuality and more as either bisexuality or latent homosexuality. Interestingly, many historicized this phenomenon, and saw such a character as a residual cultural phenomenon from a more intellectually and materially impoverished past; in other words, he was a distinctly *orientalista* imagining.

The second point here concerns racialized notions of sexuality, again alluded to earlier. While many authors have noted how, in spite of the eradication of the worst excesses of structural and class-bound racism at the time of the Revolution, many black men and women continue to desire white men and women for partners so that their children will be *adelantado* (advanced) (see McGarrity 1992: 193). For white and black men, it is easy to hear of distinctions still being made, for instance, between *una negra para singar* (the black woman who is good to fuck) or *una negro para salir* (the black woman who is good to go out with on a longer-term basis). I would agree with Fox (1973: 278) that there is little difference in a sexual morality based around 'race'. It may be that white Cubans and some black Cubans, under certain circumstances, impute to other darker-skinned Cubans a moral code which they perceive to be the mirror-image of their own simply because it helps them to define more clearly their own imagined morality. Nevertheless, we also have to recognize that many black Cubans, male and female, also play on these stereotypes.

When we look at these internal imaginings around sexuality in the context of tourism and material needs, we find many young Cubans, black and white, male and female, actively reworking racialized notions of the romantic and passionate Latin lover fused with the rampant African Caribbean virility and hypersexuality. Fed, as we shall see, by their need to attract foreigners, many young Cubans of all colours lay claim, notably in the presence of foreigners, to attributes that might otherwise be culturally undervalued and assigned only to a particular race. *Virilidad* (virility) and *sin vergüenza* (shamelessness) were reworked and negotiated by many so that the imagined attributes/devilishness of the *negra* and *negro* become in certain instances the valued heritage of Cubans of all skin colours. It is this generalized image, I was told, that draws many male and female Western tourists in Cuba into sexual relationships with young Cubans: images and tales of sexiness, lack of restraint, and, in certain instances, low prices from those 'selling sex' are well known by many male and female visitors to the island. The fact that a greater proportion of the more visible sellers of sex and hustlers were darker skinned could be attributed, as some locals pointed out, to the fact that many of the male and female sex-tourists from Europe tended to go for the more 'exotic' native (in other words, darker-skinned Cubans), drawing on pre-existing cultural and racialized notions of sexuality. However, in order to understand more fully the ways in which men and women, black and white, become involved in sex tourism, and how maleness becomes imagined under such circumstances, we must have a greater understanding of some of the material and ideological circumstances under which they labour.

STATE SOCIALISM, ENDEMIC SHORTAGES AND THE INTERNATIONAL DIVISION OF LABOUR

While there has been a copious amount of literature examining the changing position of women and women's labour in Cuban society

(Casal 1987; Dominguez 1987; Martínez-Alier 1989; Pérez-Stable 1987; Rosenthal 1992; Smith 1992; Stone 1981; and Stubbs 1987; 1993; 1994), there have been few attempts that look at the changing position of men. Nevertheless, the few which have been attempted have offered valuable insights into the ways in which the Revolution has affected the lives of men: of men and women's imaginings of maleness (Fox 1972; 1973; Lewis et al. 1977; Forrest 1999). Oscar Lewis's vivid, posthumously published account of four Cuban men talking about their pre- and post-revolutionary lives is an excellent account of a group of men coming to terms with momentous changes in their personal and public lives, the dislocations, and competing material and cultural influences within which they battle to make sense of their lives as men and as Cubans (Lewis et al. 1977). Moreover, the account shows how these largely working-class, heterosexual (I assume) men, both *negro* (black) and *blanco* (white), were attempting to come to terms both with their position within an increasingly professionalized workforce, and in their relations with women at a time when the latter were being encouraged by the state to assert their position in the public domain.

For Oscar Lewis's four men, changes in the social positioning of women were hugely important in how men imagined themselves as men. For many, as Fox (1973) observed, the creation of secure employment meant that for the first time the vast majority of Cuban men were able to realize their patriarchal aspirations of becoming the family 'bread-winner', a position previously available only to the urban bourgeoisie and rural landowners. Yet, in seeking to raise the public status of women through public works and formalized wage labour, the state simul-taneously denied many of these men the opportunity to enact this position. Nevertheless, important inroads were made towards forging greater equality between the sexes, and this has been well documented (see above).

By the 1990s, however, many commentators – Cuban policy-makers, critics and ordinary citizens alike – were still insisting that sexual equal-ity remained a long way off. Ultimately, it appeared as though the revolutionary Cuban state had failed to eradicate hierarchical sexual differences. The problem remained as to within which domain the battle was to be fought. Whereas in the earlier decades of the Revolution the ideological and material drives were thought sufficient to increase women's participation in the public domain through waged work, political activities and so on, the focus by the 1990s had shifted on to the failure of men (and some women) to change and to keep up with this vanguard action. For many, *machismo* remained as a stubborn leftover from an inglorious past, in spite of attempts by the state to overcome the material and political factors assumed to underpin such chauvinism. Importantly, and equally problematic, many Cuban women were insistent on pointing to fellow women as the greater perpetrators of *machismo*; towards female *machistas* (chauvinists) who encouraged their sons, husbands and brothers to engage in many of the non-violent (but also sometimes violent), ultimately discriminatory acts of chauvinism or *machismo* (against other men and women). Similarly, many more educated Cubans were apt to point out that women were still far more likely to dabble in *brujería* (witchcraft) and *santería* (the West-African-originated religion based on a fusion of localized African religions and Spanish Catholicism), and so on. For the state, its critics, and many left-wing and feminist commentators, then, a socialist political and economic system had been insufficient in attempts to overturn the so-called 'cultural' aspects of sexual inequality.

In some restricted sense these sorts of 'culturalist' arguments are useful if we are to avoid crude universalist or materialist assumptions. Yet, if we cast more than just a cursory glance at the broader material and political conditions under which *machismo* is said to have stubbornly maintained its presence, the 'culturalist' argument is found wanting. First, from the outset the Cuban revolutionary state has offered its citizens a profoundly ambivalent sexual ideology which I have chosen to call the 'ideology of complementary equality': the idea that women are equal to men, but profoundly different in nature (in other words, they complement one another). The symbol of the women's federation (FMC), a female soldier in uniform with a rifle slung over one shoulder while holding a baby, is just one poignant example, illustrating strength and heroism while also reinforcing the view in the popular imagination of women as mothers and carers. As Molyneux points out, referring to socialist states in general, 'despite the Communist Manifesto's call for the abolition of the bourgeois family, and the association, in the eyes of its enemies, of communism with anti-family policies, the family is regarded [by the state] as an institution of vital importance' (Molyneux 1985: 47). In Füredi's (1986) materialist critique of the former Soviet Union we are told that this importance of 'the family' lay squarely in the failure of government attempts to socialize labour and raise productive levels in all areas of the economy.

Although not so burdened by such atavistic sexual morality as in the former Soviet Union, Cuba has none the less been subject to the very same material forces evident in most past and present socialist states. The twists and turns of the Cuban Revolution are too numerous to mention here, but it is worthwhile to set out a more general material context in which studies like those of Lewis and my own some three decades later take place (see Eckstein 1994 for a comprehensive overview). Suffice it to say, after forty-two years in existence, socialist Cuba gained (and has to some extent lost) a respected health and education system, full employment for those many men who had known only precarious seasonal agricultural labour and insecure capitalist wage labour, certain welfare provisions, aspects of local participatory democracy, greater equality between the 'races' and sexes, and greater sharing of the country's wealth among its citizens.

However, with the USA cutting off all diplomatic ties and imposing a trade embargo in the early 1960s (the severity of which has steadily increased over recent years), Cuba became increasingly economically dependent upon the USSR and its allies. In 1968 the 'Revolutionary Offensive' had nationalized all small businesses, and the market ceased to operate, replaced instead by what has been described as a rather chaotic system of priority allocation. It was a system not too dissimilar to that which operated in the USSR and Eastern Europe up to the late 1980s, which allowed some sectors of the economy to thrive while others languished (see Füredi 1986). Sugar remained the country's chief export, and the socialist regime was unable to raise the island's productive forces sufficiently to develop and diversify its economy accordingly. From time to time the regime variously used moral and material incentives to entice and coerce workers within the production process (see Gonzalez 1974; Eckstein 1994; Kapcia 1989; 1992), but productivity and industrial development remained poor.

In common with the then existing socialist states, consumer goods remained chronically scarce and of poor quality (much of it imported from the Soviet Union and Eastern Europe), wages remained low, the black market thrived, and there was a distinct lack of long-term healthcare and support for the elderly or disabled (which inevitably fell on women). The cultural and literary spheres became, and remain, dominated by the Communist Party, with debate being encouraged only within the strict parameters set by the Party. For many of the educated urban young, inadequate (in both numbers and quality) housing, lack of freedom of movement internally and externally, increasing awareness of the economic and social problems experienced by the country's main economic and political sponsors in Eastern Europe, and a lack of toleration for a vibrant and independent youth culture all added to the general disquiet over the Revolution's present and future direction well before the abrupt economic collapse in the early 1990s, which I will return to shortly.

COLLAPSE, SOCIAL SHIFTS AND THE RISE OF TOURISM

In 1990, with the impending collapse of the USSR, 'The Special Period in Peacetime' was announced and austerity measures introduced. Since then (and, some would argue, well before this date) the state has been withering away, although not under the circumstances envisaged by Marx. What has ensued, to borrow from Trotsky, has been 'a struggle of each against all'. The state had tried, with some success, to build on popular support against the USA's increasingly punitive measures by mobilizing the population during its push to mechanize agriculture, eradicate the diseases associated mostly with poverty, and to educate its youthful population. However, by the mid-1990s nobody, not even the state, was pretending to be building socialism. Instead, it was a simple question of economic survival by a rather impotent state unwilling (and to some degree unable) to acquiesce to US and global demands to overhaul its political and economic system; in effect, to dismantle the whole state socialist apparatus.

Nevertheless, the state had started to loosen its control over cultural practices in the fields of art, theatre, music and film. Homosexuality became increasingly tolerated, the US dollar was legalized, and stores previously open only to diplomats and the Party elite were now open to all those with dollars to spend. The introduction of self-employment for non-professionals (*cuentapropismo*) created new opportunities for petty commodity production, and a huge grey area in which legitimate (under Cuban law) activities merged with black market deals (illegal activities). In Havana, ordinary Cubans mingled relatively freely with foreign diplomats, tourists and other western residents.

There was, of course, a flip-side to these new-found freedoms. Leisure facilities previously geared to ordinary Cubans were now allocated exclusively to the tourist sector. A simultaneous growth in the material and social aspirations of the youth, fuelled by the presence of affluent tourists, lay in stark contrast to a state unable to meet those aspirations. A correlative dollarization of the local economy was fostering a growth of social inequality based upon the possession of US dollars rather than, as had previously been the case, sex, race and regional differences. Moreover, Havana and the mushrooming tourist resorts saw a huge rise in prostitution, black market activities and small-scale begging. Such was the desire by many to leave the country that tens of thousands risked their lives during the massive seaborne exodus in 1994 known as the *balseros* crisis. Thousands are estimated to have perished. Most of those who remained were forced to supplement their meagre state income and rations by searching for ways of obtaining hard currency (for the purchase and repair of basic consumer goods such as household domestic appliances, and even for food, clothing, and, in more extreme cases, shelter). As O'Connell-Davidson notes, 'for a large number of Cubans ... the pursuit of dollars has become a far more meaningful economic activity than that which takes place in formal work settings' (O'Connell-Davidson 1996: 40).

Fully aware and acknowledging these failures, and no doubt aware of its lack of control over taxable, hard currency private revenue, the country's state and Party-run newspapers and journals were replete with articles appealing for restraint, patience, patriotic duty. Titles included 'Between the shop and the soul', or 'The matter is to choose between money and ethical behaviour', or 'To have or not to have: is that the question?' Readers were presented with the argument that self-respect and dignity, happiness and virtue, and so on, are all contrary to the spirit of acquiring material goods: 'there is no poverty sadder than the poverty of the spirit, and the exhibiting of a lack of moderation', as one contributor put it. The discussions, many of which were very open and frank, ran alongside a plethora of radio and TV programmes, and were prompted by a state concerned, for a number of reasons, with the rise of prostitution and the more loosely defined *jineterismo*. In the imagination of many Cubans, *jineterismo* had become by the mid-1990s an activity symbolizing the current plight of the country in general.

For the purposes of this argument, what is unique about the Special

Period is that the traditional domestic route to some degree of material security through domestic networking, or *sociolismo* as it has often been called (roughly translated as 'buddy socialism'),[3] has become much less attractive as many professionals and state officials found themselves more impoverished than unskilled manual workers (most professionals and ordinary Party members are prevented or strongly discouraged from profiting in the new, albeit restricted, domestic free market). So, whereas in the past some Cubans might have been drawn to well-connected fellow citizens such as particularly highly placed professionals or government officials, or ex-socialist-bloc visitors and residents (usually devoid of *substantial* hard currency purchasing power themselves), they might now be focusing their attention on western tourists.

A good example of the current predicament many Cuban men have found themselves in is to be found in the script of the popular Cuban play called *Marketing*, which ran in Havana in early 1996. Here the audience is introduced to two former high-school contemporaries – Juan and Javier – who are becoming reacquainted after their chance meeting. As their reacquaintance gathers pace they are joined by a third school friend called Pedro, who we discover washes cars for a living (probably an illegal but tolerated activity). After some time Javier offers Juan, currently a qualified engineer working at a screw production factory, a new job in his hotel helping with the *camión del sancocho* (refuse truck). Pedro hears this, and congratulates Juan by saying wistfully, *'Camión de turismo, que clase de suerte!'* ('A tourist truck! What luck!') Javier corrects him – *'Sancocho'* – but Pedro reiterates, *'Turismo'*.

For Juan and Pedro, work in the tourist industry, however lowly, is better than the jobs they are currently doing or have been trained to do. Flushed with excitement, Juan asks Javier if there is also a job to be found for Pedro, but he does so in a tone very different from the relaxed and informal manner in which he had been conversing. He initially addresses Javier as *compañero* (comrade) Molina (Molina being Javier's surname), but then quickly changes this to *señor* Molina.

Judging from the laughter around me, the bitter irony of this dialogue was immediately evident to the audience. The short scene and dialogue raised a number of important issues. First, we are faced with the recognition of new social hierarchies at the local level. Having first used the term *compañero* as one would have done in the recent past, drawing upon the notion of egalitarian comradeship, Juan quickly realizes that under the present circumstances it would be more appropriate to use the form of address *señor*; considered in revolutionary Cuba as a bourgeois manifestation of inequality, associated with hierarchical rather than egalitarian forms of respect. Javier, though, has assumed the prestigious position of the manager of a state enterprise. It is a position which takes him into the world of international tourism where *señor* is still the common form of address in Spanish, and it causes Juan to change his tone to that which he thinks is more appropriate to the 'new Cuba'.

Secondly, we learn that the modern industrial division of labour, which awards prestige and status to professionals such as Juan, has to some extent been turned on its head; Juan is ecstatic at being offered a job dealing with the waste disposal truck for the simple reason that it is connected, however tenuously, with the tourist industry – a growth industry. It is an industry that has achieved an almost mythical status in many areas of the local popular imagination as a place where Cubans can, to some extent, solve some of their immediate and long-term financial and material needs, and perhaps even fulfil ambitions for foreign travel or emigration. It is an arena, moreover, that many young Cuban men and women enter into on an informal basis, via sexual relationships or simple friendships with foreigners, and outside the realm of formal employment within tourism.

JINETERISMO AND THE NEW GUIDES OF THE INTERNATIONAL PROLETARIAT

This brings me to an earlier scene in *Marketing*. Prior to the arrival of Pedro and Javier, Juan has been alone on the Malecón, staring out across the horizon, with the song *'Se fue'* ('She's gone') by Pablo Milanés playing in the background. He is interrupted by the arrival of Javier, who discovers that Juan's girlfriend has recently left him for somebody else. As Javier tries to encourage Juan not to lose heart, we learn that the woman had become involved in the tourist industry, albeit in a rather different capacity to Javier.

Whether called *amiguita del turismo* (friend of the tourist industry), *montadora de caballos* (horse rider), *guía de turismo* (tourist guide), or more commonly *jinetera/o* (literally, a woman or man who rides horseback), we are introduced to one of the few routes ordinary Cubans have to relative prosperity or even to make ends meet: to make friends, whether on an intimate level or not, with a foreigner. Juan's girlfriend went off with an Italian. The fact that he is a manual 'worker' or 'labourer', as opposed to a professional, might be said to reflect her poor taste or her weak position, in that Cuba values its professionals very highly. However, because *this* worker is Italian suddenly elevates his status beyond that of a Cuban professional (such as Juan). In addition, when Javier euphemistically calls her *montadora de caballos italianos*, Juan's seemingly unconnected point – that he also knows of a fair-haired Cuban woman who went off with a Haitian man – reflects the depth of this sense of reversal of fortunes (Haiti being perceived in *orientalista* imaginings as the country at the bottom of the international pecking order, its inhabitants being desperately poor, 'black' and 'primitive').

Both the dialogue and the audience reaction suggested that many Cubans interpret Cuba's changing position within the post-Soviet world as the start of a new internationalism, whereby internationalism loses its proletarian and mutual assistance connotations, and instead comes to mean that the country's people (in this example its womenfolk) are sold or sell themselves to foreign workers of all nationalities (the latter formally equal allies in the fight against capitalist exploiters). Cuba's inclusion in the world market in the form of state promotion of the tourist sector has decidedly changed the country's position within the international division of labour. Rather than providing workers for the international sugar industry, the refining of Soviet crude oil, and assorted medical, military and educational services to a number of third world countries and to the former Soviet bloc, its citizens are now called upon to welcome western tourists. The bitterness and absurdity felt by many about the repositioning of Cuba internationally comes across in the ironic use of the term *Guía del proletariado mundial* (Guide of the world proletariat); used consistently in the past by the state and Party to refer to Lenin, it is now applied with humour to people like Juan's ex-girlfriend.

Marketing draws on satire, and the ironic use of terms like *Guía del proletariado mundial* may be just Cuban street banter, heavy with the use of double-entendres. Nevertheless, this is highly illustrative of fast-changing times when many Cubans like Juan feel as though the world has indeed been turned upside down, with Cubans now close to the bottom of the international pecking order. For Cubans to perceive themselves as falling at the bottom of the heap, behind even Haiti, indicates to some extent their current sense of impotence. For lighter-skinned Cubans, it illustrates their original sense of a racial and cultural superiority (see above) frustrated by material deprivation. Others may choose to look to Cuba's expertise in biotechnology and medicine, or see tourists as unsuspecting naïve people there to be used, humoured and exploited in some capacity. Yet what is undeniable is that the growth of tourism, the easing of a ban by the Cuban state in 1979 of visits to Cuba by Cuban exiles and migrants, and the more recent legalization of the US dollar, have all made Cubans more aware than ever of the vast inequalities of opportunity and material wealth that surround them.

For the Cuban state *jineterismo* has created a massive political and economic dilemma. On the one hand, the government, whose legitimacy to some extent has been based upon ridding the country of its informal status as 'America's brothel', is keen to distinguish between *jineterismo* and prostitution. On the other hand, however, ever desperate to rein in hard currency for service provision and payment of foreign debts, all activities where dollars change hands outside areas controlled by the state are seen as 'disloyal' competition with the 'legitimate' state tourist industry, and attempts have been made to curtail all such activities, often using the very same emotive metaphors based upon prostitution and pimping.

Similarly, foreigners and many locals often attempt to explain their liaisons in terms that would minimize the significance of the cash or gift component in any encounter or relationship, where possible distinguishing between *jineterismo* (acceptable) and prostitution (unacceptable).[4] So, while *jineterismo* means many different things to different people at different times, in many senses Cubans often simply try to define *jineterismo* in terms of what it is conventionally perceived of as *not* being: *prostitución* (prostitution). Lumsden, for example, suggests that *jineterismo* is really 'a way of intermittently relating to tourists rather than a full-time occupation' (Lumsden 1996: 141). Yet to *jinetear* was seen by many of my informants as including frequent and relatively straightforward sex for cash transactions as one would expect from conventional interpretations of prostitution, as well as one-off sexual acts, long-term, long-distance sexual relationships, platonic friendships, and so on.

What is certain, though, is that *jineterismo* is not a unified social phenomenon: it has no boundaries other than those imagined by different Cubans in their many different contexts. As Hart (1998) noted in her look at aspects of client and sex-worker relationships in Spain, there is a multitude of reasons why clients and prostitutes enter into and maintain these types of relationships. We may be able to establish with some degree of certainty that the broad phenomenon of *jineterismo* is underpinned by the frustrated material needs of many of the urban youth, and the desperation felt by their older family members and compatriots,[5] and that women and men are often differently affected. But it becomes decidedly more difficult to locate power and impotence – in effect, inequality – within the arena of sex and gender. The ways in which observers traditionally interpret power relations based upon *a priori* notions of a weaker female (victim) and stronger male (perpetrator) becomes highly problematic.

VICTIMS AND HUNTERS: THE PROBLEM OF LOCATING POWER IN GENDERED DISCOURSES

In her Alicante-based research Angie Hart warns us that 'clients [males] were not always oppressors, and sex workers [females] were not always oppressed by them. Power was often contested; individuals manipulated each other' (Hart 1998: 150). This is not to take the radical relativist stance of totally decentring power; as Hart is at pains to note, for many prostitution (and we could add *jineterismo*) exists in the first place largely, albeit not exclusively, *because of* 'inequalities of gender, age, ethnicity and class' (Hart 1998: 138). Nevertheless, if we look at some of the language behind *jineterismo* things do become somewhat uncertain. From the verb *jinetear* – to ride horseback – *jinetera* (female) and *jinetero* (male) are hardly images of exploited and passive victims. *Jineterismo*, like the verbs with which it is often used such as *poner una multa* (to place a fine on someone, in this case, tourists), *pescar* (to fish or catch something, also tourists) or *cazar* (to hunt), conjures up images of strength rather than of weakness. The action of riding horseback is a proactive pursuit – that of commandeering the horse, letting it do all the hard work while the rider reaps the benefits of its strength and speed.[6] In addition, while people who call themselves or others *jinetero/a* might wish to obtain a decent income by other means instead of having to resort to foreigner-centred activities, what can we say about the many

Cubans who fall in love with a foreigner as they would with a fellow Cuban, yet at the same time reap some material benefits? A sexual relationship between a Cuban and a foreigner cannot be indicative of the former's status as *jinetero/a*.

In the state and general public domains, various reasons were put forward as to why there was such as proliferation of prostitution and *jineterismo*, and what the Cuban state and its citizenry ought to do about it. What concerns me here is how the various activities subsumed within *jineterismo* were addressed through a 'gendered', or, more accurately, 'sexed', lens; the activities of men and women were *assumed* to be different simply because it was either a man or a woman carrying out the action. Often this assumption, variously held by both from the Cuban state and many domestic and international commentators, appeared to be founded upon a belief that a woman, by virtue of being female and her foreign contact being male, must be the victim in any encounter. This is a position dramatically illustrated in the words of dissident Cuban exile singer Willy Chirino's song *'La Jinetera'*: 'Behind the smile of the *jinetera*/Eva is crying for her Adam.' In a similar vein we are told that *Marucha*, the *jinetera* described in Pedro Luís Ferrer's song 'Marucha la Jinetera', 'has a pain in her soul', that 'on her cross there are more tears than smiles', that she was raped, as a child she was left without dolls, her father abused her mother and sisters, and that she herself was put into prison surrounded by *marimachas* (lesbians). Similarly, in her account of *jineterismo*, O'Connell-Davidson scorns those male sex-tourists who see the local young women as *caliente* (hot), 'so hot, they'll go with you for a bar of soap; so hot, they don't care how old, obese or unappealing the man is' (O'Connell-Davidson 1996: 46).

Paradoxically, it is generally acknowledged among Cuba's urban population that *jineterismo* found its early 'practitioners' in Cuban adolescent males and adult men forming liaisons, sexual or otherwise, with women travellers, diplomats and tourists from the Soviet bloc and the West prior to the mass tourism of the 1990s. A number of independent academic accounts accept this to be the case (see O'Connell-Davidson 1996), yet there remains very little focused literature on the subject. In those few accounts of male sexual *jineterismo* emanating from official state bodies references were made only to 'young' underage 'boy victims' seduced by older foreign men.[7] Similarly, the attorney-general of Cuba makes a similar association when he talks of new laws aiming to deal 'with those cases in which minors are used in acts of homosexuality and prostitution', begging the question, *why* specify homosexuality and prostitution if the problem is underage sex, irrespective of gender and sexual orientation?

Nevertheless, men were generally assumed to be at worst perpetrators of this exploitation of women, or at best treated ambivalently within both the academic and state-sponsored literature. We have already noted O'Connell-Davidson's comment above. Cuban newspapers stretched the boundaries of *jineterismo* to extraordinary lengths, alerting the populace to the re-emergence of the dreaded *proxeneta* (pimp). Yet, many of the activities listed included activities as diverse as hotel porters receiving bribes, illegal taxi drivers, someone who introduces tourists to hotels or private rented accommodation, and so on. Some articles even went so far as to mention other seemingly unrelated activities (albeit ones for which dollars are charged). Once again, like the difficulty in assigning identities or labels to the women we might call *jineteras*, the somewhat individual and unstructured manner in which these 'pimps' operate lead many who attempt to interpret such activities to jettison the term pimp altogether. Instead, in keeping with the loose sense of the term *jinetera*, the pimp becomes, in various discourses, the *jinetero*. He too is 'riding' or 'fining' the foreigner, even if his activities do not necessarily directly involve sexual activity. But what of those men whose activities are primarily centred upon sexual intercourse with foreigners? The remainder of this chapter looks at some of these relationships in the context of the current Cuban economic and political reality.

PINGUEROS AS SEXUAL EXPLORERS OR SEX-WORKERS? THE FUTILITY OF DEFINITION

One young, white professional called Juan Carlos recalled his 'brief flirtations with *jineterismo*' in typically ill-defined terms. Although he had a girlfriend at the time, he told me how a university professor had seduced him, offering him a meal in a top tourist hotel, and later urging the young student to masturbate with him outside in the hotel grounds. Later, he recalled his more recent relationship with a young Chilean woman called María, whom he had met while she was on holiday in Cuba the previous year. As far as Juan Carlos was aware, María had no idea of his homosexual activities. They got on very well, and their platonic friendship was sealed through countless letters and more visits by María to Cuba. Juan Carlos was convinced that she was in love with him, and although he had strong feelings for her, these were not particularly sexual. However, when Juan Carlos's partner obtained permission to migrate to the United States, his desperate lover contemplated a sexual relationship with María (whose father worked in the Chilean foreign ministry). He thought that since he had had 'sexually successful' relationships with women in the past, he would be able to do so again, albeit this time for a rather different purpose. Although some of his friends, aware of his sexuality, urged him to take this route, Juan Carlos's eventual victory in *el bombo* (the US citizenship lottery) put an end to the idea.

Although the story is unique in content, it was not uncommon to hear similar stories of nominally homosexual men becoming involved in heterosexual relationships with foreign women (often younger men seducing older foreign women), or nominally heterosexual Cuban men forging relationships with homosexual foreign men. With regards to the latter, it was not uncommon in Cuba, as in other countries, for would-be straight young men to be induced or seduced into having sex with an older man as part of a night out (Lumsden 1996: 140). In many senses this could be simply that some men were attempting to meet certain material demands in much the same way as the so-called *bugarrón* was imagined to meet his frustrated (and otherwise heterosexual) sexual urges. Conversely, as Juan Carlos pointed out, these sexual (in the case of the *bugarrón*) and material desires (in the case of the *jinetero*) also provided some men with an opening for same-sex sexual activities; activities that hitherto had been considered socially and selfconsciously unacceptable. This is not to suggest that we can uncover some key or 'causal factors' behind such sexual activities and desires; no one 'key' would fit all, let alone a single individual over time. Nor am I trying to uncover culturally, historically or individually essentialized 'sexuality'.[8] Rather, I am simply pointing out some of the cultural and material conditions under which some Cuban men have sex with foreign or well-connected Cuban men.

Central to our understanding of these sexualized relationships is the disappearance almost overnight of those public spaces where the urban youth, homosexual or heterosexual, could meet, dance and drink. As noted earlier, cafés, bars, discothèques and hotels were put off-limits to ordinary Cubans and geared to the hard-currency tourist sector only, ostensibly to contain a mushrooming informal sector that lay outside the state's control. Those few discothèques that Cubans could enter, for example in the Hotel Deauville, were places where young men and women could meet friends, dance to popular western music and, significantly, meet tourists. It was the association with *jineterismo*, together with its popularity with gay Cubans, that, some of my informants insisted, led to the closure of the hotel's discothèque some time in the mid-1990s. This precipitated a shift of its Cuban clientele *en masse* to Club Zanzibar in district of Vedado (this club was also closed in late 1996).

To some extent Club Zanzibar was a microcosm of all the contradictions and changes occurring in the contemporary urban Cuban society of the 1990s; emerging spaces for gay people, cultural liberalism and modern western popular music became juxtaposed with a vast increase in petty corruption, social inequality and, most importantly, the sexual economy between foreigners and Cubans. It was a place where men, sometimes calling themselves *pingueros*, hung out in the late evening (both inside the club and on the street outside). From the noun *la pinga*, meaning dick or cock, the term *pinguero* appears to be a recent invention, and it still seemed in 1996 to have little popular currency outside these particular environments. There was, however, an underlying atmosphere of celebration of things foreign (western), and with it the dollar and the *pinguero*, at least by the club's managers and some Cuban visitors. The songs performed there, by the singer Barry Tatica, often referred to *italianos* or *jineteros*, *pingueros*, *gays* and *guaniquiqui* (slang for money), and to the 'fining' and 'hunting' of tourists. There was an expectation by mainly young Cuban men in the club that foreigners (or, more rarely, wealthier and older Cuban men) were there to pick up young Cuban men, whether for a night of sex or a longer-term relationship, or just for companionship and friendship. There was also an expectation that those with the material means (again, mainly foreigners) would buy the drinks and or provide the $2–3 entry fee, irrespective of whether further contact ensued.

On my first visit to the club it was immediately evident that if, as some people insisted, all the Cuban men at or immediately outside the club were *jineteros* or *pingueros* (i.e. looking for sexual relations with foreign men for some sort of material gain), then 'supply' hugely outstripped 'demand'. It was also evident that while some younger locals would have had little trouble attracting the attention of foreigners for sex, if that is what indeed was on offer or in demand, it was evident that the older or less conventionally attractive Cubans present could not have hoped for the same amount of attention or response. It soon became obvious that the reasons young Cuban men went to the club were diverse, often differing from visit to visit. Indeed, it could be said that many of those who came to the club appeared to be there simply to meet friends, chat, and get into the club to dance and enjoy the music.

Perhaps one of the more interesting features again revolved round sexuality. One homosexual informant, who claimed he never went near these types of places due to what he perceived to be the crassness and superficiality of the people, told me with typical Cuban definitiveness that most *pingueros* were homosexual. He added that either they publicly denied it because of the continuing stigmatization of homosexuality, or they hadn't come to terms with their sexuality and were there to 'explore'. However, I was also told the reverse by another, who claimed that most of the *pingueros* in general weren't homosexual or even bi-sexual, but went there to meet foreign men 'because they wanted the latest fashions … and sleeping with a foreign man was the one way they can get their new pair of Nike training shoes'.

In many respects, then, this male-to-male sexual *pinguerismo* differs little from the broader, multifaceted phenomenon of *jineterismo* per se, except in one important sense: its ability to provide (homo)sexual openings for some men. Moreover, I would suggest that the often ambiguous, often highly contentious local and 'official' (state and Party) discourses surrounding those activities and desires also highlight the depths of division, upheaval and social change that lie at the very heart of contemporary Cuban social relations. Indeed, if, as is my intention, we are to draw broader conclusions here about the complex imaginings of maleness within the changing nature of Cuban social relations, then an analysis of the values and images ordinary Cubans attribute to *jineterismo/pinguerismo* becomes invaluable. Same-sex experiences and desires, for example, become enmeshed within the practices and language of *pinguerismo*, and an infinite variety of other sexualized, racialized, hierarchical, global *imagingings* of maleness and Cubanness. In this sense, then, it is utterly futile to determine the extent to which Cuban men frequent clubs like the Zanzibar to 'hunt' and 'fine' a foreigner who 'happens to be' male (whether for a long-term commitment, or just for a beer), or to sleep with a man who 'happens to be' a foreigner and able to meet material aspirations as well as sexual ones. On the contrary, examples like these urge us to problematize even further the notion of 'fixed' identities, although they do so by also urging us to look at 'material' and 'cultural' factors as well as 'sexual' desires, assuming, of course, we can even begin to distinguish between the two.

CONCLUSIONS

> Whereas the politics of identity implies that the personal itself is a key site of political struggle (for example against sexism or racism) my argument is that perhaps the most important political battle of the contemporary era is that to defend personal and private space from politicisation and rationalisation. This is not a conservative, individualist or narcissistic approach, but on the contrary the only means of avoiding one. It is about reasserting what politics is properly about: the collective struggle against material exploitation and inequality to achieve equal public rights for private citizens. (John MacInnes 1998: 136)

My purpose here has been simply to caution against turning to localized or universal definitions of 'maleness' or 'masculinity', and against too narrow a focus on the dynamics of localized 'gender relations', in order to understand the intricacies of social inequality and the means by which this can be overcome. This is not to say some men aren't chauvinists at certain times, or perhaps throughout their lives, or that some men aren't devoid of chauvinistic thoughts and behaviour. Nor is it to say that some women can't be chauvinists or that some women aren't the recipients of horrific violence by some men and other women. However, it is to say that given, among other things, the extraordinary difficulty of analytically separating 'the man' from 'the masculine', 'sex' from 'gender', and the chauvinistic 'phallus' from the entirely innocent 'penis', we ought to shift our focus more towards the broader social relations and structures within society. *Imaginings of maleness* within a dynamic, layered, sociocultural and economic context within which a man or a boy only ever thinks of himself as a man or boy relationally and contingently may help us readjust our focus away from the caricatured *macho* individual (always an easy target in the current postmodern political void), and back to the broader structures of society and the globalized capitalist economy.

NOTES

1. Attempts to distinguish between 'hegemonic' and 'marginal' forms encounter *exactly* the same problems.

2. *Juventud Rebelde*, 28 January 1996.

3. See also Shalapentokh's (1992) account of life in Brezhnev's USSR.

4. See Hart (1998: 174) for a critique of tendencies to treat prostitution per se as a blanket category. This tends to produce essentialisms of the 'other', in this case prostitution (a tendency that also occurs in accounts such as Lumsden's [1996] and O'Connell-Davidson's [1996]).

5. One report, commissioned, but not made public, by the Union of Young Communists (UJC), indicated that most of the *jineteras* or prostitutes that they interviewed lived in substandard housing with an extremely low joint household income.

6. See also Loizos (1994: 74) and Cornwall (1994: 117) for similar comparisons in Greece and Brazil.

7. *Juventud Rebelde*, 2 June 1996.

8. The debate over the specific characteristics of Cuban homosexualities in the feminist journal *Signs* between Arguelles and Rich (1984; 1996) on the one hand, and Lancaster (1986) on the other clearly illustrates the futility of constructing unitary, albeit regionalized, bounded sexual models (see also Forrest 1999). See also Carrier (1992) on the tendency to *occidentalize* 'the Western experience' (a tendency, for example, found in Kulick's account of Brazilian *travestis* [1998:229]).

REFERENCES

Alcoff, L. (1997) 'Cultural Feminism Versus Post-structuralism: The Identity Crisis in Feminist Theory', in L. Nicholson (ed.), *The Second Wave: A Reader in Feminist Theory* (London: Routledge).

Arguelles, L. and B. R. Rich (1984) 'Homosexuality, Homophobia, and Revolution: Notes Toward an Understanding of the Cuban Lesbian and Gay Experience, Part 1', *Signs: Journal of Women in Culture and Society*, 9(4): 683–99.

— (1986) 'A Reply to Lancaster', *Signs: Journal of Women in Culture and Society*, 12(1): 192–4.

Butler, J. (1990) *Gender Trouble: Feminism and the Subversion of Identity* (New York: Routledge).

— (1997) 'Imitation and Gender Insubordination', in L. Nicholson (ed.), *The Second Wave: A Reader in Feminist Theory* (London: Routledge).

Carrier, J. (1992) 'Occidentalism', *American Ethnologist*, 19(2): 195–212.

Casal, L. (1987) 'Images of women in pre- and postrevolutionary Cuban Novels', in C. Mesa-Lago (ed.), *Cuban Studies 17*, University of Pittsburg Press.

Collins, P. H. (1990) *Black Feminist Thought: Knowledge, Consciousness, and the Politics of Empowerment* (London: Routledge).

Connell, R. W. (1995) *Masculinities* (Cambridge: Polity Press).

Cornwall, A. (1994) 'Gendered Identities and Gender Ambiguity Among Travesties in Salvador, Brazil', in A. Cornwall and N. Lindisfarne (eds), *Dislocating Masculinities: Comparative Ethnographies* (London: Routledge).

Cornwall A. and N. Lindisfarne (eds) (1994) *Disclocating Masculinities: Comparative Ethnographies* (London: Routledge).

— (1995) 'Feminist Anthropologies and Questions of Masculinity', in A. Ahmed and C. Shore (eds), *The Future of Anthropology: Its Relevance to the Contemporary World* (London: Athlone Press).

Dominguez, V. R. (1987) 'Sex, Gender and Revolution: The Problem of Construction and the Construction of a Problem', in C. Mesa-Lago (ed.), *Cuban Studies 17* (Pittsburgh, PA: University of Pittsburgh Press).

Eckstein, S. E. (1994) *Back from the Future: Cuba Under Castro* (Princeton, NJ: Princeton University Press).

Forrest, D. (1999) *Bichos, Maricones and Pingueros: An Ethnographic Study of Maleness and Scarcity in Contemporary Socialist Cuba*, Unpublished thesis, University of London.

Fox, G. E. (1972) 'Cuban Racism', in I. L. Horowitz (ed.), *Cuban Communism* (2nd edn) (New Brunswick: Translation Books/Rutgers University).

— (1973) 'Honour, Shame, and Women's Liberation in Cuba: Views of Working-class Émigré Men', in A. Pescatello (ed.), *Female and Male in Latin America: Essays* (Pittsburgh, PA: University of Pittsburgh Press).

Fraser, N. (1997) *Justice Interruptus: Critical Reflections on the 'Postsocialist' Condition* (New York: Routledge).

Füredi, F. (1986) *The Soviet Union Demystified: A Materialist Analysis* (London: Junius Publications).

Gonzalez, E. (1974) *Cuba Under Castro: The Limits of Charisma* (Boston: Houghton Mifflin).

Gross, R. and N. Levitt (1998) *Higher Superstition: The Academic Left and its Quarrels with Science*, (Baltimore: Johns Hopkins University Press).

Hart, A. (1998) *Buying and Selling Power: Anthropological Reflections on Prostitution in Spain* (Boulder, CO: Westview Press).

Kapcia, A. (1989) 'Martí, Marxism and Morality: the Evolution of an Ideology of Revolution', in R. Gillespie (ed.), *Journal of Communist Studies*, Special Edition: Cuba After 30 Years: Rectification and the Revolution (5)4.

— (1992) 'The Fourth Congress of the Cuban Communist Party: Time for a Change?', *Journal of Communist Studies*, 8(1): 180–6.

Kulick, D. (1998) *Travesti: Sex, Gender and Culture Among Brazilian Transgendered Prostitutes* (London: University of Chicago Press).

Lancaster, R. N. (1986) 'Comments on Arguelles and Rich's Study', *Signs: Journal of Women in Culture and Society*, 12(1): 1988–92.

Lewis, O., R. M. Lewis and S. M. Rigdon (1977) *Four Men: Living the Revolution: An Oral History of Contemporary Cuba* (Urbana, University of Illinois Press).

Loizos, P. (1994) 'A Broken Mirror: Masculine Sexuality in Greek Ethnography', in A. Cornwall and N. Lindisfarne (eds), *Dislocating Masculinities: Comparative Ethnographies* (London: Routledge).

Lumsden, I. (1996) *Machos, Maricones and Gays: Cuba and Homosexuality* (Philadelphia, PA: Temple University Press).

McGarrity, G. L. (1992) 'Race, Culture and Social Change in Contemporary Cuba', in S. Halebsky, J. M. Kirk et al. (eds), *Cuba in Transition: Crisis and Transformation*, Latin American Perspectives Series, 9 (Oxford: Westview Press).

MacInnes, J. (1998) *The End of Masculinity: The Confusion of Sexual Genesis and Sexual Difference in Modern Society* (Buckingham: Open University Press).

Martínez-Alier, V. (1989) *Marriage, Class, and Colour in Nineteenth Century Cuba: A Study of Racial Attitudes and Sexual Values in a Slave Society* (2nd edn) (Ann Arbor: University of Michigan Press).

Molyneux, M. (1985) 'Family Reform in Socialist States: The Hidden Agenda', *Feminist Review*, 21: 47–66.

Moore, H. (1994) *A Passion for Difference* (Oxford: Polity Press).

O'Connell-Davidson, J. (1996) 'Sex Tourism in Cuba', *Race and Class*, 38(1): 38–48.

Pérez-Stable (1987) 'Cuban Women and the Struggle for "Conciencia" in C. Mesa-Lago (ed.), *Cuban Studies 17*, University of Pittsburg Press.

Rosenthal, M. G. (1992) 'The Problems of Single Motherhood in Cuba', in S. Halebsky and J. M. Kirk et al. (eds), *Cuba in Transition: Crisis and Transformation* (Latin American Perspectives series, No. 9), Oxford: Westview Press.

Rubin, G. (1975) 'The Traffic in Women', in R. Reiter (ed.), *Toward an Anthropology of Women* (London: Monthly Review Press).

Shalapentokh, D. (1992) 'Love-making in the Time of Perestroika: Sex in the Context of Political Culture', *Studies in Comparative Communism*, 25(2): 154–73.

Smith, L. M. (1992) 'Sexuality and Socialism in Cuba', in S. Halebsky, J. M. Kirk et al. (eds), *Cuba in Transition: Crisis and Transformation*, Latin American Perspectives Series, 9 (Oxford: Westview Press).

Stone, E. (ed.) (1981) *Women and the Cuban Revolution: Speeches and Documents by Fidel Castro, Vilma Espin, and Others* (New York: Pathfinder Press).

Strathern, M. (1988) *The Gender of the Gift* (Berkeley: University of California Press).

Stubbs, J. (1987) 'Gender Issues in Contemporary Cuban Tobacco Farming', *World Development*, 15(1).

— (1989) *Cuba: the Test of Time* (London: Latin American Bureau).

— (1993) 'Women and the Cuban Smallholder Agriculture in Transition', in J. H. Momsen (ed.), *Women and Change in the Caribbean* (London: Indiana University Press).

— (1994) 'Cuba: Revolutionising Women, Family and Power', in B. J. Nelson and N. Chowdhury (eds), *Women and Politics Worldwide* (New Haven and London: Yale University Press).

Wade, P. (1995) 'The Cultural Politics of Blackness in Colombia', *American Ethnologist*, 22(2): 341–57.

CHAPTER 5

Deconstructing Domination: Gender Disempowerment and the Legacy of Colonialism and Apartheid in Omaheke, Namibia

NIKI KANDIRIKIRIRA

> Power relations and domination between people are the principal basis of analysis and action ... Not only must we analyse the power relations between men and women and within these groups, but also between adults and young people, heterosexuals and homosexuals, dominant cultures and oppressed, and between rich and poor, among others ... The concept of 'diversity with equity' is embodied in the acknowledgement of the multiple identities of people and the need to build equal relations ... this is not a struggle of women against men, or young people against adults, but rather a question of everyone taking on their responsibility for deconstructing domination and building equal relations ... It implies attempting to influence ways of thinking, feeling, acting or interacting ... and, through a process of deconstructing oppressive and exclusionary ways of being and behaving, constructing democratic ways of living here and now. (Campanile 2001)

§ This chapter celebrates the resilience of a Namibian community struggling against the profound impact of apartheid that 'damaged the very core of society, rupturing families, dispersing and fragmenting communities, undermining indigenous value-systems, racialising every aspect of life' (WISER 2001). It shows how distorted masculine identities, often expressed in sexually exploitative or violent relations with girls and women, are part of a legacy of systemic societal discrimination based on race and ethnicity. The chapter suggests that work on gender cannot focus only on men as oppressors and women as victims, but should facilitate a community's analysis and understanding of its own situation and support it in rebuilding functioning family, social and institutional systems based on social justice.

Having set out to address deteriorating adult–child relationships and children's misbehaviour, fifteen communities and five schools in Aminuis,[1] Namibia, embarked on a journey of reflection and discovery that created a critical community consciousness of the inter-relationship between ideologies of racial, ethnic, gender and age superiority. Through an analysis of the construct and impact of systemic racial discrimination they not only recognized the parallels with systemic exclusion practices in their own cultures but how these had been exploited by the apartheid state to further its ends in the domination of a people based on the colour of their skin.

As an eighty-year-old woman from Tsoasis village put it during the analysis of a PRA on child development:

> While it is true apartheid damaged us, we cannot blame everything on apartheid, it has been eight years [since Independence] and still we perpetuate the abuse, neglect and violence as black people on black, on our own children. We have to look at our own culture ... we are not innocent, we also discriminate. They [white people/the apartheid state] took opportunity in our divisions. We have to understand what it is about our own culture that perpetuates this shameful situation, stop looking to blame others. We don't know what our society would have been like had we not experienced apartheid, but we know we are not innocent, look at the way we treat the San,[2] look at the way we treat our children, look at they way you treat us women [*laughter*]. It is shameful. We cannot just look back and try to blame others; we have to take responsibility, take action to put it right.

At the outset of the process, adults sought ACORD's[3] assistance in addressing the problem of anti-social, self-destructive children. Adults were blaming and victimizing children who were perceived as taking advantage of the new Namibian democratic constitution, the Convention on the rights of the child and rights-based policy to challenge adult authority and do what they wanted. Children, full of aspirations for a different future in the new Namibia, blamed adults for conspiring to deny them their newly acquired rights and demanded rights without taking on the responsibilities that came with them. However, their engagement with ACORD implied that they were already starting to understand that they needed a deeper analysis of the situation since they had contacted ACORD specifically because of its work using PRA and gender analysis with local farmers' unions.

Despite Aminuis being an isolated rural community far from the urban social, political and economic stresses that exacerbate the emergence of gangs and gang rape in the townships of South Africa, the people of Aminuis have not escaped such problems. They too are caught up in the dynamic that has resulted in social relations that encompass the possibility of violence and abuse as a demonstration of power. This manifests itself locally in a number of ways. The rape of girls in school hostels is perceived by boys and men not as an act of violence but as a form of entertainment that affirms their masculinity. Sexual violence is named and celebrated among boys in terms such as 'hunting' (rape in Aminuis) and 'the tournament' (gang rape). Such violence against girls is sanctioned through adult inaction; hungry children are beaten for stealing food but 'hunting' goes unpunished. Boys in Aminuis exhibit self-destructive behaviour – drinking, fighting and threatening suicide if not provided with the products they need to acquire status and affirm collective identity. Exploitative relations between older men and schoolgirls go unchallenged and are accepted by the girls, many of whom have babies as teenagers. Many unwanted children are abandoned to the care of grandparents, relatives and school hostels, with fathers abdicating their parental responsibilities. Education and development processes focus on preparing women and girls for single motherhood and to manage the social dysfunction of men. Male gender identity is increasingly defined by men's power to sexually exploit and oppress women, to have multiple sexual partners, many children, and demonstrable wealth at the expense of family and child welfare. Irresponsibility and unaccountability are considered admirable among men. Gender identity is also defined by men's power relationships with other ethnic groups.

Research throughout Africa on abuse in schools confirms the findings and analysis of the Aminuis community and indicates an endemic problem of abusive gender and age relations. As Fiona Leach noted: 'Sexual abuse of girls in schools is a reflection of gender violence and inequality in the wider society. Domestic violence against women and children is commonplace, as is rape and forced sex within relationships. Women are considered as "belonging" to men and hence accorded lower status'

(Leach 2001). In comparing the research carried out in Namibia, Zimbabwe, Malawi, Ghana, Uganda and South Africa, the parallels between the findings are frighteningly consistent.

Like many other communities emerging from apartheid and colonialism, the people of Aminuis are faced with what has been termed the 'youth crisis', 'the lost generation' (Mokwena 1991), the 'crisis of capitalism' and the emergence of a normative culture of violence. 'So prevalent and widely tolerated is such violence that it has come to be perceived almost as normative and to a larger extent accepted rather than challenged ... abuse and violence against women that manifests as an intrinsic, pervasive facet of gender relations' (Voegelmann and Eagle 1991). Voegelmann and Eagle (1991) asked the question how to overcome 'abuse and violence against women that manifests as an intrinsic, pervasive feat of gender relations', given the context that 'so prevalent and widely tolerated is such violence that it has come to be perceived almost as normative and to a larger extent accepted than challenged'.

Although most research has focused on the impact of this violent culture on women, a recent study in south Johannesburg by CIETafrica (Andersson et al. 2000) found that both male and female youth experienced similar levels of sexual violence until the mid-teenage years when the incidence for girls starts to increase at a sharper rate. In the context of Aminuis, although it was clear girls took the brunt of the abuse, male-on-male violence, oppression and enforced expectations of masculinity were also very apparent.

In many of the studies of violence in post-apartheid Africa, this crisis of normative violence has been related to the emasculation of black men by the racist state. Studies of violence in inner cities in Britain, USA and South America also reflect clear relationships between the emasculation of black men and the level of violence, and dysfunctional gender, age and family relations (Hurt 2000). While black men certainly do not have the monopoly on violence and gender violence the evident linkages between racism and sexism imply that the racist ideology systematically undermines black male self-worth and manipulates division, mistrust and dysfunction in order efficiently to oppress black people.

Chris Dolan's work (this volume) refers to the expectations of masculinity and the ways the state and others can deny men the opportunity of fulfilling their masculine roles, either as a weapon of war or as a means of disempowering civil society. To achieve this end the manipulation often takes advantage of the ethnic divisions in society, playing on ethnic and racist stereotypes that are believed by both the dominant and the oppressed. The model of masculinity held up as the expected norm creates, in relation to particular ethnic identities and culture, a variety of vulnerabilities for men as they are denied the opportunities and resources to achieve it. Women suffer the consequences of men's frustration and society is faced with dealing with increasing dysfunction in gender and familial relationships. Men who manage to fulfil the expected norms often become a target of other men's aggression.

This implies that in order to deal with sexism and gender violence one has to provide men with the opportunity to understand the way that patriarchy is manipulated by systems of exclusion such as racism, ethnocentrism and class and the impact this has on their capacity to fulfil the masculine roles and responsibilities assigned to them by the gender constructs of their culture. Through understanding the vulnerabilities created by this they start to understand how fighting sexism is not merely an issue of women's rights aimed at disempowering men, but is a struggle against those who would control societal relations, to maintain power through ethnic, religious and class hierarchies. If this can be achieved the concept of gender takes on new meaning; it is no longer about women but about human rights. It is about joint action against poverty and oppression, deconstructing domination and building equal relations not only between women and men, but between races, ethnicities, classes and ages.

A CRITICAL JOURNEY

National campaigns in Namibia against gender violence often focus on women as victims, preparing them to take control and to protect themselves. One media campaign, 'Fathers Take Responsibility',[4] aimed to shame men into correcting their behaviour. However, depicting them as uncaring, selfish individuals, without reference to the context in which they had developed such behaviour, resulted in defensiveness among men, including those working on gender in development.

The Total Child programme of Aminuis had the opportunity to take a different route; the community had identified a problem in child–adult relationships. The entry point of children cut across ethnic, gender and age boundaries. Everyone had an interest in trying to address the problem, whether they were teachers, parents, grandparents, carers, relatives, nurses or children. They trusted ACORD; most staff were from the community, had been students in local schools and had a track record of working on women's participation. Together they embarked on a learning process, with ACORD catalysing processes, the community researching, analysing and deciding on action, and ACORD then responding with support when the community, or sections of it, requested it.

With remarkable honesty, the community carried out forty-two participatory appraisals involving more than 1,000 people. ACORD facilitated the process, ensuring that whole villages, teachers, school hostel staff and schoolchildren were able to participate. The different community actors investigated the issues of child-rearing, child development and adult–child relationships. Each of the groups came up with its own perspective. Aware that manifestations of child and women abuse were the inevitable consequence of the power differential inherent in a racialized patriarchal society, and that previous attempts at drawing attention to this had created defensiveness, ACORD catalysed a process that aimed to establish an agreement on the context in which the problems being faced were encountered. More than fifty workshops were held and provided an analytical framework[5] for understanding the power differentials in the community. These started from a common experience, 'Understanding Racism', and led on to understanding the constructs of sexism, ethnocentrism and adult–child power relations. Using this framework to analyse their PRA findings, the community developed models of how each ideology of superiority and exclusion manifested itself in Aminuis. In order to do this the perceptions of the different stakeholder groups had to be discussed and challenged. As they entered into dialogue, children, traditionally silenced, had to find a route for their voice and analysis. This they found in forum theatre.

The journey was a painful one, each group developing defence mechanisms, attributing blame, accusing ACORD of taking the side of children and making things worse. But the level of community ownership protected the process from derailment. They had asked for our intervention; no community, school, adult or child had to participate (despite the education ministry offering to make it compulsory for staff), and ACORD staff were answerable to a representative school and community committee.

At the height of the analysis, schools uncomfortable with the outcomes (due to the fear of tarnishing their reputation in relation to the progressive anti-discriminatory education policy) were given the chance to withdraw from the programme, but none did. Reassurance was offered by letting the community define the pace and direction of the process. ACORD developed the capacity to respond to a wide range of community-initiated strategic processes.

The results of the PRA were initially received with resistance, shame, victimization and blame. But through their participatory analysis process, community members came to understand that their gender identities and relationships were a composite of sex, age and ethnic social constructs within the specific historic, political and economic contexts of colonialism and apartheid. They realized that the nature of these oppressive relations was systemic, that each reinforced the other and that manipulation of the black male identity by the apartheid state had been efficient in undermining their family and gender relations, and had reinforced ethnic division. Consequently it was realized that the problems of child–adult relationships and youth behaviour could not be solved by attributing blame, but rather by joint action to contradict the ideologies that sustain systemic discrimination. As they progressed from analysis to action, many requested that ACORD facilitate the social exclusion analysis again, so that they could refine their analysis and check their assumptions.

THE IMPACT OF APARTHEID IDEOLOGY

The community's analysis of the impact of racist ideology reflects current research into the relationship between the emasculation of black men by the apartheid state and the alarming increase in sexual violence (Voegelmann and Eagle 1991; Voegelmann 1990; Vetten 1997; Mokwena 1991; Voegelmann and Lewis 1993). What was different in Aminuis was that the understanding of this dynamic emerged from people's own research and analysis, and this led to the community examining the relationship between the dysfunction of children and youth and the fundamental cultural norms of patriarchy in gender, age and ethnic hierarchies, and taking action. They started to understand how deeply apartheid had impacted on their social and family dynamics and the concept of transference (power constructs that allow the suppressed anger of the oppressed to be unleashed on 'weaker' groups who cannot retaliate, e.g. women, the San and children). They realized that the power to enact this transference was derived from the existing power imbalances in their own culture and society. And that many of the mechanisms developed to cope with the excesses of apartheid have been assimilated into their culture as normal practice and are being transferred to their children as described below.

Men's absence from family life   Under German colonialism and apartheid the forced removals of black people to marginal land and lack of economic investment and development in the communal areas undermined their livelihood strategies. Many men had little choice but to leave the rural areas to look for additional income. Pass laws prohibited their families from moving with them and they found themselves living alone in single quarters,[6] mining dormitories and on isolated farms, working for white people.

Exaggerated masculinity   Whenever possible, men escaped the oppressive environment of the workplace and headed for home where their culture and place in the patriarchy would validate them as real men again. But on their return their self-esteem was further damaged when they found their wives and mothers coping with traditional male gender roles. In an attempt to reassert themselves they exaggerated their maleness, focusing on the aggressive and controlling aspects, and becoming sexually unaccountable. Their resentment and frustration was unleashed in their homes on their wives and families.

Emasculated by the apartheid system, men sought to reaffirm their masculinity. Denied traditional family life and the opportunity to achieve status through education, careers or position men took up the options open to them: sex and money. Their sense of self-worth and masculine identity became defined by having many lovers, many children and demonstrable wealth.

Women, traditionally suppressed, managing shifting gender boundaries and themselves impacted by racism, were faced with compounded discrimination and were in no position to challenge men. To avoid confrontation, men intimidated women into never questioning their behaviour or movements and became unaccountable.

Domestic violence Accusations of women's infidelity and disobedience, and the consequent beatings, became more and more common. Women, insecure in their new roles, submitted to the distortions in the gender identity of their men, suppressed their indignation and unleashed their frustrations on other women and, more often, on the children in their care.

Although wife-beating is traditionally unacceptable, men closed ranks and kept quiet as each coped with the frustrations of returning home to confusing gender relations and fear of being cuckolded. Old people, unsure of the new dynamic, distanced from their offspring and dependent on their remittances, did not challenge them. As domestic violence became commonplace some men argued that the abuse of wives is 'cultural'. Boys in schools boasted about the physical control of their girlfriends through violence. As a young man attending gender awareness training with !Nara,[7] explained: 'It's our culture, a woman must do as she is told, if my girl gets home from school after me I beat her, where was she?' All boys in the Aminuis PRA exercise thought that the use of violence to control their girlfriends was justified by their culture. They also argued that girls needed to be taught a lesson, 'they sleep around with older men, they are loose and so ask for it'.[8]

Abdication of the responsibility of fatherhood The mobility and anonymity afforded to men and youths living outside their community for the purpose of work or education permits them sexual freedom. Girls are socialized from a very early age to look for wealthy husbands who will help their families to escape poverty. Encouraged by their parents to attract a wealthy man, they often fall prey to older men dislocated from their wives and families. Such liaisons with older men rarely lead to the marriage or economic security aspired to.

The local assumption that male–female relationships are primarily sexual, compounded by traditional taboos that prohibit discussion about sex and sexuality, leads to all relationships being conducted in secret, providing a window of opportunity for older men to exploit girls, mistrust between older and younger females and many pregnancies with unidentified fathers who deny responsibility. Girls unable to care for the babies leave them in the rural homestead to be cared for by grandmothers or the wife of the baby's father.

The strategy of sending youth away as an investment in future economic security has backfired, but as the pressure on the rural homestead increases younger and younger children are sent away. Society has started to rearrange family relationships to cope with the fathers' abdication of responsibility. A recurrent finding in the participatory appraisal, much to the amusement of women, children and even men, was that the only responsibility fathers had was to buy shoes!

Wealth defines success   Forced removals and the subsequent lack of land reform means that black people barely subsist on the marginal lands they occupy. They aspire to formal employment as a way of escaping poverty. In a country with one of the highest income disparities in the world and where apartheid has denied black people access to other forms of validation,[9] the accumulation and demonstration of wealth has become the main indicator of success: cows, cars, jewellery and branded products. Unable to compete with older, wealthier men (the 'sugar daddies'), boys resort to forcing themselves on girls, to get what they want, to teach the girls a lesson and to defy the older men.

Systems of favouritism and neglect in the home have created an understanding among children that access to resources is equated with love and caring. This serves further to encourage girls to accept relationships with older men who could provide them with gifts and attention, a practice that boys reflected on as defining girls as materialistic, opportunistic and loose.

Divided families   As the pass laws relaxed in the late 1980s, wives, in an attempt to stabilize marital relations and reduce infidelity, followed their men to the towns and farms. The rural homestead became the domain of the old and the very young, supported by San labourers. The old people, unable to cope with the increasing number of young children, send them away to school as soon as possible. Women, faced with increasing poverty and having to care for the children of other women, have established systems of favouritism towards their own or chosen children. Hierarchies of favouritism, neglect and abuse are common, some based on traditional status hierarchies (boy heirs), others newly founded. In the domestic arena women favour, deny, neglect or abuse as they choose without contradiction. Men, dislocated from their traditional roles in child-rearing, claim they can do little to protect the neglected and abused. To enter into discussions on domestic issues would be yet another attack on their masculinity. Witnessing but unable to react openly, they find other reasons to punish their wives for neglecting their (singular) children.

Institutionalized children The state provides subsidized hostels for children from six years old to matriculation, which serves further to dislocate the family. In 1997 67 per cent of Omahake's children lived in hostels. The transfer of childcare to the hostels reduces the physical burden on the homestead and in some cases, but not many, succeeded in transferring the cost of childcare to the fathers. In the hostels, where facilities and supervision are inadequate, the staff underpaid and untrained in childcare and development, children find themselves in a microcosm of the world outside. Hostel staff, having internalized discriminatory ideologies and practices, subject children to physical abuse, humiliation and denial of basic needs in order to victimize and control them. Men seeking opportunities with young girls or wanting to steal from or to bully younger people go in and out of the hostels without challenge as the adults paid to care for the children turn a blind eye.

In schools, teachers are confronted with progressive education policies that promote learner-centred education strategies and rights-based relationships, but have no experience or role models of how to make such democratic systems work. They feel disempowered without the 'stick'. As they continually contradict themselves in trying to implement the new, fearing loss of control and then resorting to the old ways, children are confused by the inconsistency between policy and practice. Violence, intimidation and humiliation remain commonplace means of discipline despite a curriculum and policies that espouse rights and respect.

The early and prolonged institutionalization of children denies them access to traditional systems of initiation into adulthood which have not been replaced. They deal with the emotional and physical aspects of puberty and developing romantic relationships without guidance and model themselves on the adults around them.

Ethnic hierarchies and the assimilation of racist myths In the workplace, black men treated as minors faced discrimination and humiliation. Disempowered and denied their masculinity, they lost their status, dignity and self-esteem; many repressed their resentment with alcohol and relieved their frustration through violence and aggression among themselves. This reinforced racist stereotypes of black people. Victimized by white people, who pointed out that they were acting irresponsibly, just as they expected black people to act, they themselves started to transfer the stereotypes that white people held about them to each other. As they assimilated racist messages, discrimination and oppression were transferred into the existing exclusion systems of patriarchy and ethnic hierarchy.

Ethnic stereotyping and oppression have become acceptable norms as black people absorb the apartheid state's manipulation of historic divisions. A hierarchy of ethnicities has emerged among black people, based on the very same negative assumptions, stereotypes and values of the white oppressors regarding black people. The livelihoods-based ethnic hierarchies of the past were reinforced regardless of contemporary livelihood strategies. Even as farm workers, the Herero would be the foremen, the Tswana would be the skilled labour and the San would be the labourers, considered non-human and to be used at will.[10] Independence from apartheid has brought little change for the San; whether they work for white or black people, the abuse, exploitation and discrimination remain the same. San workers remain unpaid bonded labourers, eating leftovers, wearing discarded clothes and living in broken cars or makeshift shelters. Whole families find themselves bonded to families of the dominant ethnic group, bullied and humiliated into subservience, devalued as human beings. San women are sexually exploited by other ethnic groups but never married or recognized by them. And although, when very young, the children played together, they are taught their differences and as they grow they learn their place in the hierarchy. Those San children who manage to attend school drop out in the lower grades due to discrimination and bullying. The few who manage to cope in school do so through assuming the names and culture of the dominant group and denying their own.

San men, having no 'lower' ethnic group on which to to transfer their frustrations, spiral down into self-loathing and self-abuse, turning upon themselves and their women. Finding solace in alcohol, they 'confirm' a reputation for being drunken, untrustworthy people who have little or no self-respect. San women, too, faced with discrimination and increasing domestic violence, and denied the opportunity to feed and care for their families, take to alcohol. The ethnic myth that San people are incapable of being responsible citizens has been internalized not only by San but also by other ethnic groups who need to consider themselves superior as a means of coping with their own oppression as black people.

Silence and inaction Adults, in unspoken recognition of their own disempowerment as black men and women and their individual roles in the destructive coping mechanisms they have become entrenched in, remain silent and rarely challenge each other on behalf of children. Through action and words adults transferred negative self-images of being black or belonging to a 'lesser' ethnic group and distortions in gender identities to children. Gender–ethnic role models for children are thus established. The resulting sense of low worth among children affects their behaviour towards themselves and others.

THE CONSEQUENCES FOR THE EMERGING ADULTS OF NEW NAMIBIA

In reaction to what they perceive as an adult conspiracy of indifference, exploitation, neglect and abuse, children have developed self-destructive anti-social behaviour. Vulnerable to exploitation and abuse from each other as well as adults, they have developed their own coping mechanisms by imitating their elders. Unsupervised and frustrated they turn to alcohol, violence, theft and sex. Then looking for an opportunity to feel good about themselves and to transfer their anger and frustration, they discriminate against each other by ethnicity, gender and status.

For boys, status is defined by their bloodline and, more and more importantly, their access to demonstrable wealth. This not only indicates the success of their parents but also allows them to compete with older men for girls. Urban youth inspired by Afro-American culture through music and films bring consumer fashions to the rural areas. Young rural boys demand Nike, Adidas, Police and other big-name consumer goods. In the hostel environment, ignored by adults, the need to belong to the in-group is fundamental, and mothers and grandmothers, unable to afford the 'names', are threatened with suicide and violence. Although not directly excluded, San youth are indirectly denied the opportunity of belonging due to the economic impact of racism and ethnocentrism on their families.

The inter-relationship between racism, sexism and adultism that creates distortions in the development of gender–ethnic identities among adults has been assimilated by the youth and children. Young people argue that many of the practices imbibed are part of their traditional culture. Exploitative and abusive relationships between boys and girls, ethnic hierarchies and different status groups are accepted as normal by adults, confirming to children that such attitudes and behaviour are acceptable.

The 'hunters'   Boys focusing on defining their masculinity through demonstrable wealth, the number of lovers and the oppression of women and 'lesser' ethnic groups, find themselves in competition with older men for the attention of their female peers. The boys, denied access to the multiple relationships that would symbolize their manhood, cannot challenge older men so blame and victimize the girls. They accuse them of being loose and resort to sexual violence and bullying.

This has led to the establishment of a ritual in the hostels called 'hunting'. As individuals or in groups they break into the girls' hostels covered in blankets as disguise, and climb into any bed with any girl. Threatening the girls with sharp implements and sometimes cutting off their underwear with razorblades, they rape them. For boys this is an evening's entertainment, celebrated in their dormitories or back at home by bestowing on the best 'hunter' the title 'Jagter Nommer Een' (Hunter Number One). For girls it is an evening of humiliation and shame to be endured in silence.

Boys 'hunt' and abuse girls in the schools with little or no reaction from adults who, over many years, have come to see it as normal behaviour – 'boys will be boys'. Many teachers and parents themselves were the 'hunted' or 'hunter' in their school days, and they rarely take the psychological impact on the girls into account. Even if girls report it, they are not counselled; at best they are taken to the nearest clinic. Meanwhile even those boys who are caught are only reprimanded for hanging about and sent back to their hostel or off the school premises. The worst punishment for 'hunting' noted during the PRA was watering trees, despite the fact that physical punishment is meted out in the case of theft of food, running in the school or even singing at the wrong time in a school event.

In the hostels of Aminius, boys disassociated from traditional systems of initiation into adulthood, denied parental care and guidance, bullied by teachers for other misdemeanours but met with silence on sexual violence, living in squalid conditions with limited food, shelter and care, are learning to act out the societal dysfunction that has been commonplace throughout South Africa and Namibia. Where young black boys daily experience themselves as oppressed and impotent, their frustration about this marginalization is likely to take expression in the domination of girls, and of the San.

> Gender relations cannot be separated from class and race structure, particularly within the southern African context, violence against women has to be viewed in this specific context. One of the most striking features of South African society is its stratification along class, race and gender lines. If one accepts that violence and abuse against women is a manifestation of power imbalances inherent within patriarchal relations, how does this inter-relate with other hierarchical structured relations. It seems that women bear the brunt of men's need to assert power. (Voegelmann and Lewis 1993)[11]

The rights challenge – a way forward? At independence in 1989, black men expected to reinstate themselves as the power holders in ethnic patriarchal structures. What they did not expect was a constitution that enshrined the rights of all; having reclaimed their rights and dignity as back people, black men found themselves renamed the oppressors of women and groups like the Herero, the oppressors of San. The contradiction between a democratic rights-based constitution and their aspirations for reclaiming patriarchy and ethnic hierarchy started to manifest itself in their behaviour.

For the more dominant ethnic groups, the security found in their ethnic identity was intrinsically related to their gender identity. For the less dominant groups, in order to engage men in the discussion about gender power relations and the adult abuse of power over children, it was necessary to explore the constructs of the gender ethnic identity. Through analysing the impact of institutional racism on their own attitudes, behaviour and relationships, men were able to understand the systemic nature of an ideology of superiority, the impact this had on both the oppressed and the oppressor, the cost to everyone involved and the strategies one would employ to deconstruct it. Once they had reached this level of analysis, it was possible to introduce sexism and adultism[12] as related ideologies of superiority and enter into a dialogue about the consequences of manipulation by the apartheid state on their social relations. They understood the multiple identities of people and the need to build equal relations, that theirs was not a struggle of women against men, or young people against adults, but rather a question of everyone taking responsibility for deconstructing domination and building equal relations. The Total Child programme was built on this understanding and set out to influence ways of thinking, feeling, acting and interacting, and, through a process of deconstructing oppressive and exclusionary ways of being and behaving, to construct democratic ways of living.

The new education system exposed children to information on human rights, children's rights, the constitution, and gender and ethnic relations. Children started to challenge adults and demand their rights but without changing their own discriminatory behaviour and without accepting responsibility for rights maintenance. For example, youths argued that they did not need to assist in wood collection and preparing food since they had a right to food. They intimidated their elders, citing cases of parents being imprisoned or divorced by their children for disciplining them.

The glaring contradictions between the constitution, education policy and rights legislation promoted through education and the media, and societal and institutional norms confused children and adults alike. Adults who had grown up in an environment of rights infringement felt disempowered and perceived children's rights as a threat to their control over family life. They blamed the government for denying them control and victimized the children who were developing defiant behaviour patterns. Teachers struggled with their own feelings of inadequacy as they tried to implement the new rights-based, learner-centred education policy[13] that abolished corporal punishment and promoted discipline from within.

Children were taught their rights in the classroom and then were faced with their infringement in school and at home. Adults, confused by the messages they were getting from children and the media about children's rights, swung between inaction based on their misperception that they had been disempowered, and the abuse of their power, resorting to corporal punishment, humiliation and denial of basic needs.

Faced with contradictory messages and shifting boundaries, children perceived these swings between a lack of response and harsh discipline as a conspiracy of abuse and indifference and reacted accordingly. In subconscious attempts to force adults to reset boundaries, they pushed the limits of acceptable behaviour, imitating negative adult role models, carrying out 'courageous' and often erroneous acts, putting themselves and others at risk. When confused adults did not respond or resorted to age-old disciplinary methods, they felt betrayed and confused. Many children left with relatives and placed in hostels lost contact with their parents, then once or twice a year the parents would arrive and demand unconditional respect based on their age.

The responses of both children and adults to this situation set in motion a cycle of misunderstandings that fed the untruth that the old and the young have different aspirations. However, the PRA showed in nearly every case that the aspirations of old and young were mutually reinforcing and were not in conflict, and that the two groups were simply failing to communicate with each other.

TAKING ACTION

Following the participatory research and analysis, the community of Aminuis set out to overcome the legacy of apartheid policies and to start a programme of action, 'To promote dialogue between the stakeholders in children's development towards the protection and affirmation of children. And to promote action among adults and children against social exclusion (exploitation, sexism, ethnocentrism and adultism) and towards empowering individuals, communities and institutions to embrace human rights as a framework for the socialisation of children, citizenship, social transformation and justice.'

Having been able to deal with some of their discomfort with the findings of the participatory research, through analysing the legacies of apartheid and colonialism, they were ready to take a critical look at the parallels in ethnic and gender relations. In the same way that they had constructed a model of racism, they set about constructing models of sexism, ethnocentrism and adult power over children. In groups of men and women, Herero, Tswana and San, they started to understand the nature of social exclusion and how it had led to the situation they were facing.

'Hunting' was seen as not just boys being boys but as a reflection of the distortion of the male ethnic–gender identity manifesting itself among the youth.

Children were assisted to reflect critically on issues of power and participation. In small groups after school they concerned themselves with understanding how things happen, who has power and who does not, and systemic forms of discrimination such as sexism, racism and adultism. In a process that aimed to help them develop a critical awareness of the society around them and how that society works, they were introduced to experiential learning processes on affirmation and cooperation, conflict resolution, gender roles, racism, being together, anger and conflict, becoming assertive, beliefs and values, optimism and rights with responsibility.

In the process of analysing their participatory research, the community realized that children's perceptions of the situation were very different from their own and that they needed to understand them better and to challenge the cultural norms that limited the children's opportunity to enter into dialogue with adults.

The teachers with ACORD organized for children and teachers to attend forum theatre camps where they would develop the skills to articulate their perceptions and establish a dialogue with adults. The plays developed were very provocative, many focusing on the exploitation of children by adults. In the participatory research and in follow-up questionnaires with children, there had been a constant denial of teacher–girls sexual relations, but as soon as they had the right medium the children acted out the seduction and exploitation of girls by teachers. They expressed their concerns over the reaction of families to sexuality, teenage pregnancy and HIV, the abuse, exploitation and neglect of children, child labour enforced by teachers, corporal punishment and humiliation as a form of discipline, the disrespect of teachers for parents, the abuse of girls by boys and 'hunting'.

The plays were performed in schools and villages to teachers, parents, grandparents, community leaders, youth and children and provoked much discussion. With time, as the players developed their theatre skills, they were able to improvise dialogue, with spectators joining the play to act out alternative scenarios.

Forum theatre gave the girls an opportunity to act out how they felt about 'hunting'. And for the first time village youth stood up and publicly acknowledged that 'hunting' was indeed rape and that it caused pain and trauma in girls and women, affecting their lives in the long term. Adults and children decided to take action to stop it. While men still visit the hostels, the extent of 'hunting' by boys has decreased radically. In the last year there have been no reported cases of 'hunting' by senior schoolboys in the primary school and the number of cases in the secondary schools has decreased. Where it has occurred, girls have taken action to report it and the schools and parents are developing appropriate responses.

Communities set about trying to understand the rights of the child. Workshops and experiential learning processes were held to create awareness and understanding of the relationship between rights and responsibility, and children's rights and human rights.

Strategies for change Members of the community recognized that in order to change attitudes and behaviour they needed to address all of the discriminatory practices in parallel and develop a rights-based approach to child socialization and education. From their own analysis they had come to understand the government's education policy and commitment to human rights, children's rights and women's rights.

They identified a wide range of strategies to bring about change:

- Teachers, hostel matrons and community volunteers (Family Visitors) were trained in counselling. Teachers were also trained in redirecting children's behaviour, in leadership and participatory management, in group dynamics, and in experiential facilitation techniques that would provide them with the skills necessary for dealing with children in a non-oppressive way, contradicting the legacies of the past. They organized camps, workshops and extra-curricular activities for children to promote attitudes, skills and knowledge towards non-discriminatory social relations that included gender, ethnicity, racism, sexuality, child empowerment, self-affirmation and equality. Teachers encouraged peer-group management of social and anti-social behaviour both in the community and in institutional environments.
- Resource centres were set up to provide teachers and children with more information on socialization issues such as racism, sexism, managing bullies, guidance counselling, HIV, participatory management and development education, consumerism and fair trade.
- Firesides were constructed in schools to reflect traditional meeting places where children and adults could meet on common ground to explore issues of concern through the use of plays, puppets, storytelling and so on.
- Children embarked on participatory research and action projects in their schools through which they learned how to establish collective

decision-making processes, to negotiate with adults to achieve their objectives and access their support, to make informed decisions and take responsibility for their implementation, monitoring and maintenance.

- Child-to-child projects for schoolchildren were organized in which they made toys and books for pre-school children that promoted non-discriminatory social relations and a sense of self-worth.
- Forum theatre, English and debating clubs were formed in the schools to continue to explore issues of concern and to establish dialogue between the stakeholders.

The chief of the Herero community proposed that the programme take account of the early socialization of children, since children were already socialized in gender, ethnic and age relations before they arrived at school. The community carried out an investigation into the way they socialize children, reflecting on how and at what age they taught children to discriminate on the basis of ethnicity and gender. From this study a Family Visitors' pilot was established in all participating communities. Volunteers were trained to facilitate critical inquiry, using a social exclusion analytical framework, into rights with responsibility, child protection awareness and facilitation techniques for family and community counselling processes. The Ministry of Woman's Affairs and Child Welfare with Unicef and the Ministry of Basic Education provided them with knowledge and skills in early childhood development.

Breaking the silence The situation in Aminuis is not unique. The dehumanization of the black population of Southern Africa has been distressingly efficient, not only in establishing self-reinforcing discriminatory, abusive and oppressive relations but also in establishing a culture of silence and tolerance of abuse.

The people of Aminuis have broken that silence. In developing an analysis of the wider problem, men and boys were able see their behaviour as destructive, not because they had seen themselves portrayed that way, but because they had started to understand the context in which such behaviour had become part of their normal day-to-day life and to question their criteria for being a 'man'.

Although it will take time for behaviour to change, there are many indicators that attitudes have shifted and there is less acceptance of discriminatory behaviour. For example, children report that once school principals have stood up and publicly challenged ethnic bullying the situation improved dramatically. Children of different ethnicities are starting to play together in the villages. Women lead discussions in village meetings. Women and youths challenge male assumptions, and manage the reaction by employing humour. Village men discuss publicly how to deal with men who continue to abuse their wives. San people are starting to challenge discriminatory comments and behaviour in village meetings and relations. San children returning from forum theatre camps become active and visible classroom and school participants. Communities have set up multiethnic kindergartens and home-based childcare groups.

Boys are starting to redefine their masculinity, writing and performing rap songs and dramas against 'hunting' and the abuse of girls. They have renamed 'hunting' as rape. Boys have not 'hunted' at primary schools for a year. In junior secondary schools boys and girls are being counselled about 'hunting' and sexual harassment through processes involving both their families and the schools. Girls reporting harassment and exploitation by older men (including teachers) have engaged the support of their fathers and families who have worked with them to hold institutions to account and to demand appropriate action. School leadership and school boards are learning how to manage cases of sexual harassment and deal with rape through involving the police. At the outset of the programme the school community wanted to make a gate in the back of the hostel so that staff could enter in the early hours without being intimidated by male night visitors, now older girls in the hostels have been given the keys and responsibility of securing the hostels at night.

The teachers in Aminuis, having recognized that ideologies of superiority are built in fiction rather than fact, have posted signs in the staffrooms saying, 'Stop living as though the lies were true'. They recognize that collusion through inaction is as destructive as practising discrimination and abuse. Inaction and no response are being replaced by action through dialogue.

CONCLUSION

Research suggests that the damage to the masculine identity of Southern African black men has been immense and that the consequences for women and children and society in general are devastating. The manipulation of the male gender–ethnic identity by the state forced black men to define themselves negatively in relation to white people while denying them the opportunity and resources required to fulfil traditional masculine roles. This has resulted in attempts to reclaim their status by oppressing women and children.

While in Namibia and South Africa this was an explicit policy, the same dynamic can be witnessed in many other countries, especially but not exclusively in regard to black people. For example, the manipulation of gender–ethnic identities in the conflicts of Uganda and Sierra Leone has led to the use of gender violence as a weapon of war. By raping other men's women, abducting and mutilating their children and raping their fathers, husbands and brothers, states and rebel forces strike at the heart of patriarchy. Men denied the opportunity to provide for or protect their families are either subdued and frustrated into alcoholism and domestic violence or take up arms to reclaim some sense of worth. Either way the manipulators win and society loses. There is then an argument for establishing a gender discourse with men and women that explores the vulnerability created by patriarchy (the nexus of sexism and ethnocentrism).

As far back as Fanon in the nineteenth century, researchers, academics and psychologist have articulated the relationship between racist and sexist constructs, but research and development programmes still continue with a gender discourse that polarizes women as victims and men as oppressors. While development policies, strategies and awareness processes continue to focus on defining one's identity against another's, there will be little movement in gender relations. 'Gender' will be synonymous with 'women'. Meanwhile, men will be prejudged and left to develop destructive mechanisms to cope with racism, sexism and the patriarchy that confines them to aspiring to unattainable ideals of masculinity.

The process of deconstructing ideologies of superiority is a complex one. It is no use for researchers and academics to explore and articulate their findings; people have to work through the analysis themselves. They have to identify the mechanisms that construct, maintain and manipulate oppressive ideologies. This takes time, energy and commitment, but the people of Aminuis embarked on this journey. The children checked their assumptions: Are all black people dirty rapists? Are all white people good and kind? They explored who had told them this and where they found the reinforcement of these messages, they looked at

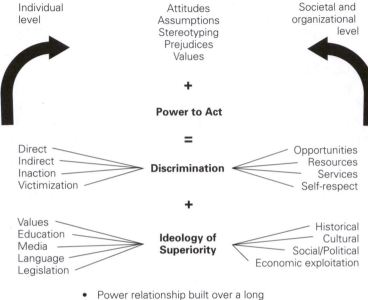

Individual
level

Attitudes
Assumptions
Stereotyping
Prejudices
Values

Societal and
organizational
level

+

Power to Act

=

Direct
Indirect
Inaction
Victimization

Discrimination

Opportunities
Resources
Services
Self-respect

+

Values
Education
Media
Language
Legislation

**Ideology of
Superiority**

Historical
Cultural
Social/Political
Economic exploitation

- Power relationship built over a long period of time;
- Systematic economic exploitation;
- Consequence of unbroken power by powerful groups over less powerful ones;
- It enters the culture of both groups;
- To some extent it is internalized by both;
- It helps oppressors to feel good about themselves;
- It is self-reinforcing

=

**Social
Exclusion**

Figure 5.1 Model of social exclusion

the media, their textbooks, their traditional stories, their history written and oral, the language people used, the laws, the political systems, the economic exploitation and the manipulation of consumer-based popular culture. Once they discovered the race-based fallacies, they then turned to look at their assumptions about women and men. Meanwhile, the adults were doing the same. They looked at how they had bought into the very ideologies that oppressed them and socialized children to accept the expectations assigned them by their race, ethnicity, status and gender and how this had impacted on their relations with each other, creating layer upon layer of exclusion and injustice. Reflection led to dialogue and to action. This involved nothing dramatic but a critical way of thinking, influencing and being that established the value of human rights above all as the basis for action, interaction and decision-making.

A DFID adviser described the Aminuis process as 'mass therapy'; maybe it is, for it reflects the pattern of a therapy process – naming, denial, analysis, understanding, deconstruction, dialogue and construction. But even in the early days he was convinced it would work ('in future one would be able to tell on first meeting that this person had grown up in Aminuis'), but he was concerned about how one would set about it in a systemic way to reach enough people. The answer is to use the same routes as those used to implement the ideology – the education system, the media, the legislature, history books, religion, socialization processes – but this time to create a milieu for the critical analysis of the cultural, social, political and economic structures and systems that perpetuate exclusion.

NOTES

1. Aminuis is some 400 km from the capital Windhoek and sits on the edge of the Kalahari Desert on the Namibia–Botswana border. Surrounded by commercial (pre-, dominantly white-owned) farms, it was created as a reserve for the Tswana people. Today it is populated by three main groups the Herero (traditionally pastoralist), who are dominant in numbers and culture; the Tswana (traditionally agriculturalists and small stock farmers); and the San and Kalahari (traditionally hunter-gatherers).

2. A hunter-gatherer group that faces extreme discrimination as an ethnic underclass.

3. The Agency for Cooperation and Research in Development – Multimedia Campaign on Violence Against Women and Children.

4. The Multimedia Campaign on Violence Against Women and Children.

5. Social Exclusion Analysis developed from *Understanding Racism and Developing Good Practice*, OSDC, Basic model, Annex 1.

6. Dormitory-style accommodation built to house black men in areas where the apartheid regime required a labour force.

7. !Nara Institute for Participatory Development, Windhoek.

8. Herero youth, 14 Rietquelle School, Aminuis.

9. Black people were not allowed to advance their careers beyond teaching and nursing.

10. The WIMSA library in Windhoek contains a wealth of research on and by San.

11. 'Jackrolling' in South Africa (Wood and Jewkes 2001), the 'tournaments' of urban Namibia and the 'hunting' of Aminius have similar characteristics as an assertion of masculinity and a way of punishing women seen as a threat. 'These women think they are better than anyone else, they look down on us, they prefer men who have money and drive in nice cars. When these women get jackrolled it's okay, she likes big men so let them give it to her' (Mokwena 1991).

12. The relationship between adults and children based on the notion that adults are superior and have the power to act on their negative assumptions about children and youth.

13. 'Towards Education for All'.

REFERENCES

Andersson, N., S. Mhatire, S. Naidoo, M. Mayet, N. Mqotsi, M. Penderis, J. Onishi, M. Myburg and S.Merhi (2000) *Beyond Victims and Villains. The Culture of Sexual Violence in South Johannesburg*, Report for the Southern Metropolitan Council, CIET.

Campanile, V. (2001) 'Feminism at Work: A Case Study of Transforming Power Relations in Everyday Life: Puntos de Encuentro', in *Institutionalizing Gender Equality: Commitment, Policy and Practice, a Global Source Book*, Oxfam GB, KIT publishers, The Netherlands.

George, E. (2001) Scared at School: Sexual Violence Against Girls in South African Schools. Human Rights Watch USA. www.hrw.org/reports/2001/safrica

Hurt, B. (2000) *I am a Man: Black Masculinities in America* (video documentary).

Leach, F. (2001) 'Conspiracy of Silence? Stamping out Abuse in African Schools', *Development Research Insights Special* (August) (Brighton: IDS/DfID).

Mokwena, S. (1991) *The Era of Jackrollers: Contextualising the Rise of Youth Gangs in Soweto*, Paper presented at seminar, a Project for the Study of Violence, University of Witwatersrand, Johannesburg.

Vetten, L. (1997) 'Roots of the Rape Crisis', *Crime and Conflict*, 8 (Summer): 9–12 (Centre for the Study of Violence and Reconciliation, University of Witwatersrand, Johannesburg).

Voegelmann, L. (1990) 'People and the Violence in South Africa. Violent Crime:

Rape', in B. McKendrick and W. C. Hoffman (eds), *People and Violence in South Africa* (Cape Town: Oxford University Press), pp. 96–134.

Voegelmann, L. and G. Eagle (1991) 'Overcoming Endemic Violence Against Women', *Social Justice*, 18(1–2): 209–29.

Voegelmann, L. and Lewis, S. (1993) 'Illusion der Starke: Jugendbanden, vergewaltingung und kultuur der gewalt in Sudafrika', *Der Uberlick*, 2: Gang Rape and the Culture of Violence in South Africa: 39–44.

WISER (Wits Institutute for Social and Economic Research) (2001) Flagship research projects: http://www.wits.ac.za/wiser/research.htm and www.wits.ac.za/wiser/research.htm

Wood, K. and R. Jewkes (2001) 'Dangerous Love? Challenging Male Machismo', *Development Research Insights*, Special Issue.

CHAPTER 6

Men in Women's Groups: a Gender and Agency Analysis of Local Institutions

HELEN HAMBLY ODAME

§ This chapter explores the minority membership of men in rural women's self-help groups. The context of this study is a major development project in Siaya district, western Kenya. Rural women's organizations in Siaya have experienced significant rates of collapse. The study of group membership, activities and governance reveals how relations between and among women and men shape institutions at the local level. Men were identified as playing roles described as 'go-betweens', 'co-workers', 'opportunists' and 'agitators'. Government policy and non-governmental organizations underestimate the influential roles played by men in women's groups, thus reducing the management and leadership potential of women and the sustainability of collective action.

It is widely acknowledged that gender-blind approaches to rural development made women invisible despite their significant contributions to agricultural production and environmental management. However, women and development approaches have made men invisible in key circumstances. One such shortcoming of WID/GAD policy has been to underestimate, both empirically and theoretically, the role of men in women's self-help organizations. Rarely noted in the literature, the presence of men in women's groups invokes the existence of patron–client relations in rural society. Little is known about the roles men assume in women's groups although this inquiry is relevant to addressing issues around institutional development and sustainability of collective action in rural areas.

This chapter begins with some reflections on the topic of gender and institutions, specifically in the context of rural Africa. The main challenges to present-day thinking in gender and development where local institutions are concerned are identified. The situation in Kenya concerning government policy towards rural women's groups is then addressed, followed by specific reference to the rise and fall of women's groups in the context of a major development activity in Siaya district, western Kenya. The apparent roles assumed by male members and leaders of women's self-help organizations are illuminated. Finally, the chapter concludes with a discussion of relevant policy considerations and issues for future research.

GENDER AND INSTITUTIONS IN RURAL AREAS

As rural sociologists have observed, nowhere in the world is rural society homogeneous (Kloppenburg 1991). What is referred to as the 'local level' or 'local institutions' are highly heterogeneous contexts, with diverse individuals and organizations whose needs, interests and activities vary widely and reflect both cultural and historical conditions. Feminist scholars argue that power relations in society are structured so asymmetrically that women and men rarely receive equal and/or equitable treatment and representation (Nicholson 1986). Given the ever-changing roles and relations which women and men experience in their lifetimes, it is impossible to generalize the multiple subjectivities that constitute the concept of gender. Therefore, gender analysis investigates dynamic roles and relations in society to account for the disparities that exist between men and women, and among women and men themselves (Connell 1987; Young 1988). It is through this capacity to address both unity and difference that the concept of gender gains its analytical strength.

Feminism, as applied to organizational studies, has examined the historical evolution and consequences of women in the workplace and management (Mills and Tancred 1992; Acker 1996). This literature has grown extensively, sometimes under the pseudonym of 'diversity' featuring now in most textbooks on organizational behaviour and human resource management. Less frequently, however, issues of women, organizations and management are explored in light of the postcolonial discourse and developing country context (Calas 1992).

Generally, gender studies have opened up organizations and conceptualized them not as material or technical entities but as social constructions and cultural systems. The literature still focuses heavily on 'women and workplace' issues, including sex segregation of occupations, and gender inequalities in recruitment, workload, pay and career development. While the 'embeddedness' of gender is substantiated in this research, more attention to non-industrial, non-western environments is needed. This is especially important if gender relations are understood as socially constructed attitudes and behaviour, that can, and do, change through the empowerment of women and the liberation of men from roles and relations that they may no longer desire or tolerate (Whitehead 1985; Plewes and Stewart 1991; Cornwall and Lindisfarne 1994; Connell 1995). In this respect, organizations are relevant as the context, means and outcome of women's empowerment. They are viewed as conflictual environments, and not as ahistorical, culturally or politically neutral partners or 'entry points' for development projects. Indeed, Tenga and Peters (1996) refer to the right to organize as 'the mother of all rights'. Organizations influence how poor, rural people address basic needs through a collective activist movement, thus challenging the narrow 'practical *versus* strategic needs' debate of past WID/GAD approaches (Hambly 1992: 145–7).

Recent feminist research on organizations in developing countries suggests two things: first that the size of the organization does not matter, and, second, that individuals and their actions and roles in the organization do matter to theory and practice. Goetz's (1997) discussion of 'getting institutions right for women' illustrates the first point. She proposes a framework for a gendered archaeology of organizations derived from the analysis of a wide variety of organizational contexts, each of which is found to be different. It is argued that a general prescription for policy or projects to address 'women's interests' will not sufficiently change the gender biases of institutions. Goetz sees change in local and global societies occurring through implicit political struggle by male and female feminists to reshape institutions in their specific context. This means that each organization, no matter how small or large, is a playing field of institutional change, including what organizational sociologists refer to as de-institutionalization (Powell and DiMaggio 1991). Through cumulative and repetitive critiques of organizations lies the transformation of institutions to support improved gender relations.

In the second area of feminist organizational analyses, attention is paid to issues such as membership, leadership and power, with a focus on structure (rules) and role-specific aspects of organizations. Resistance to change is inherent in the power structures of organizations under pressure to change (Clegg 1994). Feminist research offers cases where institutions use legislation at both the national and local level, and organizations employ various procedures and policy tools to reinforce the lack of political and economic change, and to serve as systematic checks against improvements in gender relations (Mbeo and Ombaka 1989; Miller and Razavi 1998). This includes the identification of men as members of 'women's groups' in development projects (Harrison 1997). In their review of the feminist organizational studies, Calas and Smirich (1996) point to new ways of seeing individuals whose complex subjectivities and interactions redefine fundamental concepts of organizational behaviour such as leadership and use of power. Herein is the continuing challenge to feminist organizational research: to revisit the concept of gender, especially the critique of men and masculinity. Analyses that advance from assumptions of male competitiveness and female collaboration are needed to problematize leadership and power in organizations, particularly in the neglected contexts of non-industrialized, developing country organizations.

WOMEN'S GROUPS IN KENYA

Women's groups' activities are viewed by the government of Kenya as key indicators to gauge the involvement of women in national and local socioeconomic development (Republic of Kenya 1994b: 256). As vehicles for self-help and income-generation, women's groups are 'one of the most significant efforts by rural women to take their affairs in their own hands' (Republic of Kenya 1994b: 38). By the mid-1990s, there were an estimated 23,614 women's groups in Kenya, both registered and unregistered, with a membership of 968,941 (MCSS 1991). A neglected aspect of women's groups in Kenya is that men may and do comprise a minority of their membership.[1]

Women's groups, although organized at the local level, operate in an increasingly complex institutional environment where they are required to maintain relations with other organizations such as NGOs or the Kenyan state. Government and non-governmental organizations consider women's groups in Kenya as important organizational structures or channels through which development assistance is transferred to the local level. At the local level in western Kenya, state relations with women's groups are mediated by the district office through a process of mandatory registration and reporting.

The first official registration of women's self-help groups dates back to the early 1930s with an intensification of this process after Independence in 1963 (Hay 1976; Staudt 1991). Many of the groups formed were directed towards improvements in women's social welfare. Agricultural activities were long conducted under the banner of home economics groups. In western Kenya, the overall movement of women's groups was slower, as compared to activities closer to the capital, Nairobi (Wipper 1984). However, by the 1980s the District Focus for Rural Development approach to decentralized public services and the move of the Kenyan state towards a multi-party system reinvigorated the registration process for women's groups and the purview of their activities by the district offices.

Registration of women's groups in Kenya involves recognition of the group and its members by the location-level authorities (i.e. the chief and the location-level government official for the Department of Social Services). It requires the completion of forms which record the names of the group executive and the proposed objectives and activities of the group. After submitting the forms and paying a one-off registration fee, the group is approved and registered with the district office. Through this process, the state ensures that every group has an entirely female executive committee made up of the chair (often referred to as the chairlady), treasurer and secretary. The district office requires this information to monitor the women's groups. Such monitoring is conducted in collaboration with local administrators (i.e. chiefs) who provide updates on the women's groups in their location. This registration process also validates a minority male membership in women's groups: regulations allow 20 per cent of the members to be men (MCSS 1991). The actual situation and implications of mixed membership in the women's groups involved in this study are discussed below.

An analysis of state guidelines for group registration and discussions with local officials suggest that official government policy is less concerned with membership of women's groups than with their activities. For instance, groups involved in economic activities as well as savings and loans programmes are designated for 'general control and oversight' by the Kenyan state in accordance with the 1991 policy guidelines. In contrast, groups involved in welfare activities such as adult education, healthcare and tree planting are expected to be supervised by the sponsoring government or non-governmental organization responsible for that particular programme or activity (MCSS 1991). According to the state, this division of responsibility is needed to avoid the inadequate registration and supervision of groups that arise when they are formed without the involvement of the authorities. An implication of this policy guideline is that registered women's groups involved in economic activity are potentially subject to supervision and interference by the district authorities.

Siaya district in western Kenya is indicative of the tremendous increase in the number of women's groups now registered in the country. Records at the district office reveal that over the past three decades the number of registered women's groups has grown steadily. As illustrated in Figure 6.1, only forty-two groups were registered in 1979, whereas in 1992 there were at least 2,105 groups (Republic of Kenya 1994a: 34).

Analysis of district data confirmed that the location of the women's groups correlated with the frequency of official registration. In other words, the closer the women's group was to the district headquarters, the town of Siaya, the more likely the group was to be registered with the district office. This situation is due to two reasons: first, registration allows state authorities to monitor group activities (and therefore control them through this monitoring process) and it was easier for civil servants

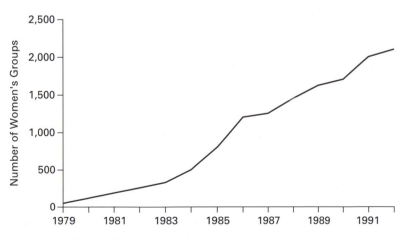

Figure 6.1 Increase in the number of women's groups in Kenya in the 1980s.

to reach those women's groups based near district headquarters as opposed to more distant groups. A second explanation was that women's groups could access the headquarters registration more easily if they were geographically closer to the district office. It was therefore important to our analysis to keep in mind the geographic distribution of women's groups and the 'reach of the state' when examining the experience of women's groups.

EVIDENCE FROM SIAYA DISTRICT IN WESTERN KENYA

Collective organization in agriculture is a long-standing practice in many parts of the world. Development policy and programming have adopted the 'group approach' on the basis of ensuring a more efficient and effective distribution of public services, the partnership of local agencies in projects, and for improving the likelihood of project sustainability.

The CARE Agroforestry Extension Project (AEP) is a case in point of an agricultural and social forestry project targeting women's groups to reach individual farmers. Since 1983, the AEP promoted agroforestry in western Kenya through assistance to 3,000 small-scale farm households through 300 women's groups.

Through the 1980s and early 1990s the AEP was considered 'one of the most successful attempts at disseminating simple and appropriate agroforestry technologies in Kenya' (Cook and Grut 1989: 22). The reputed success of the AEP suggests that evidence exists to support the premise that local institutional development took place and women's groups played a major role in this process. This hypothesis was tested against data from field research during 1991 and 1995, incorporating a return to sites and individuals surveyed in 1991 (Hambly 2000). This time-series dimension was essential to the analysis of project benefits (the focus of the research in 1991) and their sustainability (the focus in 1995). In addition to interviewing farmers and women's groups involved in the project, non-project farmers were also interviewed in order to compare the experiences of farmers in and outside the project.

Women's group activities Essentially, women's groups were found to be involved in more than just agroforestry for wood-fuel and soil and water conservation, which were the main AEP activities. As Table 6.1

shows, the major activities included purchase and resale of grains and legumes (maize, sorghum, beans and groundnuts), and to a lesser extent crop production on farmland cultivated by the group. Only a fraction of women's groups were active in tree nursery and tree-planting activities, although four active AEP groups were selling agroforestry products (polewood, timber and fruits) from trees planted during the 1980s. The crops produced or money earned were directly divided among group members, or the money earned from the sale of group produce was reinvested in the group's savings and loans activities. The majority of non-project or 'other groups' to which AEP farmers belonged in 1995 were mainly involved in savings and loans activities. Only 17 per cent of those savings and loans groups ($n=^6/_{35}$) were associated with other organizations at the local level, such as churches.

Both wealthier and poorer farmers join women's groups in order to gain access to certain opportunities and resources. Observation of group activities suggests that many of these economic activities also offer unquantifiable benefits to farmers, including opportunities to socialize with neighbours, friends and family. Therefore, it would be unwise to imply that the social function of women's groups can or should be separated from their economic function. Nevertheless, farmers' responses when asked why they join women's groups reflect their desire to gain access to three key resources: capital, labour and arable land, in that order.

With respect to access to capital, some further attention is required because it was found that many women's groups involved in agroforestry have simultaneously saved and invested their returns in savings and loans activity. In this study, the term 'capital' refers to the investment or savings generated or contributed by members of the women's groups, from which members can obtain loans. These arrangements were effectively 'rural banks' for women's group members although they were paid little attention by the project.

Our findings suggest a complex system of savings and loans operates among group members. Returns from agricultural and agroforestry activities are saved in the group account. This may be a bank account or, for smaller amounts of money, funds held by the treasurer of the group. Income could be earned by the women's group and later invested in other activities or distributed among members at the end of the calendar year. These funds could be divided equally in proportion to

Table 6.1 Major activities of AEP women's groups (as a percentage of groups engaging in each activity)

Major activity	1991 AEP farmers (n=38) AEP groups		1995 AEP farmers interviewed (n=41/54)*			
			Active or partially active AEP groups		Other groups	
	no.	%	no.	%	no.	%
Agricultural and tree crops production and/or marketing	22	66.6	5	45.5	15	21.7
Tree nurseries and tree-planting only (no marketing)	9	27.2	3	27.2	2	2.9
All types of savings and loans	–	–	2	18.1	35	50.7
Group/wage agricultural labour	2	6	1	9.1	6	8.7
Political and religious campaigns	–	–	–	–	4	5.8
Singing/praying/cooking at funerals	–	–	–	–	4	5.8
Fishing/smoking and selling fish	–	–	–	–	2	2.9
Handicrafts (weaving/pottery)	–	–	–	–	1	1.4
Total	33	99.8	11	99.9	69	99.9

* In 1995, eleven AEP farmers were not involved in any group and two did not reply. Farmers may be members of up to four other groups in addition to the AEP group (if it still existed in 1995).

Source: Author's in-depth group interviews and farmer surveys, 1991 and 1995.

the work accomplished by members, and paid directly to the group members. Some of the activities earn no direct economic returns; these are contributions made to religious projects or political campaigns and could include donations for building a church or certain church facilities, or sometimes contributions to the campaign of a local politician. These 'investments' accounted for the smallest percentage of women's groups' use of capital.

Most importantly, the findings concerning women's groups' 'informal banks' indicated that savings could be the source of investments and possible loans for individual group members, both women and men. This was a major motivation for group involvement reported by project and non-project farmers, especially women farmers. The savings and loans activities could take two distinct forms. One was cash held in the group account, from which loans could be made to group members at 20 per cent per annum interest. Non-group members can also 'apply' for loans, but at a higher interest rate (typically 30–50 per cent per annum). The second form of activity was loans made specifically for funerals.

Some savings and loans activities of women's groups are also investments that provide farmers with insurance against future emergencies. In Siaya, farmers refer to groups that engage in this activity as m'asira, or 'funeral groups', because they loan money from their savings for the benefit of bereaved group members. Funeral groups rarely collapse due to misuse of funds because there is a strong cultural sanction against stealing money associated with death and bereavement. Yet the meaning of these women's groups to farmers must also be reinforced by the necessity of having activities for dealing with an emergency. It was also noted that funeral groups have the most specific objectives and the least formal characteristics. They meet only when there is a death in a member's family. Over half these groups have no name other than 'funeral group' and often no permanent executive committee except for a secretary/treasurer who records the contributions and holds or distributes funds among the members. Both male and female members of the groups acted as secretary/treasurer in these cases. It was also noted that few of these groups were registered with the district office; therefore, many such groups were outside state purview.

In general, this information about women's groups and their activities in Siaya District suggests greater diversity and complexity than previously acknowledged. Evidently, most farmers (70 per cent) engaged in the agroforestry project were involved in more than one women's group in order to meet the different needs that they experience both as individuals (e.g. as widows) or as a group (e.g. as a family). Agroforestry was combined with other activities such as savings and loans. Involvement in women's groups was of interest to both wealthier and poorer farmers, although poorer farmers were especially interested in savings and loans opportunities.

Women's group collapse Women's groups in Siaya district that participated in the AEP from as early as 1984 experienced a fairly dramatic rate of collapse. Unfortunately, no official 'survival rate' for women's groups in Siaya is available for comparison. The Ministry of Culture and Social Services (MCSS 1991: 5) did, however, recognize an 'unacceptably high rate of failure' among women's groups. Given that 67 per cent of the groups interviewed in 1991/92 had collapsed by 1995, the rate can be considered to be quite high by any measure.

From the outset of field research, the fall of women's groups in the AEP was seen as relevant to the implementation of the project and efforts to strengthen local institutions that would be supportive of agroforestry. What was not known was why women's groups had collapsed, or why some survived. In the analysis, women's groups were

Table 6.2 Number of women's groups, by division, 1991–95

Division	Groups interviewed in 1991	Groups active in 1995	Groups inactive in 1995	Groups partially active in 1995
Boro/Uranga	7	0	5	2
Rarieda/Madiany	7	1	6	0
Bondo/Usigu	6	4	2	0
Ukwala/Ugunja	7	0	6	1
Yala/Wagai	6	2	3	1
Total	33 (100%)	7 (21%)	22 (67%)	4 (12%)

Source: Author's in-depth group interviews and farmer surveys, 1991 and 1995.

classified into one of three categories: active, inactive and partially active. Groups were considered to be inactive if they no longer met as a group or conducted collective activity. Partially active groups met less than once every six months. Their agroforestry activities were weak or nearly non-existent, but the group still met. In contrast, active groups met at least once every three months (typically, once a month) and maintained, as a group, activities related to agroforestry that had been initiated while they were participating in the AEP. Table 6.2 provides a summary of this classification of women's groups, sorted by division.

More than two-thirds of the women's groups interviewed in 1991 and active in the AEP since 1988/89 had collapsed by 1995. These findings suggested some variation across the ten divisions in Siaya District.[2] Bondo had the highest proportion of women's groups still active in 1995, three years after the AEP had ceased its extension and technical inputs into women's groups. Unlike the correlation of the location of the groups with their official registration noted above, location had no effect on women's groups in Boro division, which, although closest to the town of Siaya, were not necessarily less likely to collapse.

The term 'group collapse' is relevant to this study as an indicator of what studies on the sociology of organizations have referred to as *de-institutionalization* (Powell and DiMaggio 1991). In this case, women's groups that once had defined structure, governance and activities ceased to exist as organizations. Collapsed groups do not meet on a regular basis or carry out any type of group activity, agroforestry-related or otherwise. It was noted, however, that this does not necessarily mean that the group had dissolved a group bank account, or resolved possible disputes over collectively held funds and resources. As well, some past leaders of collapsed women's groups held on to or used to their individual advantage group assets or equipment (e.g. trees, donkey carts, wheelbarrows, seeds, watering cans). Finally, group collapse does not mean that the group is de-registered with the district office. The author found that 41 per cent of women's groups that had collapsed since 1991/92 still appeared (under a partial or full name) in the state register in 1995.

There was never only one reason for a group's collapse; all twenty-two AEP women's groups that had collapsed cited at least two major problems. The various reasons provided by farmers individually and through focus group discussion are listed in Table 6.3.

Farmers, both inside the groups and AEP and outside them, discussed a range of opinions and actual reasons as to why women's groups fall. For instance, in discussions concerning relations within the women's group as a reason for group collapse, AEP farmers said problems arose because internal differences were exacerbated by other, externally related problems. For instance, misuse of group-held resources was often found to relate to poor communication with the AEP or interference by 'outsiders' (chiefs, local politicians, the NGO and so on).

Surviving women's groups Not all of the thirty-three women's groups involved in this study collapsed. Seven were still active in 1995 and in interviews with them the team sought to understand why women's

Table 6.3 Number of actual and perceived reasons for group collapse[1]

Reason[2]	Actual	Perceived	
	AEP groups (n=11)	Other AEP farmers (n=29/54)	Non-AEP farmers (n= 37/42)
Greed, misused or stolen resources	8	9	10
Infrequent meetings; low turnout	8	3	0
Poor relationship with the AEP	7	4	n/a
Death/absence of group coordinator	6	4	0
Interference by officials/politicians	4	3	0
Imbalances in group work	3	4	1
Lazy members	3	3	0
Time-consuming activities	1	1	5
Lack of money and inputs	0	2	1
Weak/uneducated leaders	0	1	0
No answer/ don't know	0	11	4

Notes: 1. Reasons identified were either 'actual' (as reported by actual group members) or 'perceived' (as reported by other farmers observing these groups). Neither group of responses is expected to represent the 'only truth' of why groups collapse. 2. Some groups/farmers provided more than one answer; n/a = not applicable.

Source: Author's in-depth group interviews and farmer surveys, 1995.

groups survive, and to what extent the groups had continued their involvement in agroforestry-related activities after the AEP ceased its assistance to them. In fact, all these groups still operated tree nurseries of varying sizes. They also reported that their members had benefited from access to tree seedlings, on-farm tree-planting and the sale of tree seedlings (four cases only). Beyond this point, generalizing about the seven cases is problematic as each had specific characteristics that contributed to its resilience. There were only two common characteristics identified in the in-depth analysis of the several cases of surviving women's groups: (1) the role and style of group leadership; and (2) the extent to which the groups achieved and continued to achieve benefits from their collective activity. These benefits could be in the form of products such as crops or cash distributed to individual members, access to group labour, transport or natural resources such as arable land. As mentioned earlier, small-scale revolving savings and loans activities were practised by all surviving AEP groups, but this form of activity was more typical of groups categorized as 'partially active', rather than active and surviving women's groups. The intangible benefits enjoyed by surviving women's groups (for instance, trust or loyalty among group members, protection from external interference, and social – including religious – interaction with friends or family) were observed to be the inseparable basis for tangible benefits.

These two factors – group leadership and benefits – also seemed to work together to support the self-image and purpose of the women's groups. To explain this point further, it is useful to describe two of these women's groups.[3]

Case 1: Okiero Women's Group   The Okiero Women's Group was set up to respond to the CARE AEP's call for women's groups to join the project in 1984. The group is located only 7km from the AEP headquarters. The seventeen group members include five men. Selina Achieng, the oldest member of the group, is seventy-one years old. She and her son Christopher Otek, who is thirty-nine years old, have always been 'executive' members of the group. Otek is the coordinator, but officially his wife, Margaret, is the chairlady and Selina is the group treasurer. In the past eleven years, the group has cultivated and sold vegetables and cereals and used the surplus food for catering at funerals. They report that they can make more money processing and selling the surplus food at funerals than through any other type of marketing activity.

In 1991, interviews with Okiero Women's Group showed it to be one of the most successful women's groups involved in agroforestry in the district. In 1990, the group produced 4,000 seedlings of several tree species during the long rainy season. The group still operates a tree nursery, but produces only 700 seedlings per year. The 12 farmers participating in the main interview reported that they had planted out more than 1,000 trees since 1991. Having all the seedlings they currently need, the farmers are eager to find new ways of selling the seedlings they produce in their tree nursery.

On land still registered in the name of the dead husband of Selina Achieng, the group has planted several fairly well-maintained alleys of maize, *Leucaena* and *Glyrricidia*. The group also has two zero-grazed cows that provide milk for sale. The group obtained the cows from a church project in 1993. In addition to their involvement in the AEP, Okiero Women's Group also received and repaid a loan from another CARE activity in Siaya, the Women's Income Generating (WIG) project. The group used this money to buy and sell maize and sorghum. This was a successful enterprise, although the group did not reveal the level of profits realized. The group has a savings and loan arrangement for its members. Each member donates 10K/sh (less than US 15 cents) every fortnight towards the group account. When the group meets, each person pays 10K/sh to the member who hosts the meeting to cover the cost of tea and porridge served to the group members. If a member misses the group meeting or any type of group work, he or she is charged 10K/sh which is given to the organizer of the meeting.

During all three visits to the Okiero Women's Group, Christopher Otek dominated the discussion. He said, 'Some years ago the group was feeling so nice, but recently it has become discouraged.' He stated that the group 'is well known for its skill in nursery work and that it is even known to the government'. Several visitors have been brought to the tree nursery because the group devised its own way of growing tree seedlings using banana leaves for pots. Even researchers from Kenya Forestry Research Institute (KEFRI) came to take cuttings from the trees. Another member of the group, a fifty-five-year-old man, interjected a comment that members of the group were growing bitter. 'We know the gifts for what they are,' he said. This comment was a reference to a promise from KEFRI that the farmers would be paid for the tree cuttings taken to Nairobi. Another group member added that a church project had reminded them that money given to the group to purchase a dairy cow was only a loan which has to be repaid with a female calf or in cash. The cow often requires veterinary medicine that the group cannot afford and the members are not in agreement that it is paying for itself.

Three-quarters of the members of the Okiero Women's Group belong to other women's groups. 'The more groups you are in, the more you gain,' said Otek. One NGO is going to plant sunflowers and 'will give me a machine to process the oil'. The money comes from Britain, he has heard. Alcoholics Anonymous has also started a *posho* (flour) mill project nearby, and Margaret, the group chairlady and Otek's wife, is the cashier at the mill. Otek is pleased about this because the business is running well.

The research assistants found it difficult to interrupt Otek and direct questions to other members of the group, including Selina Achieng, the team's contact AEP farmer. At the end of one visit, Otek said in English, 'Come to me if you have more questions, I know, the others don't know.' A research assistant felt challenged by another remark from Otek: 'CARE people are not serious; they do not listen to people's problems.' He gave the research assistant a list of items he wanted delivered to the CARE headquarters in Siaya. The items ranged from a biogas unit to pesticides. Otek estimated the total cost of this list came to 125,000 K/sh or US $4,200.

Case 2: Uhuru Women's Group Walter Otieno was born in 1927 and has lived all his life in the village of his birth. Otieno has been a member of the Uhuru Women's Group since it was set up in 1969. It was less active in the 1970s than in the 1980s. It joined the AEP in 1984 after learning from the chief that a new project to support farmers was being started. At the beginning of the 1980s, Uhuru Women's Group had twenty-six members, twenty of whom were women. In 1995, it had only twelve members, seven of whom were women. The others had gradually dropped out of the group as they realized that the tree nursery activities were small-scale and that, as one group member commented, there would be no cash handouts.

Otieno is the coordinator of Uhuru Women's Group. His wife is the chairlady of the group. Otieno is a prosperous farmer who owns twenty head of cattle, three of which are zero-grazed cows. He hires three full-time labourers to help him on his farm; they are also members of the women's group. Nearly two acres of his farm are planted with trees, plus a one-acre woodlot. He continues to replace the trees he harvests with indigenous species of trees as well as eucalyptus and cypress for timber production. Otieno owns the land on which the Uhuru Women's Group has its tree nursery. The nursery is large in comparison with most women's groups' tree nurseries observed in Siaya district. It is approximately a quarter of an acre in size and is on well-drained soil less than 500m from a stream. A pile of manure stands nearby to use in the seedbed. In the late 1980s, the group used to produce several thousand tree seedlings and thousands of vegetable seedlings per season. Production is now less than 300 tree seedlings and 500 vegetable seedlings per season. The reason for this reduced activity, according to Mama Salome, one of Otieno's three wives and who was inherited from his brother, is that some group members are lazy. They planted only a few trees on their farms and never became leaders in agroforestry like Otieno and his family. Mama Salome is fifty-three years old and has always been the chairlady of the group. Two young men and a woman (all under thirty years of age) asked the research team for information about small-scale commercial enterprises such as oilseed production and processing. Otieno responded to the young farmers' comments that group members do not see trees as a means for earning cash income.

Uhuru Women's Group started as a family group. In 1995, one-third of the members belong to Otieno's extended family, others are neighbours and friends. Relations within Uhuru Women's Group 'have gone up and down', related Mama Salome. In 1995, they were better than in the past, remarked the group treasurer, an elderly woman who is Otieno's neighbour. They were quite bad in 1992 when, during local elections, Otieno's brother, who was then coordinator of the Uhuru Women's Group, was beaten and some months later died. The tree nursery was vandalized and many seedlings were destroyed or stolen, animals were killed and the group was afraid to come together to work. Otieno commented that his brother had been labelled the 'opposition's prefect' and said that if local politics had not interfered with the group, everything would have worked out well.

Mama Salome remarked that 'our group is well known in the area and until 1992 we felt safe'. The group had a good reputation with the AEP and understood that the project had withdrawn from most groups in the area. However, the group still had various items of equipment from the AEP (stored at Otieno's house) and in 1994 Otieno had obtained a few hundred polybags for tree seedlings from CARE and the Forest Department.

When asked about their future plans, Uhuru Women's Group members presented several ideas, the most popular of which seemed to be the purchase of a tractor and wagon and an oxen-plough. Otieno has two oxen that he is willing to contribute to a proposed group oxen-plough activity. The tractor, group members felt, could also be good for business, especially for hauling water, sand and other construction materials. One of the older women said men were dominating the group with their 'tractor ideas'. She said the women in the group preferred to buy and sell maize, sorghum and millet. Nevertheless, Otieno said, the group would not rush into new activities until the members were certain that there would be no political interference.

These narratives of two women's groups in Siaya are employed to illustrate the influence of leaders and benefits of group survival. The narratives also suggest that there may be more than one leader or sets of leaders in these groups. There is an 'official' executive (always a woman) and what can be referred to as a 'shadow executive' (usually a man). Of equal importance is the male membership of women's groups. In these examples, both Otek and Otieno are not 'officials' of the group, but they are leaders. The 'official' women leaders recognize the role of these men in the groups. However, the style of leadership in the two groups is different. Whereas Otek's domination of group discussion often did not allow other members to comment on the leadership of the group, the members of the group led by Otieno participated freely in discussions and debate over group activities.

Clearly, the cause of group collapse proves to be a process of decline based on a combination of complex partner relations and dynamics within the group. It is also apparent that, given the nature of the group membership and leadership, group activities and external group/project interactions were strongly influenced by gender relations within the women's groups.

MEN IN WOMEN'S GROUPS

The role of men in women's self-help groups is a relatively recent area of gender and development research. Previous research on women's groups in Siaya has tended to underestimate the character and influence of the male minority membership. For instance, Achola (1991) recognizes that men are members of women's groups, but reports that they are 'recruited' only for skills such as book-keeping or leadership experience or to carry out certain tasks 'traditionally done by men'. Furthermore, despite more than a decade of activity in Siaya district, the Farmers' Group Community Support Programme (FGCSP), supported by IFAD (the International Fund for Agricultural Development) and implemented by several government ministries, has a similarly narrow viewpoint: 'Men rarely hold office however, although they may act as the spokesman for the group in its dealings with its official clan. Many of the men are husbands of the women members. They may provide land to the group or assist in some of the heavier production-related tasks' (FGCSP 1995: 7). Such statements indicate a clear need for researchers and development policy-makers and planners to be made aware that gender relations in women's groups in Siaya implicate not only women, but also men.

During fieldwork in 1991, the author found an average 25 per cent male membership in thirty-three AEP-assisted women's groups in Siaya district (Hambly 1992). In 1995, the average membership of men in both surviving and collapsed groups was only slightly lower, approximately 21 per cent of the total membership. Only one group reported having never had men as group members. Some groups had a male membership of up to 42 per cent (the median was 27 per cent). These figures were higher than the government's 20 per cent limit on male membership of women's groups (MCSS 1991; Republic of Kenya 1994a). In recent years, CARE is more open about the fact that male membership in its renamed 'farmers groups' is approximately 35 per cent.

If the mixed membership of women's groups is viewed from a perspective informed by gender relations, the number of men is only one of the concerns within the overall analysis. Other social relations, including age, marital status and socioeconomic standing of the men in women's groups, are also relevant considerations (Young 1993). Are the men in women's groups more influential because they are older, relatively wealthier than the women group members, or married to women group members? It was found that although the age of the fifty men who were members of the women's groups ranged from thirty to seventy-five years, more than half the men were sixty years old and above. This result should, however, be seen in the context that men of working age (twenty to fifty-six) are often not resident in the district.

Regarding the socioeconomic status of the men, it was difficult to apply the measure used to determine the socioeconomic status of AEP and non-AEP farmers because not all the individual members of the women's groups studied were interviewed and their farms visited. However, on the basis of available data, group visits and observations of AEP-assisted farmers, we determined that the significant relation was the marital status or family relations of men in women's groups. It was found that 84 per cent of the men in the women's groups were married to, or relations (mainly sons/nephews) of women in these groups.

Other studies of gender relations within organizations inform us that the number (quantity) of men in women's groups may be less influential than the role (quality) of specific men (Goetz 1995; Macalpine 1995). We can now add that in the case of rural self-help organizations in Siaya, men's age and marital status in relation to individual women in the group are highly relevant factors in explaining group behaviour or dynamics.

Furthermore, the analysis of surviving or collapsed women's groups found that men are most influential when they are 'shadow executives'. Men call themselves 'chairman' or, more frequently, 'co-ordinator', occasionally 'patron' and even 'organizing secretary'. Typically, such leaders are often married to or sons of past or current 'official' executive members of the group, all of whom must be women according to government regulations. Discussions with local-level government officials confirmed that chiefs or assistant-chiefs, as well as local civil servants, knew that men assume 'shadow' roles in women's groups. However, they said that in many cases other group members (both men and women) 'wanted it this way'.[4] While this was the opinion of mostly male district officials, some comments from female farmers (individually and as groups) confirmed that men were recognized by women to behave or belong differently within the group. The reflections of a research assistant after interviewing seven groups are illuminating:

[O]ne of these groups had a major argument when some members were accused of 'eating' what CARE and other NGOs like IFAD brought to the group. It was said that men in the group helped the women members talk to CARE ... women said they would miss these outside links if men were not in the group. 'Men will always be going out and around and getting ideas,' said one woman farmer. Another remarked, 'The only way for the group to do better is by having these ideas.' In another group where money earned by the groups was 'eaten' and the group quit their tree nursery, the Chairlady said, 'Men in the groups are good if their interests are for the group and not for themselves.'

In other interviews, the opinion was expressed that women's groups 'appear more serious' to local authorities and to husbands when they have men as members. In one such case, the group coordinator of a surviving women's group, a male teacher, explained that both women and men work harder and more 'professionally' (his words) when there is a male coordinator. He then went on to remark that 'When CARE dropped other groups, we received a loan', which he believed was the reason for the AEP's willingness to accept and recognize his leadership role in the group.[5]

Examination of the role of men in women's groups in Siaya District suggests that men have a different presence from that of women. Their influence is partly as leaders, but also as non-executive members. Four specific roles were identified.

1. Men as state/NGO 'go-betweens' It was stated in six group interviews that men often acted as liaisons to the AEP and other external organizations. A man was useful, one group chairlady explained, because 'he can go around and find the ones who can assist us'. Typically, men may manage relations with the local chief and assistant chiefs. They may speak on the group's behalf at location-level meetings and, according to several respondents, take the lead in registering the group with the district office or opening the group's bank account. This role carries considerable power and does not simply imply administrative tasks but political interaction.

2. Men as co-workers Men were reported to be valuable members of women's groups because they might have access to resources valued highly by resource-poor women. One example is the role of men as operators of oxen-ploughs. In four cases (two AEP groups and two non-AEP groups), the oxen-plough earned considerable revenue for the group (US $75 per day). All the members could also benefit from access to the oxen-plough, and the money earned from it contributed to the group's savings and loans activity. It was also noted that oxen-ploughs provided an opportunity for female farmers in the group to sell their labour, cultivating by hoe the furrows dug by the plough. The payment for this work would go directly to the member instead of into the group savings. Typically, this work was combined with simultaneous planting (by line or broadcast seeding).

A second way in which male group members made important contributions to the group was by providing land (especially land with access to water) for cultivation. The group would grow trees and crops for sale and pay 'rent' to the farmer owning the land. Similar arrangements could be used to access transport, including fishing boats and donkey carts. Only in a few cases was land provided free of charge to the women's group. In one case, the elderly farmer contributing the land had been designated the group 'patron'. In another, the farmer had no particularly influential role.

Finally, it was noted that in some cases women's groups invited younger men, who were referred to as 'sons' (eighteen to twenty-five-year-olds), although they were often not closely related kin, to join in some activities. These men often had designated roles in group activities; for instance, they might help with certain tasks such as fishing, producing charcoal or transporting produce to markets.

3. Men as opportunists Labour is a major need of all farmers, male and female, in Siaya district, and women's groups provide a relatively inexpensive source of labour. The labour of women, someties in combination with oxen-ploughs, is often preferred because their physical strength is combined with knowledge and skills when performing certain tasks such as planting and weeding. Some widowers or monogamous husbands said during the group interviews that they had joined women's groups to gain access to the labour and knowledge of the group. Men may behave opportunistically when they benefit more from the group labour than they contribute.

Members of several groups blamed men's interference in the generation and allocation of income received from group activities for the collapse of groups. In one particularly extreme case, the male co-ordinator of a group had pressured members to contribute their savings to a female politician whose campaign promises included obtaining 'matching grant' support for women's groups in the division. The candidate was defeated in the elections, the funds invested by the group disappeared and the group eventually collapsed.

4. Men as agitators One of the women's groups examined in depth had been quite active in the AEP between 1983 and 1991. However, in 1992 the husband of the group chairlady retired from his job in Nairobi and became a full-time resident on their farm. The group members described him as a tremendous 'pest' who constantly demanded that the group reorganize itself and its activities (mainly tree-planting and buying and selling sugarcane and maize). The man went so far as to complain to the chief that members of the group were cheating on their contributions to the group savings and loan activity. After some time, the members gave in and made the man the 'organizing secretary'. The group collapsed in 1994 after the man's wife, the chairlady, died. When this former group leader was interviewed with other former members present, he was adamant that the group could be reactivated, with new members if necessary. The man's role was more destructive than constructive because of his interference and mishandling of group funds, leading to the subsequent abandonment of the group by other members.

Given this range of men's roles in AEP women's groups, it can be seen that the roles may be *political and/or practical* in nature. The political role of men in women's groups is most obvious when they act as liaisons to external organizations, local officials or the political campaigns of politicians. These are power-based roles often involving control over resources such as capital, labour or land for the benefit of a single man (and not necessarily a man and a wife, or a son and his mother). On the other hand, the practical roles of men in women's groups are exhibited when men act as co-workers or facilitators of access to resources such as arable land and information. The problem for women's groups in Siaya district is how to maximize the practical role of men in groups while minimizing their political role. Some farmers argued during the interviews that the activities of women's groups could not expand without men's interference and assistance. For this reason, they said, 'women-only' groups were not necessarily more desirable, and they were unrealistic. These findings further reinforce the view that rural women's groups can hardly be considered homogeneous in their interests or their membership, and that their activities in Siaya cannot be seen as uninfluenced by gender relations.

CONCLUSION

In summary, examining the diverse roles of men in women's groups sheds light on the rise and fall of the groups. In many respects, the analysis of AEP women's groups in Siaya reinforces a point made some years ago by March and Taqqu (1986):

> Informal associations simultaneously promote women's political influence and economic contributions on the one hand and their subordination, victimisation or exclusion on the other. The internal dynamics of women's informal associations explain neither the origins of nor the variations in women's position; these can be better accounted for in light of the linkages between formal and informal spheres. But an appreciation of informal organizational patterns makes women visible and marks their influence in a way that theories focusing narrowly on formal organizations cannot. (March and Taqqu 1986: 121)

While women's groups involved in the AEP blend the informal and formal dimensions of traditional and contemporary organizations, the case of the AEP suggests the significance of understanding the ways individuals interact in and interpret group structure. In contrast, national policy obscures the role of men in women's groups in Siaya, and international development agencies reinforce the deficiency.

These findings further contradict the ethnocentric, Weberian belief that an organization operates without regard to the persons within it. The Kenyan government and AEP focused on the structure of local organizations, not the interpretations and meanings of the groups held by individual members and leaders. This enabled us to define what women's groups were and how they were led and managed. A women-only focus on rural organizations in Siaya would otherwise neglect male and female farmers as agents of change, and resisters of change.

The evidence from Siaya confirms that neither rural men nor women are passive or powerless social actors. However, women, as compared to men, face considerable difficulties in obtaining and maintaining fair and inclusive social relations and political representation. Women farmers can use their knowledge or take action against inequitable social structures. They can, for instance, welcome men into groups to obtain access to information or resources that would otherwise be difficult to obtain. Individually, women may exit group activities when systemic problems associated with male 'shadow leaders' or misused group resources are no longer tolerable. Also, individually and as a social group, women in Siaya take action to protect themselves in situations over which they have little or no control. Women farmers are thus circumventing the restrictive aspects of a project and opposing dominance of their own knowledge and identities. Women farmers in the AEP were participating in the project, but controlling their participation (Jackson 1997).

In conclusion, by addressing the concepts of gender relations and human agency by both women and men in the analysis of institutions at the local level, organizations cannot be situated as mere partners or entry points for development projects. In the case of the AEP, women farmers in Siaya were targeted by the project, but at the same time they used the project to pursue their livelihoods beyond the bounds of the AEP and its effects. Women sought solidarity with men if required, and negotiated male dominance of group activities. Their actions continued despite, as well as because of, the existence and limitations of social, political and economic structures. These areas deserve further research to build the critical analysis of gender in women's groups.

NOTES

1. Women's groups have long been involved in agricultural research and development activities in Kenya. These organizations may also be referred to as 'community groups' or 'farmers' groups'. The term 'women's groups' is deliberately used in this chapter for two reasons: (1) the majority of members of rural self-help groups examined in this study are women; (2) the project examined in the study was initiated specifically with the intention of supporting 'women's groups', although it adopted the terminology 'farmers' groups' as the project evolved. The project's 'repackaging' of women's groups as farmers' groups is shown to be relevant to the analysis of the survival and/or collapse of the groups.

2. Siaya district has since been divided into two separate districts, Bondo district in the southern region and Siaya district to the north.

3. These descriptions come from interviews with individual farmers in the group, the group itself and researchers' field notes following the interviews or during feedback to the farmers. All names have been changed.

4. The local officials who reported this comment and similar statements included the district social services officer (in 1995), three location community development assistants (LCDAs) who are location-level staff of DSS (in 1991 and 1995) and the head of the FGCSP at the district office. All these respondents, except one LCDA, were male. Only the head of the Farmers' Training Centre in Siaya reported that male membership in women's groups generally had a negative effect on group structure, process and activities.

5. In this particular case, CARE continued to support the women's group until 1993, and the group was still partially active in 1995. However, its agroforestry activities were vastly reduced, from 9,200 seedlings produced in 1988 to a few hundred seedlings in 1995. Its membership also fell from seventeen members in 1988 to ten in 1995.

REFERENCES

Achola, M. A. (1991) 'Women's Groups in Siaya District: Objectives, Constraints and Achievements', in G. S. Were, C. A. Suda and J. M. Olenja (eds), *Women and Development in Kenya: Siaya District* (Nairobi: Institute of African Studies), pp. 11–29.

Acker, J. (1996) 'Gendering Organizational Theory', in J. M. Shafritz and J. F. Ott (eds), *Classics of Organization Theory* (Orlando, FL: Harcourt Brace), pp. 463–72.

Calas, M. (1992) 'An/other Silent Voice? Representing "Hispanic Woman" in Organizational Texts', in A. J. Mills and P. Tancred (eds), *Gendering Organizational Analysis* (Newbury Park, CA: Sage), pp. 201–21.

Calas, M. and L. Smirich (1996). 'From "The Woman's" Point of View: Feminist Approaches to Organization Studies', in S. Clegg, C. Hardy and W. Nord (eds), *Handbook of Organization Studies* (London: Sage), pp. 218–57.

Clegg, S. (1994). 'Weber and Foucault: Social Theory for the Study of Organizations', *Organization*, 1(1): 149–78.

Connell, P. (1987) *Gender and Power* (Stanford, CA: Stanford University Press).

Connell, R. W. (1995) *Masculinities* (Berkeley and Los Angeles, CA: University of California Press).

Cook, C. C. and M. Grut (1989) *Agroforestry in Sub-Saharan Africa: A Farmers' Perspective*, Technical paper 112 (Washington DC: World Bank).

Cornwall, A. and N. Lindisfarne (eds) (1994) *Dislocating Masculinity:Comparative Ethnographies* (London and New York: Routledge).

FGCSP (1995) *Local Initiative Fund and Credit Component in the Farmers' Group Community Support Program Phase II. Siaya District, Kenya*, Unpublished report.

Goetz, A. M. (1995) 'Institutionalizing Women's Interests and Gender-sensitive Accountability in Development', *IDS Bulletin*, 26(3): 1–10.

— (1997) *Getting Institutions Right for Women in Development* (London: Zed Books).

Hambly, H. (1992) *Agroforestry: A Gender and Environment Analysis*, Unpublished MES thesis, Faculty of Environmental Studies, York University, Toronto.

— (2000) *The Implementation and Institutionalization of Agroforestry in Western Kenya: A Gender and Agency Analysis,* PhD Dissertation, Faculty of Environmental Studies, York University, Toronto.

Harrison, E. (1997) 'Men in Women's Groups: Interlopers or Allies?', *IDS Bulletin,* 23(3): 122–32.

Hay, M. J. (1976) 'Luo Women and Economical Change During the Colonial Period', in N. Hafkin and M. J. Hay (eds), *Women in Africa* (Stanford, CA: Stanford University Press), pp. 110–23.

Jackson, C. (1997) 'Actor Orientation and Gender Relations at a Participatory Project Interface', in A. M. Goetz (ed.), *Getting Institutions Right for Women in Development* (London: Zed Books), pp. 161–75.

Kloppenburg, J. (1991) 'Social Theory and De/Reconstruction of Agricultural Science: For an Alternative Agriculture', *Rural Sociology,* 56: 519–48.

Macalpine, M. (1995) 'Sameness and Difference for Women Bureaucrats', *IDS Bulletin,* 26(3): 125–30.

March, K. S. and R. L. Taqqu (1986) *Women's Informal Associations in Developing Countries* (Boulder, CO: Westview Press).

Mbeo, M. A. and O. Ooko Ombaka (eds) (1989) *Women and Law in Kenya* (Nairobi: Public Law Institute).

MCSS (1991) *Policy Guidelines on Community Group Promotion Development* (Nairobi: Department of Social Services, Ministry of Culture and Social Services).

Miller, C. and S. Razavi (eds) (1998) *Missionaries and Mandarins: Feminist Engagement with Development Institutions* (London: Intermediate Technology Publications).

Mills, A. J. and P. Tancred (eds) (1992) *Gendering Organizational Analysis* (Newbury Park, CA: Sage).

Nicholson, L. (1986) 'Gender and Modernity: Reinterpreting the Family, the State and the Economy', in L. Nicholson (ed.), *Gender and History: The Limits of Social Theory in the Age of the Family* (New York: Colombia University Press).

Plewes, B. and R. Stuart (1991) 'Women and Development Revisited: The Case for a Gender and Development Approach', in J. Swift and B. Tomlinson (eds), *Conflicts of Interest: Canada and the Third World* (Toronto: Between the Lines), pp. 107–32.

Powell, W. W. and P. J. DiMaggio (eds) (1991) *The New Institutionalism: Organizational analysis* (Chicago: University of Chicago Press).

Republic of Kenya (1994a) *Siaya District Development Plan (1994/98)* (Nairobi: Government Printers).

— (1994b) *Development Plan (1994/98)* (Nairobi: Government Printers).

Staudt, K. (1991) *Agricultural Policy Implementation: A Case Study from Western Kenya* (London Kumarian Press).

Tenga, N. and C. M. Peters. (1996) 'The Right to Organize as Mother of All Rights: The Experience of Women in Tanzania', *Journal of Modern African Studies,* 34(1): 47–162.

Whitehead, A. (1985) 'Effects of Technological Change on Rural Women', in I. Ahmed (ed.), *Technology and Rural Women* (London: George Allen and Unwin).

Wipper, A. (1984) 'Women's Voluntary Associations', in M. J. Hay and S. Stichter (eds), *African Women South of the Sahara* (Burnt Mill: Longman Press).

Young, K. (1988) *Towards a Theory of the Social Relations of Gender* (Sussex: Institute of Development Studies).

— (1993) *Planning Development with Women: Making a World of Difference* (London: Macmillan).

CHAPTER 7

Boys will be Boys: Addressing the Social Construction of Gender

MARILYN THOMSON

§ In an effort to address gender inequalities, development agencies in recent years have become increasingly interested in exploring gender relations and the cultural construction of masculinities. The entry point is often work with educational, community and cultural institutions offering activities designed to make men more conscious of how gender affects their lives, taking a life cycle approach. Work on masculinities is often concentrated in areas such as sexual and reproductive health or violence and conflict, in which the importance of gender relations is most directly obvious (Chant and Gutmann 2000).

Much of the focus on gender in development has been on discrimination against girls and women and not on how boys learn to be men and what this means for gender relations as they grow up. However, there is a body of academic literature on gender and masculinity stretching back at least two decades. For example, it was recognized in the 1980s that the construction of gender was having a negative impact on gender relations because male stereotypes were damaging and preventing young men from realizing their potential, also because young men were internalizing negative images of girls and women through the press and media (Askew and Ross 1988: 2–3).

Development agencies have only relatively recently started to integrate some of these academic theories into their own practices. For example, concepts such as the 'the pressure of masculinity' and the 'fragility of masculine identity' are often given as explanations for problematical male behaviour such as violence and sexual risk-taking behaviour (Greig et al. 2000). There is also recognition of the need to address the ways in which male children are brought up and to change the messages boys receive from parents, schools and the media about what it means to be a man. Save the Children UK (SC UK) published a set of good practice guidelines in 1994 on equal opportunities in UK and European programmes. One of these focused on gender equality and included an analysis of gender and masculinity:

> Strategies focused on combating poverty and social disadvantage must be combined with those which encourage men to seek meaning and purpose in their lives outside of the traditional versions of masculinity with which they identify. This poses major challenges to the child development and socialisation processes and to youth work and work in all contexts with boys and young men. An organisation based on children's rights such as Save the Children has no choice but to make these issues central to its agenda for the future. (Save the Children 1994: 29)

In practice masculinity did not become a central issue as was proposed, although there is some interesting research and programme work on gender and masculinity which will be referred to in this chapter. One of the key areas where masculinity is addressed in organizations working on children's rights is the socialization process at different stages in the life cycle, from the early years and within the school. There has also been a focus on the role of fathers within the family. Unicef, for example, recognizes that the role of the male in family decision-making and as caretaker of children has been largely overlooked as a topic for research and programme activity (Richardson 1995).

This chapter will examine some of the issues raised from field experience and research on masculinities as they relate to boys and gender relations. Information is presented from SC UK programme experiences in different countries, including the UK. A cross-cultural approach is a valid one as there are many similarities in the way in which socialization occurs through education, the media, the family and peer group in most countries, although the manifestation of masculinity may vary according to the cultural context.

CULTURAL IDENTITY AND SOCIALIZATION

Many of the theories on masculinity and children state that in order to transform gender roles and identities it is necessary to influence the socialization process through which individuals learn about their culture and society. For development agencies this might mean developing project work to influence different institutions that shape gender stereotypes such as the family, school and peer groups. It is particularly important to ensure that gender awareness is an integral part of projects that support early-years education and child development work. This section presents some cultural issues and practices identified in development projects although in many cases it is too early to say how far these projects have been successful in influencing and changing cultural attitudes about male gender roles and identities.

In all cultures and societies, gender stereotypes begin from the moment we are born and are identified as either a boy or a girl. This label determines how we will be treated, how we are expected to behave and our view of the world. Gender characteristics are learnt at a very young age and as we grow up we learn in our everyday interactions what is appropriate behaviour for a boy or a girl: 'Boys don't cry' or 'Don't be a sissy' are common criticisms made of little boys. This socialization can lead boys to feel anxiety, even fear, of being like the 'opposite' sex. Boys learn about the behaviour expected of men which, in most cultures, is synonymous with being physically and emotionally strong, being competitive, dominating and controlling others. This is reinforced in many ways in different cultural contexts. For example, a study of boys' behaviour in London primary schools found that they were encouraged to be tough and aggressive and that this behaviour was acceptable to teachers and parents as the norm for boys: 'aggression whether "in fun" or "for real" is associated with masculinity in this society. Aggression in boys is a reflection of attitudes and beliefs about violence generally in society and it is, therefore, related to the nature of wider society and to the power relations between groups in it' (Askew and Ross 1988: 12).

Similar examples of aggression being promoted in boys can be found among tribal communities in western Kenya and southern Ethiopia that hold rites of passage ceremonies for adolescent boys on reaching puberty. One of these consists of mass beatings of boys (aged twelve to eighteen years) to harden them and make them strong. These beatings can be quite vicious and last for several days but the boys have to show that they can withstand the pain and not cry. Bravery is a key attribute for men in these communities and, through participation in this ceremony, boys have to demonstrate that they are not cowards. There is

project work to support local organizations that address harmful practices and the rights of the child by questioning assumptions about boys
and child-rearing practices more generally with the communities involved.

A project working with young men in Jamaica (Richardson 1995)
found that the development of gender roles is not straightforward.
There is a very high number (42 per cent) of women-headed households
in Jamaica. As a result, boys often look for role models in the public
domain, they are socialized in the ways of the street and many look to
the success of the 'don men' as a model. These are men who control
local politics in poor urban areas in Jamaica, often using violence, and
who have money, power and status. Younger adolescent boys are also
influenced by older boys in their peer groups who teach them about
sexuality and ethnic values and are important role models (Richardson
1995: 27–8). These young boys can be vulnerable to many negative
influences at this stage, for example, petty crime and taking drugs, and
the process of education by the older group is not always in their best
interests. Positive peer education therefore needs to be a central component of development projects with young people in this type of
situation. However, as we will see below in relation to programme
work in Peru on HIV/AIDS, peer education does not always have the
immediate results that are expected.

The media and the classroom also influence children in the gender
stereotypes they portray which can either lead to a questioning or a
reinforcement of male and female gender identities. Development
programmes that target education and raise awareness in the media of
negative gender stereotyping are therefore a very important vehicle for
changing attitudes. However, in order to influence cultural changes, a
multi-pronged approach is needed: legislation, social policy and services,
training of professionals, capacity building of local community groups,
as well as work with the community. How far development agencies
with limited resources can be effective in supporting these changes is
open to question. Monitoring progress, for example measuring the extent
to which gender relations have improved as a result of interventions, is
often weak. Also it might not always be feasible to evaluate the impact
of projects, given that changing attitudes could take several generations,
particularly in some contexts where traditional stereotypes persist in the
wider society and are reinforced by the media and other institutions.

CHANGING GENDER RELATIONS

Development programmes operating in different countries need to take into account the changing nature of gender relations in different cultural contexts in their situation analysis in order to plan their programmes effectively. Traditional perceptions of what masculinity means are being questioned in some countries as boys and young men grow up to face a world unlike that of their fathers. Changes in women's roles and discussions about the rights of women and girls have also led to a questioning of male gender roles and relations. There are examples in some cultures of men taking a more nurturing and active role in the domestic and family sphere and encouraging their sons to do the same. Changes in family life and composition, together with greater social acceptance of some of the demands from the women's movement to end gender discrimination, mean that today children and young people in many societies are receiving different messages from previous generations. However, in some cases these messages are mixed as traditional stereotypes persist alongside changing gender relations, which can lead to confusion and contradictory messages. The dynamic nature of gender is apparent in some contexts where gender stereotypes and identities are changing along with economic relations and interpersonal arrangements between men and women. This is having an impact on the way children and young people perceive their own gender identities. The context for these changes varies but there are some common trends between countries. For example, an increasing number of women-headed families might mean that boys grow up without a positive male role model within the family. The situation in Jamaica cited above provides an interesting case study of the possible repercussions for boys' development.

The social and economic environment in which boys are growing up today is very different from that of their fathers and grandfathers, when men had a clearly defined role as the authority in the family. Increased migration to urban centres in many developing countries has resulted in changes in traditional family structures. Poverty also means that men are no longer the sole breadwinner and many have had to leave their families behind to look for work. Changes in the world economy are also having an important impact on the life options and the type of jobs available to young men. Today, they face competition from young women who are increasingly entering into what were previously considered to be male professions. Many of the available jobs, particularly in developing countries, are increasingly in the service sector or in manufacturing in the electronic and garment industries, often considered to be 'women's work' (Schacht and Ewing 1998). Development agencies working on child labour issues should therefore be taking gender issues into account when planning project interventions or advocating child labour issues, as employment options for girls and boys and their working conditions are changing rapidly with the impact of globalization.

GENDER-BASED VIOLENCE

Violence against women and girls has only relatively recently become an issue of concern to the major UK development agencies (Parbha 1999). However, available statistics indicate that gender violence carried out by men against girls and women is tragically commonplace in most countries. This violence takes many different forms: emotional and physical, sexual abuse, incest, dating and courtship violence, rape, forced early marriage, domestic violence and economic exploitation, including child pornography and commercial sexual exploitation. It is estimated that, in most countries, between 25 and 50 per cent of all women have been physically assaulted at least once by an intimate partner (Warrior 1999: 17).

In recent years there have been a few initiatives in some developing countries to examine cultural constructions of masculinity and how these lead to violence against women and children. Montoya, for example, in his study on preventing male violence, describes the male role models for young men in Nicaragua:

> Violence is a common experience for males from a very early age and is one of the principal mechanisms for socialisation. In popular culture as well as in the social sciences it is considered one of the main dimensions of *machismo* ... Men have to exercise this, particularly in front of other men, through stereotypical behaviour such as: drinking a lot of alcohol, sexual promiscuity, sports, gambling and dominating women. (Montoya 1998: 19, trans. M. Thomson)

Montoya is a member of a national men's group in Nicaragua that came together to examine male identity and the roots of their violence, particularly within the family. They run workshops to improve communication between men, which is often superficial and aggressive, and they also work with young men to influence them to change their behaviour. This experience is worth monitoring as it may provide valuable lessons for other regions embarking on this type of project. Support for activities on gender violence quite rightly have concentrated on offering critical support to women and children who have been victims of violence. However, it is important to work with men, and especially with boys, on prevention of family violence, making them aware of power relations and encouraging them to find other forms of resolving conflicts. There is a fear among women's organizations working on domestic violence that a focus on male perpetrators will lead to crucial funding for their organizations being cut as the focus moves to men. This highlights the need for funding agencies and social services to support a range of approaches; it is fundamental to continue to offer support to survivors while at the same time looking for ways to prevent the continuation of violence in future generations.

WORKING WITH BOYS AND MEN

The social construction of gender is relevant to Save the Children's work addressing violence, the role of men in the family and HIV/AIDS transmission. This section presents some of the issues around gender and boys that have been identified in SC UK's research, such as children's perceptions of men and boys and young men's attitudes and practices around reproductive health. Examples are also given of the approaches used in programmes, such as equality training in the early years, and of tools to work with young people in different cultural contexts to address gender relations and boys' specific gender needs. Some interesting issues arise from this work and need further investigation. For example, there appears to be a divide between conceptions of gender inside and outside the home, so children are receiving contradictory messages about gender. We also need to look at the links between social class, work and gender roles.

Gender in the early years   A research project carried out with children in England explored whether changes in work roles for men and women were having any impact on young children's understanding of gender differences. The finding of the study on 'Children's Perceptions of Men' carried out by Save the Children's Equality Learning Centre and the Working with Men group reveal how children are influenced by and perceive gender from a very young age. A total of sixty-two children were interviewed (aged five to eight years old, equally split between boys and girls and of different ethnic origins) and their views threw up some interesting insights into these changes and the role models that children have today.

The study found that changes occurring in the lives of children's parents and other close adults have influenced children's views of what men and women are and what they do. The results suggest that some children have moved away from traditional notions of masculinity and femininity – for example, that men are breadwinners and women are home-makers – but at the same time they are receiving mixed messages about gender roles. Many of the children, identifying which jobs and roles were gender-specific, said that they were appropriate for both men or women: 'I haven't seen a woman train driver, but I'm sure there are some' (boy aged eight). When the boys and girls were asked what makes men different from women, anatomy was always the starting point. Once physical differences had been established, most of the comments were about behaviour: 'Men make cars, girls can but they are not very good at it' (boy aged eight). 'Men are better at leading' (boy aged seven). The girls considered 'responsibility' to be a feminine attribute and a distinguishing factor between men and women, with women being more responsible. Some of the girls felt that boys were not to be trusted, although one girl thought that some boys could learn to be responsible.

The children's perceptions of roles outside the family seemed to be more developed than roles within the home and the most consistent stereotyped behaviours were mentioned in relation to the domestic sphere. So when the children were asked, 'What do the men you know like to do most?', sports, videos, computer games and driving cars were recurring responses. Some comments revealed the view that men tried to avoid housework in order to do what they enjoyed: 'My dad pretends to be poorly, so he can't do any work around the house'; and another boy commented: 'My dad's got headaches half of his life.' In some cases the interviewers thought that the children were repeating comments that they had heard adults make.

The study recommends that early-years educators should make time for children to discuss their observations about what it means to be a boy or girl and to help them identify their strengths and abilities in a rapidly changing world. Children are curious about gender and the differences they see in what men and women do but are often inhibited by adults' reluctance to talk about these issues. The study concludes that boys and girls do understand gender differences and the conflicts that can arise from these and it is therefore important that equality issues are addressed from an early age. This can be done by teachers raising gender issues in a variety of ways throughout the school curriculum and in play activities. Increasing the proportion of men in infant and primary education (as teachers, male parents or outside speakers and helpers) would also help boys feel more comfortable and more able to learn.

Aggression, violence and conflict A key area in work focusing on boys' gender identities concerns violence, aggressive behaviour and accepted social norms. The role of the media in portraying aggression is well known but the media, especially films and TV, can also be used as vehicles to question aggressive behaviour and to show alternative male identities. As mentioned previously, gender roles and relations vary from one cultural context to another; this is most apparent in conflict situations where roles are reinforced or distorted. SC UK has addressed these issues in projects with parents and carers which train them to manage young children's behaviour without physical punishment; in awareness-raising activities in relation to families and social violence; and in the rehabilitation of and support for children in conflict situations as child soldiers. Some of these projects and the issues that have arisen from them are described below.

In South Asia, SC UK is currently working with Unicef to develop a new initiative on the theme of working with men and boys. This follows a joint three-year film project called 'Let's Talk Men' which examined gender issues in order to tackle the problems of increasing violence against girls. Ranjan Poudyal, co-ordinator of the project, explained the background:

The system of patriarchy in which social structures and institutions produce unequal, hierarchical, authoritarian and ultimately violent relationships is highly entrenched in South Asia. How do you combat violence against women, when it springs from such an all-pervasive system? Since men are the main perpetrators of violence, it is imperative that they constitute a primary focus ... Within the popular media nothing, to our knowledge, specifically addresses boys, adolescents and young men concerning their masculinity and that masculinity's generally violent role models. (Poudyal 2000)

The film scripts were developed through workshops with the male film-makers who were encouraged to depict realistic situations and stories rooted in their own cultures. The first workshop encouraged the men to reflect on their own sense of masculinity and, through a life history approach, to explore the process of becoming a man and the events that shaped and strengthened their experiences of maleness. They covered different aspects of the socialization experience: roles, stereotyping, bias and masculinities in contexts such as aggression and violence against women. Some of the experiences of the film-makers discussed at the workshops and reflected in their films focused on the 'pain' of being a man in some situations and how individually they felt powerless in other situations. One of them used the metaphor of being a race horse in the family, as the only male heir, and described his feelings of powerlessness stemming from the expectations that people had of him. Although recognizing that men wield great power they also discussed the costs of the privileges of being a son, husband and father in the form of their duties and obligations.

The films, which examine different aspects of male identity, were produced in four South Asian countries (India, Pakistan, Bangladesh, Nepal) and they will be shown in schools and in community projects in order to raise issues and present alternative role models for boys. A workbook will be distributed with the films (which have been translated into the different South Asian languages) and these will be used as a learning tool for interactive workshops. It is too early to assess the impact of the film project in terms of changing attitudes but the film showings have led to interesting debates and some of the films have been nominated for awards at film festivals. The next phase of the project will include research into issues such as fatherhood, early childhood development, becoming a man and approaches to gender training with men and boys.

Another example of addressing the specific gender needs of boys and girls is work undertaken in countries that have gone through civil war or social unrest. Peace-building can often lead to a loss of identity for men and boys who have been soldiers and fighters from a young age. SC UK works with partners in a number of countries where there are conflict situations (for example, in Angola, Rwanda, Sierra Leone, Sri Lanka, Colombia and Liberia) to reintegrate boys who have been soldiers or involved in the fighting back into the community. Boys are deliberately recruited by armies and opposition groups because they are more easily manipulated than adults and can be indoctrinated to perform crimes and atrocities without questioning. Seen as more expendable, boys are used for even the most dangerous military tasks such as mine-detecting and spying. In conflict situations there is a gender division; boys are mainly recruited as soldiers, while girls and young women are more often incorporated into militia and guerrilla forces as messengers, cooks and 'wives'. The children of poor and disadvantaged families are particularly vulnerable to this type of exploitation. With few other opportunities to access basic necessities such as food and water, they see membership of armed forces and militia groups as offering relative security and an identity in very insecure and frightening situations.

Some of the project activities that SC UK has engaged in include setting up transit centres for former child soldiers while staff attempt to reunite them with their families or communities. The centres are designed to provide a typical community for the children, where they can take part in recreational activities, education, gardening and cooking. This work has helped them to recover from the nightmares and traumas of war and reunited them with other family members as part of their often difficult reintegration back into their home communities. The fundamental aim of this work has been to help them recover their status as children and to give them back some of the opportunities (for education in particular) which were taken away from them.

Save the Children has produced a number of tools for working on the issue of family violence. One of these is a manual (Warrior 1999) that presents a variety of approaches adopted by partners in different parts of the world to address violence in the family. It defines the alarming variety of forms of violence within the family using a gender analysis. It aims to increase understanding of the magnitude of the problem by providing statistics, personal stories and insights into the variety of causes, including male aggression and power relations. The manual quotes a report from the World Health Organization (WHO) which states that child abuse has become a major public health problem world-wide with an estimated 40 million children aged up to fourteen around the world suffering from abuse and neglect and requiring health and social care. Children are more likely to be murdered, physically assaulted, sexually abused, abducted, subjected to harmful practices and emotional violence by family members than by strangers (Warrior 1999: 17). In families where there is domestic violence, children are affected emotionally, not only by witnessing the violence: 'A research study of women in the UK experiencing domestic violence where there were children in the home found that in 70 per cent of cases the child was also physically abused. Similar figures are found in other regions of the world' (Parbha 1999).

Each chapter of this manual includes practical exercises to work through with staff or with young people to help them to understand and act on issues of gender violence and children's rights. We have developed resources to work on managing children's behaviour and violence within the family. The approach starts from the premise that violent behaviour is the result of the socialization that boys and girls receive in their homes and schools. We also provide practical tools to work on equality and diversity issues with children, non-violent conflict resolution and developing parenting skills for disciplining children without physical punishment. Other manuals and videos have been developed for working with teenagers to help them to develop more respectful relationships that value gender differences.

These tools and manuals must be appropriate for the age group of the children or young people. A basic approach with all age groups is to listen to what children have to say and involve them in carrying out research and, ideally, in developing and piloting tools. For example, a study was carried out in the UK into young children's views and experiences of smacking (Willow and Hyder 1998). In order to carry out the study with seventy-five five- to seven-year-olds, a community artist was commissioned to produce a story book with a central character (called Splodge) to whom the children could relate. The children were asked to help Splodge understand smacking, through a series of his questions, such as 'Why do you think children get smacked?' and 'What does it feel like to be smacked?' The story book was piloted among children and amendments were made to both the illustrations and the text according to their comments. The children were subsequently involved in the discussion groups and they suggested activities which adults could pursue to stop or reduce smacking. The report was a very strong tool to use in advocating at government and UN level for the legal protection of children against corporal punishment.

These examples give some indication of the different approaches that can be used to offer children, and young men in particular, alternative models of behaviour. Child participation is crucial, not only because it takes their views into account, but also because it provides a model showing respect for different points of view. It is also important to work with teachers and other adults in a position to influence boys' identity and relations, so that they are able to work with young people in a participatory and inclusive way.

Challenging gender stereotypes Education plays a key role in reinforcing or challenging gender stereotypes among children. Gender differences in behaviour and choice of play activities for boys and girls begin at a very young age. These continue in formal education and are influenced by adults' gender roles and expectations. In the UK there has been discussion in recent years about how boys, particularly those from ethnic minorities, are falling behind girls in their schoolwork (Figueroa 2000). Research findings suggest that by the age of seven about one-third of boys are struggling to read and five times as many boys are expelled from school as girls. Low levels of literacy and numeracy contribute to and compound the problems that groups of boys have, for example poorly educated young men are the most prominent group in crime statistics (Lloyd 1999:6).

In an effort to find out the causes and possible approaches to address boys' academic underachievement, SC UK, together with Working with Men, carried out a survey on boys' and fathers' views on reading in England (Hyder and Treffor 1999). This report highlights some of the debates as to the likely causes for the low achievement of some groups of boys in school: 'rapidly changing employment patterns which particularly badly affected the working class are, in fact the problem; or that current images about "being a man" operate counter to education, making it not "cool" to achieve' (Lloyd 1999: 6).

A central component of this project was a consultation with fathers and groups of boys of different age groups in four London schools. 'Reading for the Future' (Lloyd 1999) confirmed many of the issues raised in the literature, for example that gender socialization affects the kind of books that boys read. Studies suggest that boys are more likely to be interested in reading facts and information; if they read fiction it is more likely to be adventure stories than novels about relationships and emotions, particularly after the age of fourteen (Millard 1997). In addition, boys would not contemplate reading books that dealt with female experiences, rejecting books that seemed in any way like a 'girls' book' (Sarland 1991).

The findings of this study show that gender plays an important part in boys' reading choices; and although some boys read less fiction as they grow up many do read non-fiction. Another important finding is that boys often model their reading behaviour on their fathers' reading habits and fathers play a role in encouraging their sons' reading and other school activities. It is therefore important to involve fathers and, for early-years educators, to encourage boys to read by creating an appropriate setting where developing reading and writing skills are integrated into the types of activities that boys like doing.

The report came up with a number of recommendations for early learning centres, schools and local authorities. In particular it suggested that non-fiction books should be included and valued equally in reading schemes; that boys who have difficulties should be identified as early as possible; that there may be literacy problems behind boys' behavioural problems in the classroom; and that fathers should be actively encouraged to take part in reading with their sons and in other school activities. Following on from the study, SC UK and Working with Men ran a poster and information campaign in which famous football players promoted fatherhood and boys' reading, and produced interactive books for fathers and sons to read together.

Male sexual behaviour and reproductive health The issue of male sexual behaviour is central to work on sexual and reproductive health. Vulnerability to sexually transmitted infections (STIs), especially HIV, is associated with gender power relations which make it difficult for girls and women to negotiate safer sex. The social context of HIV transmission is critical as more and more women are becoming infected through heterosexual intercourse, and women now make up more than half of the 36.1 million adults infected with HIV world-wide (Bhatta-charjee 2000). We need to find ways to address, for example, the fact that in many cultures male promiscuity is acceptable, that there may be a greater acknowledgement of male sexual needs and pleasures and that men are expected to control women sexually. Involving young people in discussing intimate topics such as these before their sexual initiation is therefore important and requires a very sensitive approach. Sexuality needs to be looked at within the context of young people's lives, not as an isolated issue. As is illustrated below, SC UK has approached this by involving young people in peer education programmes working on sexual health issues in order to reach a wider group of young people than would be possible though traditional channels.

Gender relations are central to our HIV/AIDS work in Mozambique, where an estimated 10 per cent of the population is HIV positive and there are over half a million AIDS orphans. Children are particularly vulnerable as they become sexually active at a relatively young age and girls are particularly at risk as a result of inadequate knowledge and sexual exploitation (Welbourn 1995). SC UK's approach focuses on involving and strengthening community-level structures and creating new opportunities for women and children to participate. In order to promote safer sex and delay the onset of sexual activity, the programme aims to increase understanding of how gender relations are constructed and transmitted. Our programme staff use the 'Stepping Stones' approach, which helps individuals and communities to change their behaviour. This training package explores gender relations at a community level, working with different peer groups. The methodology consists of a series of participatory exercises, such as role-play and games, to encourage active participation and group learning. It helps them to analyse communication blocks in a range of matters that can cause conflict in relationships such as money, alcohol, sex and love and decision-making. Evaluations in communities of the impact of these workshops have shown that they have been successful in changing behaviour by improving communication in relationships. In one example, the majority of peer groups formed continued to meet after the training had finished, as one participant from a Stepping Stones workshop in Zambia explained:

The peer groups became more open to discuss sexuality, a topic which the older regarded as taboo to discuss in the presence of the young. They felt the problem of HIV/AIDS had no age limit hence the need to accept and care for those affected. The use of condoms which was strongly rejected especially by the older peers was now accepted as a good alternative to fight the disease. (Cornwall 1997: 30)

In Peru, SC UK has worked with the Instituto de Educacion y Salud (IES) since 1992. They carried out a participatory research project with young people in a working-class neighbourhood in Lima to establish gender differences in relation to vulnerabilities to HIV/AIDS transmission. The exact picture of the epidemic in Peru is unclear. There are an estimated 72,000 adults and children living with HIV/AIDS, out of a national population of around 25 million and, given that it has still not spread widely in comparison with the spread in other countries, the high incidence of reported risk behaviours among young people in Peru is a cause of great concern. Cultural constraints impede prevention efforts; notably resistance to condom use from the Catholic Church, *machista* double standards regarding the acceptability of male promiscuity and the expectation of female monogamy, and a high prevalence of bisexuality in men.[1]

The IES has developed successful strategies for working in schools to promote sexual and reproductive health for adolescents, focusing on education from a gender perspective. By looking at the different cultural manifestations and attitudes towards sexuality it has identified appropriate responses to encourage more responsible sexual behaviour among young people. Activities include education and counselling in a number of schools in poor neighbourhoods in which trained students and teachers offer information, advice and orientation to young people. Peer education helps to create a comfortable environment within the schools in which young people can actively participate and have access to information and sex education materials. The aim is to have schools become an effective place for the promotion of adolescent sexual and reproductive health and development of life skills. The project is designed to encourage a participatory approach whereby each of the schools forms a committee of promotion and prevention, chaired by its head teacher.

Health centres located in the same areas as the selected schools also participate in the project and staff have been trained on specific issues such as counselling, family planning, gender, teenage pregnancy and HIV/AIDS, with the objective of improving the quality of care of adolescent sexual health. The school–health centre link encourages the students to use the reproductive health services on offer.

There are now projects in sixteen schools in Lima and six in Chimbote, where young health promoters have been trained and provide basic information and orientation to their peers on a range of issues relating to self-care in sexual and reproductive health. They also refer those who need assistance to the local health centres. Educators reach peers (usually aged between thirteen and fifteen years) both in school and those who have already left school or who have dropped out. They have informal conversations every day with a variety of contacts, they give out IEC materials and organize games which are popular with the young people.

As part of the project, regular meetings are held with peer educators where the general problems faced by adolescents in the area and the experiences of being a peer educator are discussed. The peer educators identified some of the main problems for boys as gangs, drugs and lack of information and use of contraception. Membership of gangs is most common among teenagers who have dropped out of school. Drug-taking is common, particularly cocaine, which boys in these poor neighbourhoods often start taking at around the ages of sixteen or seventeen. Some steal to get money to buy drugs, or parents give them pocket money which they then spend on drugs. Drug use is integrally linked to gangs whose members are also encouraged to drink and smoke. Teenage boys and girls lack information about sex and sexuality and there are many reproductive health problems as a result. One boy who got his girlfriend pregnant blamed his own parents for not giving him enough advice and information. The peer educators encourage condom use but the boys generally say that they don't use them as they 'can't feel anything'. The peer educators on the whole thought that condom-use rates had not increased significantly among their friends in spite of the promotion. According to the peer educators, young people fear HIV, but they don't fear other STIs as they can be cured and there is still little understanding of the link between HIV and STIs. The average age for first experience of sexual intercourse was put at about fourteen or fifteen years, but was thought to be younger in the gangs, where one of the initiations is that a boy must have sex with a girl. Gang members also engage in commercial sex with older men, as it is an easy way to make money. Sexist attitudes persist; for example, physical and verbal abuse of girlfriends is common and the girls are forced to give money to male gang members.

The peer educators were also involved in monitoring changes as a result of their activities and in putting forward suggestions for future changes to the project. Although they had seen positive changes, they felt that there was a long way still to go to change attitudes, behaviour and gender relations among young people in these marginalized neighbourhoods, especially when helping others is seen to be a sign of weakness – to give good advice is not 'cool'. As one educator put it: it is 'bad to be good'.

CONCLUSIONS

SC UK's programme experiences and learning in different countries allow some recommendations to be made on good practice and approaches to work on gender issues with children and young people. A central element is to challenge the traditional gender socialization of boys and girls and, given the variety of institutions that are involved, this will require a multi-pronged approach. For example, using the media to create awareness of different gender issues; working with both boys and girls on equality issues; involving parents and teachers to make them aware of their own attitudes and assumptions about gender and child-rearing practices. Other good practices identified include: listening to children's and young people's views and addressing their different gender needs; expanding the gender options available to boys by encouraging them to express their feelings; exploring male gender identities through videos and film projects that encourage discussion and disseminating this information to other people through peer education. It is also important that teachers and carers work with teenage boys to foster greater self-confidence, to promote better understanding of gender differences and to encourage more respectful relationships between young people.

This chapter has attempted to show that programmes aiming to improve gender relations and inequality should not only aim to empower girls and women but must also focus on male gender identities and address the negative aspects of male socialization. However, experience has shown that changing attitudes and behaviour and promoting more equitable gender relations is a longer-term process and it might be difficult to see these changes in the lifespan of a project. Nevertheless, this should not deter efforts to address gender in our work with the next generation; this is an investment for a future in which we hope more just and equitable relations will prevail.

NOTE

1. Information on Peru project from internal reports by Douglas Webb, HIV/Aids Adviser, Save the Children Fund. See also Webb and Elliot (2000).

REFERENCES

Askew, S. and C. Ross (1988) *Boys Don't Cry: Boys and Sexism in Education* (Milton Keynes: Open University Press).

Bhattacharjee, P. (2000) 'Stepping Stones: A Participatory Tool to Integrate Gender into HIV/AIDS Work', *Development in Practice*, 10(5): 691–4.

Chant, S and M. Gutmann (2000) *Mainstreaming Men into Gender and Development: Dabates, Reflections and Experiences*, Oxfam Working Paper (Oxford: Oxfam).

Cornwall, A. (1997) *Stepping Stones Training and Adaptation Project: A Questionnaire Survey of Recipients of Stepping Stones Materials* (London: ActionAid).

Figueroa, M. (2000) 'Making Sense of Male Experience: The Case of Academic Underachievement in the English-speaking Caribbean', *Men, Masculinities and Development*, IDS Bulletin, 31(2): 68–74.

Greig, A., M. Kimmel and J. Lang (2000) *Men, Masculinities and Development: Broadening Our Work Towards Gender Inequality*, Gender in Development Monograph 10 (New York: UNDP).

Hyder T. and L. Treffor (1999) *Children's Perceptions of Men* (London: Save the Children and Working with Men).

Lloyd, T. (1999) *Reading for the Future: Boys' and Fathers' Views on Reading* (London: SC UK).

Millard, E. (1997) *Differently Literate: Boys, Girls and the Schooling of Literacy* (Brighton: Falmer Press).

Monotya, O.(1998) *Nadando contra corriente* (Nicaragua: Puntos de Encuentro).

Parbha, P. (1999) *Home Truths: Domestic Violence and Its Impact on Women and Children*, Working Paper 19 (London: SC UK).

Poudyal, R. (2000) 'Alternative Masculinities in South Asia', in *Men Masculinities and Development*, IDS Bulletin, 31(2): 75–8.

Richardson, J. (1995) *Achieving Gender Equality in Families: the Role of Males, Innocenti Global Seminar Report* (Florence: Unicef).

Sarland, C. (1991) *Young People Reading: Culture and Response* (Milton Keynes: Open University Press).

Save the Children UK (1994) *A Guide to Good Practice on Equal Opportunities in Relation to Gender Equality in UK Fieldwork* (London: SC UK).

— (1997) Gender and HIV/AIDS Guidelines for Integrating a Gender Focus into NGO Work on HIV/AIDS (London: SC UK, ActionAid and ACORD).

Schacht, S. and D. Ewing (eds) (1998) *Feminism and Men: Reconstructing Gender Relations* (New York: New York University Press).

Warrior, J. (1999) *Preventing Family Violence, a Manual for Action* (London: Save the Children Alliance).

Webb, D. and L. Elliot (2000) *Learning to Live: Monitoring and Evaluating HIV/AIDS Programes for Young People* (London: SC UK).

Welbourn, A. (1995) *Stepping Stones: a Training Package on HIV/AIDS, Community and Relationship Skills* (London: ActionAid).

WHO (1999) Violence against Women Information Pack: a priority health issue, Geneva.

Willow, C. and T. Hyder (1998) *It Hurts You Inside* (London: Save the Children and NCB).

CHAPTER 8

Why Do Dogs Lick their Balls? Gender, Desire and Change – a Case Study from Vietnam

NEIL DOYLE

§ This case study from Southern Vietnam explores three themes that are relevant to current debates on men, masculinities and gender relations in development. First, how the constructions of gender, to which both women and men widely subscribe, facilitate and constrain the individual agency of women and men in different ways and to varying extents. Second, how within this discursive landscape, which allots power and associated sexual privilege on the basis of gender, there still remains social space for considerable diversity. Looking particularly at the variety of men's attitudes and behaviour, I make the case that if men are a problem it is certainly not *all* men *all* of the time. In addition to the contrast between the consistency of gender construction and the diversity of lived realities, the third theme I want to explore is that sexual desire should not be theorized away as an entirely social construction devoid of a material component. I draw upon feminist frameworks to explore this relationship between the material and subjective aspects of masculinity. The nature of male sexual desire and its role in men's behaviour is particularly relevant to health interventions that aim to challenge existing male sexual practices.

Well, why do dogs lick their balls? It's simple – because they can. It is, of course, an old joke, but one that still makes men and women laugh, perhaps because it reflects an element of truth – how men aspire to satisfy their sexual desires when in a position to do so. After suggesting this to several friends as a title for a chapter discussing male sexuality, it seems that it appeals to both women and men. Those who locate themselves in the feminist movement liked it since it fits many of the caricatures of men they are used to. Perhaps surprisingly, male friends also seemed to find it appropriate since they could identify with the role of sexual desire in their behaviour. Needless to say it is not meant as a slur against Vietnamese men (even though maybe as a light-hearted dig at men in general). I myself found very little distance between the fears, hopes, aspirations and desires of the male informants and my own. What we had in common was much more than what differentiated us. Indeed, one common theme in male informants' narratives is the perception that there is a bond of 'sexual desire' that links men. As one informant put it after confiding to me about his weekend away from his regular partner with a sex-worker: 'Well, we're men, aren't we.'

So what has it to do with men, masculinities and gender relations in development? One of the themes of this chapter is how the construction of gender identities subscribed to by both men and women facilitates certain male sexual behaviour (not quite licking of testicles, but something along those lines). Examining both women's and men's sexual narratives of regular and irregular partners I want to illustrate how these gendered discursive formations 'enable' men to act in certain ways. This is by no means to suggest that men are helpless victims of hegemonic ideas of masculinity. Far from it, men can and do make different choices about their actions. And this leads on to the second contrasting theme of this chapter: how within the prevailing discursive landscape there is considerable social space for diversity of thought and action. Overall it is a story of both consistency and diversity.

A third theme I wish to present is how 'desire' needs to be included in an analysis of male sexuality. A description of gendered discourse tells us a lot about how men can dominate women sexually, but it does not necessarily tell us why. 'The radical feminist analysis suggests that men, consciously and unconsciously, use their sexuality in the service of their general social interest. Male sexuality is seen as one further, and, sometimes, the main weapon by which men attempt to control women and maintain male domination' (Edley and Wetherell 1995: 187). The danger of looking towards purely social explanations of sexual behaviour is that 'sex' itself can get lost among all the theory. As Vance puts it when discussing social construction theory: 'to the extent that social construction theory grants that sexual acts, identities and even desire are mediated by cultural and historical factors, the object of study – sexuality – becomes evanescent and threatens to disappear' (Vance, 1989: 21). In my interpretation of the data, women are subjugated sexually by men, but often sex is the end rather than the means. Many men perceive sexual gratification (albeit mediated by social considerations) as a key driver to their behaviour. Central to the discussion of the role of male desire must be the relationship between the material aspects of the male body and the subjective aspects of masculinity that shape the lived realities of men. Feminist writing offers a range of perspectives that can help in exploring this relationship.

An important outcome of second-wave feminism was the separation of sex from gender. However, this dichotomy itself can be problematic for theorizing the material aspects of the body.

> Just as various theories of the body seem forced to perceive the body either as wholly determining (biology is destiny) or wholly determined (the extremes of constructionism), women's experience tends to be understood as either completely innocent of patriarchal discourses, and thus capable of undermining such discourses or wholly constituted by them. The fates of women and the body are apparently (if somewhat mysteriously) inextricably linked. (Cahill 2001: 80)

So it is with men too; the fate of men and their sexed bodies are inextricably linked. What I explore later in this chapter is the nature of this linkage.

ORIGINS OF THE RESEARCH

The starting point of this research case study was a project by CARE International in three southern provinces of Vietnam: An Giang, Soc Trang and Ba Ria/Vung Tau. The project, entitled 'Men in the Know', developed sexuality training for men to promote safer sex within relationships as well as a trial of the training package with 2,000 men. The training took the form of participatory workshops that focused on two broad areas: first, imparting knowledge on the physiology of sex; and, second, challenging the sociocultural factors that shape sexual encounters (Doyle 2000). This case study uses data from the research component of the project.

CARE International's focus on men arose from a previous project; 'Assertiveness Training Skills for Women for Protection from HIV/ AIDS'. During this, participants expressed a desire for their partners to receive training in women's sexuality and safer sex in general. The desire to engage with men was an instrumental one, where the rationale was improving the lives of women rather than seeing men as gendered beings needing attention.

In the original funding proposal there is no clear, explicit model of male or female sexuality. In its opening section, the proposal states: 'men have low expectations of sexual satisfaction within permanent relationships, and a poor understanding of the mechanism of their (or their partners') bodies. Little wonder that 54% go to prostitutes for "exciting" sex on a bi-weekly basis' (CARE International in Vietnam 1998: 1). Not only is this sensationalist statistic highly questionable in the light of later research, but it clearly casts men (a category of brothel frequenters) as the health problem that needs to be dealt with. If interventions are to remain located in the 'woman as victim, men as problem' discourse (Cornwall 2000: 21), it will limit the scope for engaging with men in constructive dialogues on sexuality.

Although this research supports the view that women's health and overall happiness are at risk from the behaviour of men, it also suggests ways to engage with men in a more constructive fashion.

A NOTE ON METHODOLOGY

Guttmann, in his analysis of masculinity in Mexico, draws upon Gramsci's concept of contradictory consciousness. He describes it as a way 'to orient our examinations of popular understandings, identities, and practices in relation to dominant understandings, identities and practices' (Guttmann 1996: 14). I have also found it a useful framework within which to examine the data from Vietnam. The dominant gendered discursive formations which I will go on to describe are a form of hegemonic ideology. In contrast to this, the lived reality of people's lives produces contradictions in how people live out gender roles. In Vietnam, as in Mexico City, 'the very indeterminacy and ambiguity of social life provides an opportunity for both men and women to negotiate male identities' (Guttmann 1996: 23).

To bring out the relationship between structure and agency as well as that of biological sex and gender (as previously discussed), the methodology needs to address not only the domain of the individual but also the broader social structures and institutions within which individuals operate. Although qualitative methods tend to be more appropriate when exploring the nuanced meanings of gender and sexuality in people's lives, they are limited in the way that results can be extended across large populations.

To get both breadth and depth of understanding, the research used qualitative in-depth and group discussions together with a quantitative survey. Although 'feminists have characterised the dominant methodologies of twentieth century social science research as male centered' (Holland et al. 1999: 459), I do not see quantitative methods as being necessarily misogynistic. The fact that historically they have been used by a principally male establishment to the detriment of women is more a reflection of male dominance in institutions rather than an indication that there is something about quantitative methods that is inherently male. Indeed, 'the social survey, being very much a pragmatically developed and practical device, has no necessary identification with the ideals, aspirations or requirements of positivism' (Hughes and Sharrock 1997: 16). If quantitative data are analysed in a sympathetic way within appropriate frameworks, they have much to offer.

The survey was a probability sample of 225 men who were due to take part in the workshops, as well as 139 of their partners. Although representative of those taking part in the workshop and their partners (since randomly drawn from a list of participants), it cannot claim statistical validity as a sample of men in Vietnam or even those areas of Vietnam where the workshops took place. However, demographics show a wide range of ages and sources of livelihood which suggest that even if the sample cannot claim geographical representivity then it did at least cover a broad spectrum of Vietnamese men and women.

WHY MEN ARE ALL THE SAME

In order to examine how 'male' and 'female' are constructed across a wide sample of men and women, respondents were read a series of personality characteristics, and asked which they felt to be male, female or both. Such quantitative techniques have limitations, for example, in the way the attributes were chosen (in this case by the research team based on previous exploratory qualitative research) as well as assumptions about the complexity of representation. Even allowing for the limitations, it is clear that, across these simplistic dimensions anyway, 'man' and 'woman' are constructed by women and men in broadly similar ways.

By using biological sex as the basic unit of analysis, it precludes the possibility of examining the gendered sexual continuities and discontinuities that might exist. There is a real danger that 'by accepting these constructs as given, by not unpacking them', we are in fact colluding in maintaining false dichotomies (Lorber 1998: 16). However, this was very much the paradigm in which the research was designed – a project aiming to improve the well-being of *women* by targeting *men*. Future interventions could well consider (within the current realities of the cultures they are working within) alternatives in project design. For example, attitudinal or behavioural segmentations (that may or may not include male and female) could be used as the unit of analysis. Biological sex could then be one of several variables used to describe the characteristics of a segment rather than an a priori division of sexed bodies. Later in this chapter I present such a segmentation that although based on a sample of men shows how meaningful variations happen within – and perhaps it's fair to assume – across biological sex.

As is shown in Figures 8.1 and 8.2, women and men agree in how they associate characteristics with genders. Predominantly male characteristics are those that befit an empowered group; they include 'assertive', 'strong' and 'decisive'. Men's empowerment is extended to the sexual realm also; men are 'promiscuous'. The characteristics that are associated with women, on the other hand, are the ones that contribute to women's domination by men. Women are 'obedient', 'loyal' and 'reliable'. And in much the same way that the construction of men is extended to the sexual, so it is with women too. Men are 'promiscuous' whereas women are 'faithful'.

The differences in the way gender is constructed are clearly played out in differing attitudes to the importance of male and female virginity. Overall, a similar proportion of men and women consider that a girl should remain a virgin until she is married. Using a straightforward five-point agreement scale, the vast majority (85 per cent of men and 85 per cent of women) agree that 'a girl should be a virgin until she is married'.

Men as a group place considerable importance upon virginity for women. As an investigator reported back to the research team after an interview with a female informant: 'The first time they had sex ... At first, there wasn't any blood. He asked whether she'd had sex before.

She said no and he believed her. But then, when he saw a little blood, he sighed happily to see a sign that she was a virgin, he was really happy.' Men generally see virginity as something of value to men; to be 'given' on the wedding night: 'It is only worthwhile if a woman keeps her most valuable possession until marriage' (male informant).

There is some awareness of the inequality inherent in men's attitudes but this is very much tempered by recourse to cultural values as a way of justification. Also there are no similar sanctions put upon men. In fact the opposite, part of being a man is being knowledgeable and having sexual experience before committing to a lifetime partner.

> I have an idea, if a girl loses her virginity, her value is reduced. But when a man has sex, even a thousand times, he doesn't lose any of his value. Isn't it unfair? Saying that, I don't mean that a woman should be able to do anything she wants. For example if it was a mistake how could she avoid it? If our society was more developed and had better sex education, then a man would remain a virgin until marriage too. However, in our society, I think a man should try sex before marriage

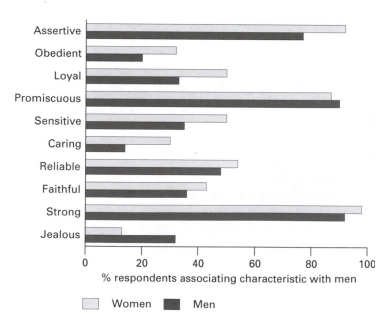

Figure 8.1 Male characteristics (men, n=225; women, n=138)

so that he can learn some experience to share with his future wife. (male informant)

To be honest, being Asian, all men are selfish, everybody wants to be able to take his wife's virginity. (male informant)

Although clearly disadvantaged by the discourse of virginity, women informants also expressed virginity as the ideal, albeit in part due to the fear of men's perceptions. 'People say that husbands are happy when they find their wives are virgins until marriage. If a girl loses her virginity before marriage, then her husband will feel jealous and hate her. Then the girl's life will be miserable' (female informant).

The impact of gender constructions goes beyond expectations of the wedding night. The construction of 'woman' as obedient and faithful limits women being active agents in their sex lives. One male informant commented: 'Women are passive. They want it a lot but don't dare to speak out, right? When a woman says yes, she means no and the opposite' (male informant).

Women also describe their own passivity, but in the face of social

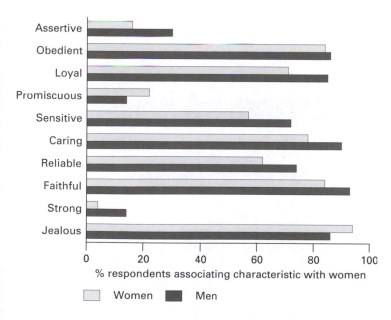

Figure 8.2 Female characteristics (men, n=225; women, n=138)

expectations there is limited scope for action. The subject position of 'woman' prevents them from expressing their own desire.

I let him have sex with me when he wants, but I never ask for it first. When my husband asks, I've got to please him, it's my duty. (female informant)

After he comes, he just stops. I'm sad. But when he pulls out of me … I just have to accept it. (female informant)

Such discursive formations also make it more possible for men to coerce women into having sex even without resorting to using physical force:

After getting married, we just had a normal relationship. But later on, I didn't feel like having sex any more. So, it was like being forced, well I'm married and have to do my duty, give him whatever he wants, serve him. Sometimes I go home tired after work, but whenever he asks, I have to give in. Otherwise, my in-laws would think badly about me. Sometimes I don't want it but don't know how to say no to him. (female informant)

One of the research team reported back to the group:

Sometimes when she doesn't want to, he pushes her, she feels like she is being insulted. When she told him she doesn't want sex, he asks her

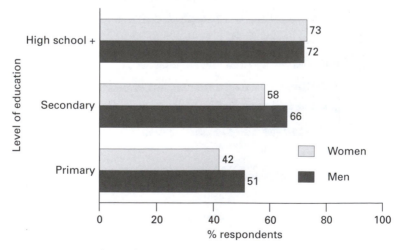

Figure 8.3 Sexual knowledge quiz score, average % correct responses, based on battery of 18 true/false statements (men, n=225; women, n=138)

if she is keeping it for somebody else, so, she gives in. But sometimes when she wants sex herself, but he didn't she just has to put up with it. (interviewer referring to interview with female informant)

The above quotes show how it is not only the construction of gender that limits or facilitates sexual roles; structural factors such as the relationship with other family members (also subject to similar discourses) can further accentuate power inequalities. This research also indicates that education is another critical structural factor.

Women are particularly disadvantaged in the area of sexual knowledge. Knowledge was measured using a battery of eighteen true/false questions on sexual knowledge (concentrating on transmission of HIV/AIDS and STDs). Overall on this measure, women have lower levels of knowledge (see Figure 8.3). The gap between men and women is greatest among those who have received only primary education or lower. A possible explanation of this could be that men have greater access to other sources of information such as non-formal networks.

There are clear differences in women's perception of character and appropriate behaviour with different levels of education. In this sample, better-educated women are more likely to challenge the established order. Education generally is associated with a more equitable attitude

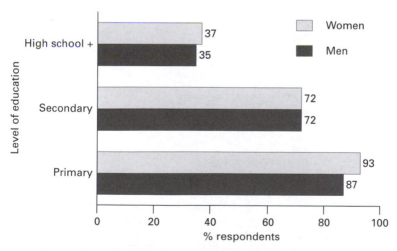

Figure 8.4 'Women should spend their time at home looking after their husbands and children', agree or agree strongly (men, n=225; women, n=138)

towards gender on the part of men also. There is a significant reduction in the number of both men and women who agree 'Women should spend their time at home looking after their husbands and children' (see Figure 8.4) and 'A husband should be able to ask for sex whenever he wants it and his wife should obey' (see Figure 8.5) with increasing levels of formal education.

Lower levels of knowledge further disadvantage women. Many women enter sexual relations unprepared and so are very much dependent upon their partners. 'When I first got married, I was so scared, I didn't know anything. I thought my husband married me to have somebody to cook and clean dishes, but he said if it was just for that, he could do it himself!' (female respondent).

Although we can identify consistency in the dominant sexual discourses, the above data show that not all women and men are marked by these gendered discursive constructs to the same extent. A broad range of factors including education, economy and intergenerational relations of power can either facilitate the creation of or reduction in social space for negotiating identities. In the next section I will highlight how such a social space allows for the negotiation of diverse masculinities in Vietnam.

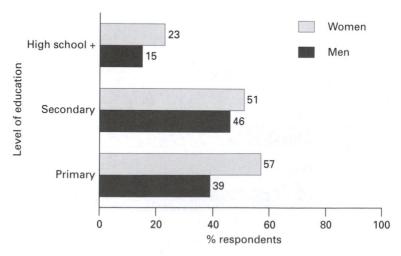

Figure 8.5 'A husband should be able to ask for sex whenever he wants it and his wife shoud obey', agree or agree strongly (men, n=225; women, n=138)

WHY MEN ARE ALL DIFFERENT

In contrast to the dominant ideology of gender, the research also shows that there is some social space in the lived realities of both men and women that allows men to vary widely in their behaviour and attitude.

One advantage of using a complex methodology is that different methodologies can bring out different dimensions of women and men's relationships. On one hand the quantitative data suggest there is considerable consensus among men and women on what gendered sexual roles are (and inevitably how men and women should act). However, this is complemented by the qualitative data which not only bring out the impact of these discursive formations but further highlight the significant social space that exists for individual agency. This is true for both women and men.

One example of this duality is that, for some men at least, men's sense of identity is in part dependent upon their partner being sexually satisfied. Men might be in an empowered position *vis-à-vis* their sexual partners, but this is tempered by a fear of 'failing to perform': 'In a sexual relationship, making a wife satisfied is very important, even the most important. That's because if you don't make your wife satisfied, she won't respect you and look down on you. Letting a woman look down is something to be ashamed of' (male informant).

In addition to this, men's privileged sexual position is also vulnerable when faced with women who are sexually assertive. Such women scare men. They threaten not only men's access to sexual satisfaction but also, on a more fundamental level, their concept of self. 'I used to study with a girl from Poland. Our Vietnamese nature is different, I felt that she was too experienced. She was more lively than me, flirting, seducing … It made me feel like I was losing my power' (male informant).

To quote Sarah White, it does seem that, for men, 'Manhood does not appear to be self-reliant and autonomous. On the contrary, masculinity seems to depend chronically on the estimation of others to be highly vulnerable to attack by ridicule, shaming, subordination, or "dishonourable" female action' (White 1997: 17).

As a way of highlighting how different men can think in different ways, a cluster analysis was carried out on the data. This kind of multivariate analysis (as opposed to bivariate) looks at the relationship

between many variables at one time rather than one at a time. Specifically, cluster analysis is a technique by which a set of objects (in this
case, men) can be grouped into a smaller number of homogeneous
groups based on a number of observed characteristics (attitude). The
net result is an attitudinal segmentation where each segment tends to
hold a similar set of attitudes. What is of interest is what different
attitudes are held in common by a particular segment as well as how the
segments differ in the attitudes they have.

In this segmentation a battery of twelve attitudinal statements was
used. By no means do they represent a list of all possible attitudes men
can have about sex. They were based on exploratory qualitative research
that was aiming to discern areas of gender inequality and are clearly
loaded towards negative aspects of gender relations. Each man was
asked to rate his agreement or disagreement with each of the statements
using a five-point scale with a neutral mid-point.

The analysis produced a solution with four segments that differed in
size. By comparing the mean average of agreement with the various
statements we can discern what are attitudes that define each segment.
Statistical tests are used to establish the validity of observed differences.
Obviously twelve attitudinal statements cannot adequately encapsulate
all the subtle intricacies of social life, but some interesting differences
do appear. I have deliberately avoided giving names to each segment
since this would overstate the determinability of the analysis. For
example, we cannot say that he is 'traditional man' therefore he believes
his wife should stay at home cooking. It is more a case of making the
point that within dominant discourse there are meaningful differences
in attitude among men that influence behaviour.

Out of the twelve statements, not all are equally as differentiating
between the segments. 'A girl should be a virgin until she gets married',
'It is not acceptable for husbands to go to a prostitute under any circumstances' and 'Both husband and wife should be faithful to each other' all
had little power in differentiating between the segments. For all four
segments the rating was positive; or, put another way, men across all
the segments agree with these statements. For some men at least there
is a contradiction between their support for marital fidelity and their use
of sex-workers.

Looking at the attitude across the four segments (see Table 8.1), the
prevailing attitudes in segments 4 and 2 are those most likely to put

Table 8.1 Attitudes across segments

Statement	Attitudinal segments and proportion of sample			
	1 16%	2 23%	3 31%	4 30%
Men are naturally unfaithful	×	●134	×	×
Sons are better than daughters	×	×	×	●13
Men are unfaithful because they get drunk and cannot control themselves	●34	●34	×	×
A husband should be able to ask for sex whenever he wants and his wife should obey	×	×	×	●123
Women should spend their time at home looking after their husbands and children	×	×	×	●123
It's OK for men to go to hostess bars once in a while with friends for a drink	●23	●134	×	×
It's natural for men to have sex with sex-workers	×	●134	×	×
If my wife was unfaithful I would leave her	×	●13	×	●13
Sex with the same person becomes boring	×	●13	×	×

Notes: ● denotes an overall mean average of agreement within that attitudinal segment; a subscript indicates tests have shown significant difference at 90% confidence level with one or more of the other attitudinal segments.

women's health and happiness at risk. In segment 4, we can clearly see how the privileged position of men allows them unfettered sexual access to their partners, as well as a gendered division of labour. Attitudes in segment 2 also tend to see a woman's place as being in the home, but this is linked to discourses that subjugate women sexually; men are naturally driven by sexual desires and so sex outside of regular relationships (for example with sex-workers) is sanctioned.

These data also show that these diverse attitudinal segments tend to have different sexual behaviours. It is no surprise that the segment previously identified as segment 2 has the highest incidence of risk behaviour – defined as penetrative sex without a condom with someone who is not their present partner (see Figure 8.6).

Segments 1 and 3 appear to reflect far more egalitarian attitudes towards women. Nearly half of men therefore do not think that women should stay at home looking after their husbands and so on. If women are the victims and men are the problem, it is certainly not all men. Historically, those working in Gender and Development (GAD) have tended to characterize men in fairly simplistic terms; this data analysis suggests that the reality is more complex, with variations not only in what men think but also in what they do.

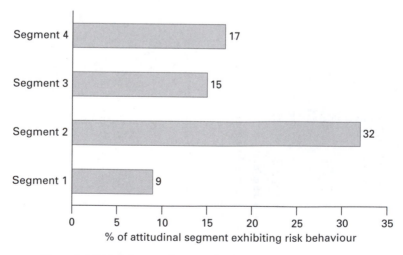

Figure 8.6 Risk behaviour by attitudinal segment (segment 1: n=36; segment 2: n=52; segment 3: n=70; segment 4: n=67)

The previous discussions, although having a part to play in debates about the construction of men in gender and development generally, also have a more immediate impact upon those working in the areas of sexual health. Central to behaviour change communication is the idea that messages are tailored to the needs and context of the target. In the light of the above, it is not enough to have a simple message to all men, especially one that casts them as a single group of brothel frequenters. Men are diverse in their attitudes, contexts and practices. Priorities need to be set about which men are most likely to be having unsafe sex and how interventions can be designed with their attitudes, contexts and behaviours in mind.

A PLACE FOR DESIRE

As discussed previously, there is a danger that an emphasis on the social aspects of sexual behaviour leaves desire out of the picture. This is not to say we should retreat to nativist or pre-social positions where we lose 'the vital purchase on the social' (Connell and Dowsett 1999: 187). but we should try to keep some of the 'sweat and the passion' (p. 192).

Rubin draws a parallel between sex and physical hunger: 'The belly's hunger gives no clues as to the complexities of cuisine. The body, brain, the genitalia, and the capacity for language are necessary for human sexuality. But they do not determine its content, its experiences, or its institutional forms' (Rubin 1999: 149). In much the same way that food, irrespective of how its various meanings are constructed, can never be dissociated from hunger, so sexual behaviour cannot be dissociated from desire.

In Vietnam, men having sex with sex-workers is closely linked to men being in groups and drinking. This is similar to other Asian countries such as Thailand (Greene 2000: 55).

> … it starts from drinking, drinking at a birthday, for example, we're just getting going and then we decide to go to a hostess bar. (male informant)

> … there were some of us who knew what to do, they showed us how to get a girl back home, back then we weren't scared of AIDS or anything (*laugh*) … so we went the whole way, it was pretty bad because

there was 5 or 7 of us with one girl, after, we paid and dropped her off ... that was the first time. (male informant)

Greene (2000: 55) cites Fordham (1995) who describes the importance to Thai men of impressing others through womanizing and spending large amounts of money. In Vietnam, alcohol and peer groups also play a crucial role but in a different way. This research suggests that these factors are important because they provide an enabling environment; they are not a reason to use sex-workers per se. If these were to be causal influences, then perhaps we could reasonably expect a sense of regret or shame when recalling experiences. For example, if men see using a sex-worker as aberrant behaviour under external influences, then 'I was drunk' or 'My friends made me do it' might be given as a justification. In contrast, the principal justification for using sex-workers is for the physical experience. In Vietnamese, men often use the expression that literally translates as 'solve physiological need' (*giai quyet sinh ly*). Overall, men's narratives of experiences with sex-workers are free from any sense of shame or regret: 'she was an expert, a professional, it was nothing to do with shared need between two people, it's just to satisfy my need' (male informant).

Commercial sex also offers varieties of sex perhaps not available with regular partners. 'When having relationship with sex-workers, we could ask them to do what we want because we pay them. Since they receive money, they do what we want, like using their mouths' (male informant). Putting aside the gender and class inequalities that the sex industry is built upon, as well as the representations of gender that further sanction paid sex, there remains a physical desire (in this case for oral sex). The act is not devoid of social significance, but the 'why' (as opposed to the 'how') of men having paid oral sex is that they like it. To go back to the original question, 'Why do dogs lick their balls?', it can be rephrased: 'Why do men use sex-workers?' The answer is that because they can; structural considerations and gender identity provide the enabling environment.

So, is there any more to understanding male sexual behaviour than, men do these things because they like to and their empowered status allows it? To answer this I will draw upon feminists who have long theorized the relationship between power and sexual desire, particularly in debates about rape.

Brownmiller (1975) identifies rape as being about power rather than sexual desire. On mob rape she stated 'sexual appeal, as we understand it, has little to do with the act of rape. A mob turns to rape as an expression of power and dominance. Women are used almost as inanimate objects to prove a point among men' (Brownmiller 1975: 124–5). This might be the case with rape, but it does not tell us about sexual desire in general. Brownmiller attempts to include all men in the process of rape. Her statement that rape is 'nothing more or less than a conscious process of intimidation by which *all men* keep *all women* in a state of fear' (Brownmiller 1975: 15) denies the highly variable prevalence of rape across cultures. Cahill (2001: 23) cites two studies that show that in many cultures men do not rape women (Schwendinger and Schwendinger 1983; Sanday 1981). This still leaves us with the possibility that (rapists aside) desire is more important than power to men.

Other radical feminists such as Dworkin (1989) and MacKinnon (1989) have taken this as a basis to extend the primacy of power over desire to heterosexual sex in general. Since social norms reinforce heterosexuality, it ceases to be a free choice for women; rape and consensual intercourse are qualitatively the same: 'for women it is difficult to distinguish the two under conditions of male dominance' (MacKinnon 1989: 174). From this perspective male sexual desire is not an end in itself but an instrument of power in a wider political project. I question this analysis on two grounds: first, this research shows that male dominance is not universal in either the way men's attitudes are shaped by dominant discourses nor in the behaviour of individual men. It would be fair to assume that such variation allows at least some women more agency over their sexual choices than the concept of forced 'heterosex' suggests. Second, there are recorded examples of gay subcultures (men who have sex with men) that exist in spite of dominant heterosex norms (St Pierre 1997).

The physical sensations of sex are not a licence for exploiting power differentials, be they class, gender or ethnicity. To draw upon Rubin's food analogy, being hungry does not justify cannibalism. So it is with men: sexual desire cannot be used as a justification for exploitation. But if we are going to engage men in debates on development and sexual health, we cannot just theorize desire away. What we need is a framework that can include both desire and its role in supporting and being supported by broader structures of power.

Grosz's analysis of the relationship between the material aspects of the body and subjectivity can help us to locate desire within broader frameworks of language and discourse. Grosz uses the model of a Mobius Strip (a two-dimensional surface that has only one side) to demonstrate the way that the interior and exterior aspects of the body are linked without clear boundaries or transition between the two. 'It enables subjectivity to be understood as fully material and materiality to be extended and to include and explain the operations of language, desire and significance' (Grosz 1994: 209). The same model can be applied to men; the subjectivity of men can be seen as being inextricably linked to the material nature of their bodies. We can avoid both the deterministic positions of 'male instinct' as well as the radical constructionism that denies a role for bodily experience. We can therefore give 'full weight to bodily experience without treating the body as the container of an historical essence of sexuality', and so 'find ways of understanding social relations as themselves sexual, not merely as framing sexuality from the outside' (Connell and Dowsett 1999: 187).

Accepting desire as important in its own right does not mean ignoring the impact it has upon women's lives. The results of this research show how male sexual desire can lead to the objectification of women – in this case sex-workers. For the men whose concern is their own desire, sex-workers are not complete people, they are objects to be used. Although this objectification through sexuality may not be part of a wider political project, such 'sexualization is one way of fixing disadvantaged persons in their disadvantage, to their clear detriment' (Bartky 1998: 47). There is an inevitable element of objectification in sexuality generally; a woman's or man's sexual gaze at a stranger does not take into account all the mental and emotional properties of that stranger. What is important is to what extent this objectification is oppressive and becomes extended into every aspect of her or his experience (Bartky 1998: 46). In a broader context it could well be the case that the 'dominant masculine sexual imaginaries are politically, legally, economically and socially legitimised through existing networks of power, whereas women's imaginings about men are not' (Gattens, 1996: 147).

Although this research focused on men's view of desire, the results also indicate some social space for women to articulate their own sexual desires. It might be considerably less than for men but it is there. If it's not to be a case of 'Leaving sex to the feminists is like letting your dog vacation at the taxidermists' (Paglia 1992: 50), the target of feminist ire should not be heterosex in its entirety but the social and political structures that lead to a narrow, masculine expression of it.

CAN MEN CHANGE?

Within the overall political project of enhancing women's status and power, the realization that there is diversity among the group 'men' must offer hope for greater equality. The social spaces as previously outlined allow for men to act in different ways within the same discursive arrangements. The results of the project, of which this research was a part, show that men and women's lives can be improved when men are given access to more knowledge about their own and women's bodies, and about the physiology of sexually transmitted infections, and when established norms are challenged.

Overall, 91 per cent of men and 93 per cent of their female partners agree that 'they are a lot happier in their relationships now' after the workshop. Men can change their behaviour for the better. As one male participant told the research team after the workshops: 'When I got back and talked to my wife I know that when she is having her period she's irritable, now I know how to keep calm and get over it. Before the workshop when my wife got angry so did I and we'd argue' (male informant).

It is not only the men who tell us that their relationships are better, women also feel that their lives are better: 'Generally ... before, at home he was not usually very relaxed. But since the workshop ... he works hard, is open and most of all in our sex life he understands more' (female informant). Again, 'For example, now ... before he didn't know ... now he knows, he massages my legs and arms and other stuff too' (female informant). But we must sound a note of caution since the research has also shown that although the individual behaviour of men can change, the overall gendered discourses of sexuality that shape sexual encounters are much the same.

> Before when I refused to have sex with him he was very difficult, but now after the workshop sometimes when I am sick or feel tired and tell him he agrees. (female informant)
>
> Before he went to the workshop, when he got home and demanded sex

I just gave in, but after the workshop he is more understanding. For example, when he sees that I am tired he won't ask at all and lets me sleep. He loves and cares more about our family. Now, in our relationship we only have sex when both of us feel comfortable. (female informant)

If women's lives have changed as a result of these workshops, it is largely because men have decided to change their behaviour. Although this must be good news, it hasn't altered the basic power inequalities between men and women. Life for women might be better but only because men (for whatever reason) have allowed it to be that way (Doyle 2000). Furthermore, although having an immediate impact there is no guarantee that these changes will be maintained when the basic power inequalities are unchanged.

A WAY FORWARD

The theme of this chapter has been exploring both consistency and diversity among men. In part the consistency refers to the dominant ideology of gender. In contrast to this I have illustrated the considerable variety of and diversity in masculine behaviour and attitudes. Although hegemonic discourses are not necessarily amenable to 'quick fixes', the actions of individual men in changing their behaviour as well as the social space where individual women and men can negotiate identity offer hope for broader social change. To engage with men, interventions will have to move away from simplistic caracitures to seeing men as gendered beings whose subjectivity and material being are mutually constituted.

Fairclough (1993) describes a process of social change as being one where people recombine discursive conventions in new ways. As women and men see the contradictions between their lives and hegemonic discourses, they use the available social space to recombine discursive conventions in new ways and so bring about structural changes in these very same discourses. Through this process, new hegemonies are developed and so social change through the actions of individuals is possible.

REFERENCES

Bartky, S. L. (1998) 'On Psychological Oppression' (1990), in M. Rogers (ed.), *Contemporary Feminist Theory* (New York: McGraw Hill).

Brownmiller, S. (1975) *Against Our Will: Men, Women, and Rape* (New York: Penguin Books).

Cahill, A. J. (2001) *Rethinking Rape* (New York: Cornell University Press).

CARE International in Vietnam (1998) 'Men in the Know', project funding proposal to AUSAID (unpublished).

Connell, R. and G. W. Dowsett (1999) '"The Unclean Motion of the Generative Parts": Frameworks in Western Thought on Sexuality', R. Parker and P. Aggleton (eds), *Culture, Society and Sexuality: a Reader* (London: UCL Press), pp. 179–96.

Cornwall, A. (2000) 'Missing Men? Reflections on Men, Masculinities and Gender in GAD', *IDS Bulletin*, 31(2).

Doyle, N. (2000) 'Pillow Talk: Changing Men's Behaviour', *Development Research Insights*, 35(21).

Dworkin, A. (1989) *Pornography: Men Possessing Women* (New York: E. P. Dutton).

Edley, N. and M. Wetherell (1995) *Men in Perspective: Practice, Power and Identity* (Hemel Hempstead: Harvester Wheatsheaf).

Fairclough, N. (1993) *Discourse and Social Change* (Oxford: Blackwell Publishers).

Fordham, G. (1995) 'Whisky, Women and Song: Men, Alcohol and AIDS in Northern Thailand', *Australian Journal of Anthropology*, 6(3): 154–77.

Gattens, M. (1996) *Imaginary Bodies: Ethics, Power and Corporeality* (New York: Routledge).

Greene, M.E. (2000) 'Changing Women and Avoiding Men: Gender Stereotypes and Reproductive Health Programmes', *IDS Bulletin*, 31(2).

Grosz, E. (1994) *Volatile Bodies: Towards a Corporeal Feminism* (Bloomington: Indiana University Press).

Guttmann, M. C. (1996) *The Meanings of Macho: Being a Man in Mexico City* (Berkeley: University of California Press).

Holland, J., C. Ramazanoglu, S. Sharpe and R. Thomson (1999) 'Feminist Methodology and Young People's Sexuality', in R. Parker and P. Aggleton (eds), 1999, *Culture, Society and Sexuality: a Reader* (London: UCL Press), pp. 457–72.

Hughes, J. and W. Sharrock (1997) *The Philosophy of Social Research*, 3rd edn (Harlow: Longman Social Research Series).

Lorber, J. (1998) 'Beyond the Binaries: Depolarizing the Categories of Sex, Sexuality, and Gender' (1996), in M. Rogers (ed.), *Contemporary Feminist Theory* (New York: McGraw Hill), pp. 15–25.

MacKinnon, C. A. (1989) *Toward a Feminist Theory of the State* (Cambridge, MA: Harvard University Press).

Paglia, C. (1992) *Sex, Art and American Culture* (New York: Vintage).

Rubin, G. S. (1999) 'Thinking Sex: Notes for a Radical theory of the Politics of Sexuality', in R. Parker and P. Aggleton (eds), *Culture, Society and Sexuality: a Reader* (London: UCL Press), pp. 143–78.

St Pierre, M. L. (1997) *Evaluation of SCF(UK) HIV/AIDS Prevention Programme for Men Who Have Sex with Men (MSM) Final Report* (SCF UK and HCMC, Vietnam).

Sanday, P. R. (1981) 'The Socio-cultural Context of Rape: A Cross-cultural Study', *Journal of Social Issues*, 37(4): 5–27.

Schwendinger, J. R. and H. Schwendinger (1983) *Rape and Inequality* (Beverly Hills, CA: Sage).

Vance, C. (1989) 'Social Construction Theory: Problems in the History of Sexuality', in D. Altman et al. (eds) *Homosexuality, Which Homosexuality?* (London: Gay Men's Press).

White, S. (1997) 'Men, Masculinities, and the Politics of Development', *Gender and Development* 5(2).

CHAPTER 9

Targeting Men for a Change: AIDS Discourse and Activism in Africa

JANET BUJRA

§ Campaigns against the spread of AIDS in Africa have recently begun to target men. This raises challenging questions not only about forms of intervention but also about theoretical perspectives which have abandoned essentialist views of men and masculinity and shifted to a perception of masculinities as plural and contingent. In addressing these concerns, I review field data from a recent study in Tanzania and look at AIDS initiatives in Africa which target men.

My aim is to explore the implications, both in theory and in practice, of the growing insistence that 'without men there would be no AIDS epidemic' (Foreman 1999: vi). The debate centres on how masculinity is defined and theorized, how it might facilitate the spread of disease and how it might change. The focus is on Africa, where HIV transmission is predominantly heterosexual. A critical review of some examples of AIDS interventions which target men is complemented by the findings of recent fieldwork on gender and AIDS in a rural area of Tanzania, part of a larger comparative study of Tanzania and Zambia.[1]

A shift in the focus of AIDS campaigns in Africa echoes changing global conceptions of gender. Essentialist perceptions of both 'men' and 'women' (which had considerable political force) are now generally rejected. With acknowledgement of the diverse social forms which gender may take, it is not 'masculinity' as a singular characteristic of men that is now at issue, but the plurality and contingency of 'masculinities'. The debate encompasses exploration of how diverse forms of masculine identity are maintained through everyday discourse and practice, though it is also concerned with their transformation (Cornwall and Lindisfarne 1994; Mac an Ghail 1996; Cornwall 1997; White 1998; Connell 1995).

Some contributors to this debate suggest that masculinity is malleable enough to encompass men's acquiescence in their own disempowerment (this has sometimes been framed precisely in terms of AIDS campaigns; see Redman 1996). For others, masculinity, despite its diversity, always entails claims to privilege, authority and the right to dominate women. While 'targeting' men is essential to decelerating HIV transmission, we should not assume that it entails any rethinking of masculinity or increased mutuality between the sexes. In seeking ways to frame public health messages that men will 'hear', there is the risk of restating the terms of a predatory masculinity in which men's objectification of women in regard to sex is paramount.

AIDS IS GENDERED

Recognizing AIDS as a gendered phenomenon was an achievement of social scientists, an element in the questioning of purely medical models of disease (Seidel 1993). However, AIDS is not gendered everywhere in the same way. The predominantly-homosexual transmission between men found in Europe, America and Australia sets up quite different questions about gender than does the predominantly heterosexual mode of transmission found in Africa and some other areas of the world. In America and Europe the emergence of AIDS fanned homophobic moral panics, against which we have to set the role of the epidemic in furthering gay pride and self-organization (Altman 1994; Davies et al. 1993; Van de Ven et al. 1999). In Africa, where all sexually active adults are at risk, the scapegoating process at first focused on a different but also stigmatized and oppressed category – women, who were less well placed to organize a fight-back or self-protection (Bassett and Mhloyi 1991; de Bruyn 1992). While AIDS in both cases raises questions about gender relations,[2] homophobia and misogyny are different creatures. Translated into social action in developing countries, 'gender' was initially taken to be synonymous with 'women' (White 1997). AIDS campaigns set up women as 'targets' for intervention and in the process presented them only as victims waiting for rescue or 'empowerment'. Attention was focused on women's particular vulnerability in the AIDS epidemic – a vulnerability that was both physiological and social (women are more likely to be subjected to coercive sex and less able to negotiate safer sex). Our project was based on the more positive thesis (borrowed from Ankrah 1991 and Ulin 1992 in particular) that women in Africa had developed networking and organizing skills that might be harnessed to the fight against AIDS, especially for their own protection. We also argued, however, that empowering women could not be achieved without an engagement with male power over women in particular contexts (Baylies and Bujra 1995). Where AIDS is transmitted heterosexually, women require men's co-operation in order to protect themselves. This is particularly the case when the main form of protection is male condoms; but it also applies to the strategy whereby women rely on male partners to be faithful. Targeting women for AIDS interventions had a limited impact. It did not always fail: risk-awareness among women was generally heightened, while success was occasionally achieved in empowering sex-workers to insist on condom use with clients (some examples are summarized in Baylies and Bujra 1995). However, while the slogan 'empower women' appeared to take gender relations seriously, it rarely entailed an inter-rogation of men's sexual behaviour.

As 'gender' was reformulated to mean 'the relations between men and women', a space was opened up to explore men's greater complicity in the transmission of AIDS. From Christine Obbo's bold but throw-away remark in 1993 that, in the African context, 'Men are the solution', to more recent assertions, including one by a male official of UNAIDS that, 'The HIV epidemic is driven by men' (quoted in Foreman 1999: viii), there has been a global shift in both the perception and response to the gendering of AIDS (Carovano 1995; Campbell 1995). At this point, the social construction of masculinity comes into focus, not in essentialist guise as a unitary 'male role', or with men perceived univers-ally as 'the problem' (Cornwall 1997), but in a new academic discourse of 'multiple masculinities'. There are both strengths and weaknesses in this literature when viewed in the context of HIV prevention. On the one hand, a recognition of the pluralistic and contingent forms that masculinity may take leads to the positive conclusion that men can change. On the other hand, there is ambivalence about the degree of potential transformation, given continuing debate about the extent to which men universally exercise power over women (albeit in a diversity of ways and some more effectively than others). There is a residual essentialism inherent, for example, in the notion of a socially dominant mode of manhood – 'hegemonic masculinity' (Connell 1987). Others

have argued that this dominant representation 'offers a discursive resource to men in general which they may choose to exercise ... It ...
creates effects without being consciously exercised by any particular
man' (Jackson 1998: 3).

A continuing insistence on men's essential dominance is here allied
(perhaps) to wishful thinking – that they might 'choose' not to exercise
it. Models of health behaviour often have this as their foundation, namely
that 'individuals can and do make decisions about their behaviour, and,
at least potentially, have the capacity to translate those decisions into
action' (Carovano 1995: 3). In a context where men *enjoy* power, in what
circumstances would they sacrifice that enjoyment? Approached for his
views on men and HIV transmission, Connell himself responded:

> In Western culture, the most honoured form of masculinity involves
> being authoritative, decisive, controlling other people, exerting power.
> This affects heterosexual relationships in damaging ways. When sexual
> conquest is the main goal, a pattern of sexuality can be created where
> women are repeatedly at risk and have limited resources to resist this ...
> Until dominant forms of masculinity are challenged and economic power
> shifts towards women, this isn't likely to end. (quoted in Carovano
> 1995: 7)

There is a range of views about how men's power manifests itself:
discursively, materially, institutionally or culturally. The study of sexuality lends itself to formulation in terms of discourse or representation.
Its focus on what is private, covert and hidden behind closed doors puts
a premium on what is said about sex, or expressed in other cultural
forms. The discursive framing of much of the literature on masculinities
(Cornwall 1997) may pre-empt a structural mapping of men's power
(over women, other men and resources), or an exploration of the limits
of men's control (Hearn 1996) – all of which provide the dynamic
social context within which masculinities are defined and played out.
Women in Africa may subscribe to a discourse that denies wives the
right to refuse sex to husbands, but they do this in the knowledge of
men's social power – their socially sanctioned violence and control over
the means to survival.

When it comes to devising strategies for change, these considerations
cease to be merely academic. If men's power is challenged, their resistance may militate against change. What practical advantage is there in

recognizing and exposing the diversity and contingency of masculinities? Should interventions be responsive to the hegemonic form of masculinity or aim to exploit difference? Connell (cited in Carovano 1995: 10) argues that: '[h]eterosexual men have a great deal to learn from homosexual men in "Western" countries [in] caring for people living with AIDS.' But would they concede this? Is it productive to challenge the social stigma attached to the public expression of men's gentler feelings (care, compassion, grief), or, in the tragic context of AIDS, to question the imperative that 'men are supposed to be strong, stern, they're not supposed to cry or show weakness' (Carovano 1995: 13, citing Hernandez)? If hegemonic masculinity dictates multiple sexual partners, and 'monogamy is not seen as an attractive way to demonstrate masculinity' (Campbell 1995: 206), how can this view be transformed in the context of safer-sex campaigns?

White concedes that 'trying to bring about change in gender relations constitutes a cultural offensive' (White 1998: 5); it is certainly critical of present modes of male behaviour and self-presentation. This criticism may be resisted by men and it may or may not be what local women want (Sweetman 1998).

In Africa, from the mid-1990s onwards, exclusive emphasis on the vulnerable (women, the young) in AIDS campaigning has begun to give way to facing down the powerful, grasping the opportune nature of such a challenge at a point when men are also vulnerable, when casual unprotected sex is a death-wish rather than an assertion of manhood. Strategies are devised to engage men more directly in AIDS campaigns. The Society for Women and AIDS in Africa, dedicated to supporting women in the AIDS crisis, now calls on 'Men as our partners in the fight against AIDS' (Dakar conference theme, www.hivnet.ch: 21 December 1998). Campaign literature demands: 'Men must be sensitised and mobilised to a greater extent for an effective response to HIV/AIDS and STDs.' The argument is rationalized in terms of men's political power: 'Since men occupy most positions of influence, their participation in advocating gender-sensitive politics and programmes is essential' (SAFAIDS/KIT/WHO 1995: 36). A recent publication, *AIDS and Men* (Foreman 1999), devotes six out of eleven case studies to Africa. Its conclusions challenge men more starkly, since, 'men determine the path of the disease ... all men should take responsibility for their sexual behaviour' (Foreman 1999: ix, xii).

Below, I look at the extent to which these themes are echoed in practice when interventions are devised and implemented.

MEN AND SOCIAL POWER IN AFRICA

Men in Africa have been under scrutiny for some time. Feminists have noted their dominance in social relations, their control over key economic resources and monopolization of political positions (Amadiume 1987; and discussion in Meena 1992). Often the debates have been essentialist and naturalist in their assumptions, posing 'men' as a monolithic category everywhere oppressing women. Others have been more nuanced, recognizing the difference that class, ethnic location or period may make to men's behaviour. On the political front, African feminists have been increasingly vocal about men's violence against women, with rape and domestic aggression being brought into the open and exposure of attacks against women who dare to compete with men in the public arena (in work, in education, in political parties and on the streets) becoming more common.[3] The brutalization of women in African societies ravaged by war has become a particularly charged issue (see McFadden 1992; Enloe 1993; Turshen and Twagiramariya 1998; Turshen 1999).

AFRICAN MALE SEXUALITY

In the context of the AIDS epidemic, some African feminists have looked critically at male sexuality, noting for example that: 'African societies in general tolerate multiple sexual partners for men, but exert moral and social sanctions on women' (Obbo 1995: 176). Rather more forthright is McFadden's unapologetic reference to 'the promiscuity of the African male' (McFadden 1992: 160). It is common to contextualize this in terms of colonial male labour migration and the emergence of a market for commercial sex in Africa (Bujra 1982; White 1990), while more recent postcolonial realities – civil war, intercontinental trade, economic crises and widening social divisions – are seen as fuelling the commoditization of sex and the opportunities for extended sexual networking (Obbo 1993; Cleland and Ferry 1995). But McFadden questions whether African male promiscuity can be explained simply 'as an involuntary consequence of sexual abstinence' (where men are separated from wives by labour migration or war), implying thereby a more voluntaristic and culpable form of behaviour on men's part, or a genetic predisposition towards 'promiscuity'.

While this stance lends itself easily to racist constructions, it should not simply be evaded by labelling it as biological reductionism. What 'evidence' we have suggests that men on average have more sexual partners than women, whether we do the counting in Britain or Botswana (Cleland and Ferry 1995; Foreman 1999; Rweyemamu 1999; Wellings et al. 1994). Surveys of sexual behaviour must, of course, be treated with great caution, depending as they do on the veracity of the claims made. Where success in sexual activity 'involves the honour and pride of men' (Mohamed Osman of Somalia, quoted in Carovano 1995: 5), a tendency to exaggerate may meet with general acceptance, while women may be inhibited by social disapprobation from making similar claims. Phillips (1994: 7) argues, for example, that in Zimbabwe: 'sex has been constructed as a subject for men. It is for men to talk about, to initiate, to pursue, to enact ... it is for women to recognise the taboos, to decline the continual advances of men, to exercise discipline in refusing their own desires.'

Cleland and Ferry (1995) make the general point that patterns of sexual behaviour vary markedly between (and within) countries in response to social mores and the availability of opportunities for sex. War provides just such an opportunity. McFadden (1992: 185) quotes Giller and Nabaganda on the bloody conflict which marked the fall of Idi Amin in Uganda: 'tens of thousands of women died at the hands of the soldiers, often following rape. They were not acts of sexually-starved men, but expressions of violence, aggression, anger, hatred and revenge; a need to demonstrate power by soldiers in an army which was being defeated' (McFadden 1992: 185). Turshen, recounting discussions in the African Women's Anti-War Coalition, reports their view that: 'men use rape as a way to dishonour and humiliate not just women, but the enemy group. High levels of rape have promoted the transmission of HIV not only in theatres of war but in the home areas of soldiers when they return to wives and local partners' (Turshen 1999: 125; see also McFadden 1992; Bennett et al., 1995).

Given global variations in male sexual behaviour, it seems reasonable to argue that context is a potent factor. The data say as much about men's varying power to limit and control women's sexuality as about their lack of control over themselves. The fact of higher male sexual activity does not automatically equate with higher risk of HIV transmission, of course, since this requires that HIV has taken hold within the population and that sexual activity is unprotected.

HOMOSEXUALITY: AFRICAN DENIAL

A key challenge to hegemonic masculinity is represented by homosexuality. The existence of homosexuality has often been denied in Africa, despite it having been documented in many places.[4] More than one African writer has noted that AIDS was at first seen as a 'white homosexual disease' that had little bearing on their lives (Kaleeba 1992; Nkosi 1999). Governments have found it useful to insist that homosexuality is an alien and non-African 'perversion'; ordinary people frequently voice the same sentiments (Kiama 1999). In some countries – Kenya, Uganda, Zimbabwe – denial is not deemed to be sufficient and homosexuality has been declared a criminal act. Occasional prosecutions take place (for example the recent high-profile case of the ex-President of Zimbabwe).[5] The view that men are responsible for the AIDS epidemic is thus initially denied in response to homosexuality, because African men could not be involved in an act 'against African tradition' (President Moi of Kenya, quoted in *Mail and Guardian*, 7–13 October 1999).

The hysterical and angry rejoinders which queries about homosexuality often provoke from African men in positions of power suggest that the notion of diverse forms of sexuality is extremely threatening (Kiama 1999). Only in South Africa has there been a different trajectory. The first AIDS cases there were reported among gay men (Abdool Karim 1998). Gays began to organize from the early 1980s, when, under apartheid, homosexuality was a crime. They took on the AIDS threat by providing counselling and medical services (Reddy 1998; *Agenda* 1998). Gay associations were swept along in the same tide that brought apartheid down and which ushered in a new constitution in which homosexuality was legalized and sexuality could no longer be held as grounds for discrimination (Reddy 1998). The gay scene had been dominated by middle-class whites, but black homosexuals were now able to associate openly. By this time, the AIDS epidemic had turned heterosexual and heterosexual transmission has now become the predominant form in South Africa.

MASCULINITIES: AFRICAN PERSPECTIVES

A denial of homosexuality may extend to a denial of the implied diversity of masculinities. But in the climate of fear about death and sexuality, there is beginning to be a change of mood in Africa. The concept of 'masculinity', as something distinct from biological sex, and fashioned through sociocultural processes, has begun to make an appearance. It goes along with the discovery of men as a new target in AIDS intervention work. Some men are becoming aware of themselves as gendered beings and of their masculinity as a contingent cultural construction, rather than something fixed and natural. They are making connections between constructions of masculinity and men's behaviour towards women (Carovano 1995, quoting Rwegera; Rweyemamu 1999, quoting Swai; Anane 1999).

The work of Chenjerai Shire from Zimbabwe, which appears in Cornwall and Lindisfarne's book *Dislocating Masculinity* (1994), is unusual in its explicit rendering of the argument. Writing of the 'Shona' people in Zimbabwe, Shire tells us that he uses the term masculinities 'To examine male preoccupations as celebrations of maleness, pluralised to render a definition as fragmented as the many domains in which men are constructed as "men" through language and space' (Shire 1994: 149). He explores the historical processes whereby the very creation of a 'Shona' identity was tied up with colonial power relations and where masculinities were constructed around 'the assegai ... the rifle' and domestic service: 'Shona men became the "boys" of the colonisers' (Shire 1994: 149). At the same time boys became men by rejecting the 'inside' space of women and conquering the 'outside' space of men. In urban areas, where men were diminished as wage labourers, they

> inhabited a masculinity that regarded women as ... whores whose presence in male spaces, such as beerhalls, evoked extreme forms of misogyny. Any form of violence was legitimised within the male space of the beerhall. Male attitudes towards women in towns were reflected in the language of the beerhall ...'it's a woman, let it be beaten' ... Such attitudes remained entrenched in male spaces. (Shire 1994: 152–3)

Shire's view is of masculinities continually made and remade within the shifting structures of social and political power. The transformation of such relations in South Africa has created a political climate where the questioning of hegemonic masculinity, framed as rampant hetero-sexuality and male social dominance, is a public issue, unlike elsewhere in Africa (Agenda 1998).

The shift to a language of plural 'masculinities', perceived as social constructions, has positive consequences for work on AIDS, for it raises the possibility that men may change their ways in changing social circumstances. In the second half of this article, I first review data from my own field research in Tanzania to ask whether the AIDS epidemic is forcing men to reflect on their sense of themselves and their behaviour, and whether, in doing so, they express diverse masculinities. I then explore some of the ways in which AIDS interventions have been targeted at men in Africa, asking whether an awareness of the socially constructed nature of masculinities makes an effective difference.

LUSHOTO

Part of our project entailed work in a rural setting in north-eastern Tanzania where the people were peasant farmers, predominantly Muslim and of a single ethnic group. Despite a long history of male migration to the urban areas of Tanzania and Kenya, the rates of HIV prevalence are still relatively low here. Little AIDS prevention work had taken place in this rural area, but most people were knowledgeable about AIDS, the symptoms of its final stages and its mode of transmission.

The fear of AIDS was already impinging on the relations between men and women in Lushoto. Men owned land and women worked it, most men lived together as patrikin throughout their lives while women married in, and men held all the important positions of political and social power. Women were not totally powerless; they sold small surpluses garnered from their harvests and thus had intermittent access to cash, while older women had a long tradition of organizing them-selves in matters relating to life crises.

The research process first involved participant observation within the community, combined with a base-line survey (N=100; 50 men/50 women). In a second phase, researchers worked with local people to make a change: to break the barrier of silence regarding AIDS and to facilitate rethinking and reorganizing to address its impact in the village. Data came from a variety of settings: individual and private interviews, group sessions, overheard conversations and everyday observation and interaction.[6] In reassessing these data in relation to what thet tell us about conceptions of masculinity, what is striking is the difference between what men said in private and what they said in public.

In private, both men and women confided that their greatest fear was of their most intimate partners, especially spouses. For men, this was a new situation, for they expected to be secure in their control over women and their sexuality. The idea that a wife could threaten this by infecting her husband was shocking: 'Will she bring me the disease?' 'You are worried that your wife might have it, that she might not be faithful to you.' They were similarly shocked by the idea of a wife taking control of her own protection, by refusing sex or demanding the use of a condom: 'A wife who asks you to use those things is not a wife but a prostitute.' 'How can a woman decide? She can't order her husband to do things!' They reported having to reinforce their authority: 'I drove away one of my wives because she was behaving badly and I feared the outcome.' Tellingly, their view of themselves as the power in the home is reasserted: 'If the "government" in your home is bad you will get [AIDS] – you need to rule your wives so that they don't go straying.' They emphasized the need for trust between partners while recognizing how dangerous such trust had now become (Bujra 2000b).

In public men are less likely to admit to these private fears. They present a front to other men of being in control of 'their' women, while the strength of this lies in it not being stated. In public, men are more likely to deflect the blame for the spread of the epidemic on to others, seeing it as an evil brought by strangers or by young people, especially young girls who run away to towns, get into 'wicked and immoral ways' and return infected to spread it to others. Religious leaders might even welcome AIDS, as in the following quote: 'It is like a Big Stick sent by Almighty God, to warn people. It is a reminder that they should avoid wickedness and stay true to their lawful marriages and to their wife or wives, or suffer a terrible death. And the youth! They are indulging in sinful behaviour without any controls, especially young women.'

In targeting young women (and young men) for blame, men are also conceding that they can no longer control their children. One village leader spoke of young people who disappear: 'They don't even bid farewell, they just run off – is there any parent who will agree if their son or daughter says they want to go?'

In all-male workshops and in individual interviews, men spontaneously rehearsed a view of themselves as men in relation to sex. They were the initiators of sexual activity, the decision-makers as to when or how sex took place; strong men did not 'negotiate' with women. They might refer to their 'uncontrollable sexual urges' that mark them out as 'real men' making it difficult for them to plan safer sexual encounters, and that certainly exclude the possibility of abstention. One man asserted that holding back required self-control, but added: 'How can a man do that and the woman is still full of desire? He can't control himself.' In a workshop one man described his hasty attempts at protection: 'But listen! I bought [a condom] just there at the bus stand [in the nearby town] – I went and I used it straight away! After the job, I found it was split!'

Older men, however, saw themselves as more able to repress desire. Sexual licence was deemed a mark of youth. One elderly man confided to me: 'Young people have high sex, and can't control themselves – they only have to see a young woman and they are ready!' There is no stigma in younger men speaking of casual sex as a mark of male prowess in front of their elders; indeed, older men took their boasting for granted, advising them to use condoms. In individual interviews, despite personal questions about extra-marital sex being asked only obliquely, men of all ages would disclose such affairs in a matter-of-fact way. Women made no such disclosures in public, though some younger women working as bar-girls in the local town were more open in private.

Men are beginning to recognize that such uncontrolled sexuality puts them at risk in the era of AIDS. They will, at least, verbalize ways that they might curb it: 'If you see this one and that one, you desire them. [But] if you want many women you must protect yourself.' In one men's seminar I heard the first mention of masturbation as an alternative mode of coping with desire (received without enthusiasm!); in another there was this proffered solution from two young men: 'We have decided to go for football instead of staying idle and finding ourselves searching for girls ... afterwards we would be tired out and go home to sleep. We won't be having that desire to go out.'

Although condoms were off-putting – they were said to reduce pleasure, among other disadvantages – men were facing up to the fact that they needed to know how to use them. In an area where condom availability was low, knowledge was sometimes thin. When the use of condoms was demonstrated by a local AIDS officer, using a penis mould, men's hysterical embarrassment and glassy eyes spoke of a most 'unmanly' loss of emotional control.

Masculinity was also expressed in men's view of themselves as leaders of the community and as custodians of its customs and traditions (*mila na desturi*). Despite this, the AIDS epidemic was pushing some to reconsider time-honoured practices and to display their qualities of leadership in a responsive rather than conservative manner. One example concerns communication between parents and their children on the subject of sexuality. A village leader summed up: 'In our customs (*desturi ya Kisambaa*) it's shameful to discuss such things with your own children. But I have come to realise that this disease requires us to break the rules of our people, and so I do advise them. It's wrong for us, but we have to do it if we want our children to live.'

Another example related to the practice of widow inheritance. At a workshop the following exchange occurred after the practice was mentioned:

Man 1 (*decisively*): Let us get rid of this custom.

Man 2: We can't just wipe it out – this is our *mila na desturi*. But perhaps people should first be tested [for HIV], both of them, before they inherit or are inherited. Of course, our *mila na desturi* are superior to those in some places – it is not obligatory to inherit – there is a choice. The woman can choose whether to be inherited or to stay alone or she can go back home …

Man 3: We may have to think of other things besides our *mila na desturi*.

In another workshop, a village leader reflected thoughtfully that wife inheritance was a way of providing for the widow and her children 'through the clan. But now, with this disease …' Men were not only talking about change; I was told that they were refusing to inherit widows where there was doubt about the cause of death of the husbands. Whether they presented themselves as upholders of clan custom or as reformers, it was as men taking decisions in their own interests and on behalf of women; no one suggested including women in the discussion, even though they could suffer from the outcome.[7]

IDENTITY OF HUSBAND AND FATHER

Finally, I want to illustrate how another masculine identity, that of husband and father, is held up to question in response to the AIDS threat. We organized a group of male and female coordinators whose twelve members were chosen in village workshops. Men chose half their own number from among male village office-holders. This group brought together men and women in a community where women were normally silent in mixed groups. We organized the first meeting with some trepidation.

Strikingly, a discussion of sexuality and health turned into a charged debate about domestic labour. One of the men blamed mothers for the bad behaviour (sexual immorality) of young people. The women were incensed and pointed out that men gave very little support to their wives. As fathers they did little to ensure that children were under control. The debate now took a surprising turn, with two men taking the side of the women. In so doing, however, they displayed two very different versions of masculinity, one more conventional, the other subversive.

The 'subversive' was a young man in his mid-twenties. His sister had died of AIDS and, in the absence of his mother, he had been the one to care for her, performing intimate tasks and tending her *in extremis*. This man had spoken out courageously in an earlier workshop: 'My sister had this illness and she lasted for three years or more, and her needs were great. All her money was finished and she got worse. She had nothing left. But I did get the right food for her, milk, eggs and so on.' At the time I noted that his brave statement was received in silence; few publicly claim AIDS victims as relatives. Whether it was the experience of nursing his sister, or for some other reason, this man had a very different view of women's lot. In this earlier workshop he had also boldly asserted: 'You know, there are many women here who, even after they have a child, they don't get good food. She is swollen with hunger. She has to look after herself, while the man who created the problem by giving her the child has disappeared into thin air!'

I observed one of the village leaders quietly reprimanding him, perhaps because he had made this statement in front of 'outsiders' (the workshop facilitators). At the coordinators' meeting he immediately endorsed the women's perspective. After detailing women's work burdens, he described husbands rolling home drunk and demanding food: 'Do you, the man, have a right to that food? But you eat it! ... I'm not saying all men are like this. But many leave everything to their wives.'

This was challenging talk in mixed company and the other men looked angry or uncomfortable. The situation was rescued by the elderly treasurer of the mosque committee who assumed a more conventional masculine role, that of elder statesman. He assuaged the women's anger by conceding men's shortcomings as fathers and husbands. It was true men left women to do all the work, taking no responsibility: 'We are dictators in our own homes.' Details of how domestic tasks should be shared now emerged:

> Let's say it reaches Saturday – it should be my responsibility to buy the soap for washing the clothes. Am I there? Or am I out? And maybe at the end of the week there are clothes to repair, the child's uniform is torn and so on – but do we involve ourselves? We don't. Saturday we say – 'it's the weekend' and we come rolling home at ten or eleven at night. Do we ask for a report on what is going on at home? No! ... Fathers don't even know their own children and have to call them 'You! what's-your-name!' [He concluded:] The government puts no restrictions on men's freedom. It doesn't insist upon their responsibilities, so it is not surprising that young men are found roaming about at night, spreading AIDS.

The women were delighted, cheering him on. The rhetorical flourishes were deceptive, however, as the elderly man again deflected blame on to 'young men'. His continuous reiteration of the word 'we' is also deceptive, for he does not mean himself. This was most apparent when he spoke of how fathers did not take an interest in their children's schooling and how they had no idea when children had failed exams. Everyone knew that his own son was completing high school, and a daughter followed the next year – one of less than a handful from this village. What he was doing was to relate biological fatherhood with a variety of ways of playing that masculine role, and implying that fathers had to change if there was to be any hope of combating AIDS.

Here, then, is some evidence of men's growing awareness that their gendered identity is in question, and that their mode of self-definition as men is linked to the spread of AIDS, directly or indirectly. More than one definition of 'masculinity' also emerges, with the key differences being defined by age/generation and by marital and reproductive status. These are not antithetical positions; it is evident that young unmarried men are simply apprentices who will eventually adopt the *gravitas* of older men. Older men play to a script of authoritative and wise leadership, young men are permitted to sow their wild oats; both modes are seen as legitimate ways of expressing manhood. But herein lies the rub, as one elderly man put it: 'If we look at the people who are dying of this illness it is young people – it is not the old [*wazee*]. They go to Tanga, Dar and other places and then we are shocked to find them coming home to die.' They are shocked as fathers and as men to find that sowing wild oats reaps death. And with all their masculine and parental authority, they cannot save the young men who 'don't listen'.

The younger man's subversive expression of a masculinity which took on women's grievances could easily be silenced. There is no fixed age at which a man graduates from the status of youth (*kijana*) to that of mature man (*mzee*), though it generally follows after marriage and the birth of children. This man had been chosen in an all-male workshop as a representative of the youth, but he was approaching thirty, was married and had two young sons. On one occasion I heard him being chided by one of his elders to the effect that he needed to leave 'youthfulness' behind now. The licence which the old grant to youth allowed for his rebellious talk to be discounted, though in fact his performances were often catalysts in challenging the status quo. They also startled men into recognizing that women have begun to form a critical part of men's audience.

In conclusion: men's control over decision-making and resources is undented by mere talk, however subversive. What does not surface in public discussion is a reckoning of men's violence against women – some between spouses and some directed against young unmarried women. Another prop of male power, the freedom to be absent for months or years in towns (and while there to engage in extra-marital sex), is also not a matter for discussion. However, when young women leave it is a matter of moral outrage (Baylies and Bujra 2000: 120–32).

AIDS has made a discursive difference in this area where the epidemic has not yet had a devastating impact; it progress might still be halted. The link between AIDS and masculinity in its various guises is coming into focus for both men and women.

INTERVENTIONS

HIV prevention in Africa has begun to target men.[8] The question is whether the impact of such interventions is enhanced by an understanding of constructions of masculinity in the relevant settings, and whether, by not confronting men's social power outside discursive practice, such interventions merely encourage lip-service to gendered mutuality.

Much research remains to be done in this area, but few campaigns entail more than condom promotion and AIDS risk-awareness training. In Lushoto district capital, for example, free condoms are provided in 'guest houses' and 'peer educators' are trained among bar-workers. While the targets may be gendered (men as clients of sex-workers), any attempt to question men's behaviour, their self-definitions or their relations with women as wives, partners or daughters is muted. The aim is to win men over rather than alienate them, and the appeal is to their instincts of self-preservation rather than to mutuality in sexual protection.

Targeting men for AIDS interventions has required creative thinking about how they can be accessed in conducive settings. In terms of HIV prevention, this has been variously interpreted to mean occupational settings where men predominate in the workforce, such as miners or truckers on long-distance routes. Work has also focused on heavily male institutions such as the military or male prisons. Finally, there are campaigns which target the sites where men get together for leisure, especially those where the consumption of alcohol or drugs lowers levels of male inhibition and where women are available to supply sex commercially. Targeting men generally means focusing on sexual relations as cash transactions, rather than on their negotiation in marital settings.

MEN ON THE MOVE

A typical example of such work is a truckers' project in Tanzania (AIDS Analysis Africa 1992a). The truckers ply the international highway from Tanzania to Zambia and they are among the most highly paid workers in the country. They are described as 'tough characters', violent, hard-drinking, free-spending and with a high rate of sexual activity: half the men in the study reported fifty or more regular sexual partners;

approximately a third were HIV-positive. As men separated from wives and regular girlfriends, their sexual demands were satisfied by bar-workers in the many truck stops along the route. The AIDS awareness programme, initiated by a medical charity with USAID funding and Ministry of Health support, focused almost solely on increasing the supply and use of condoms. In this it seems to have been successful. Apart from one challenge to sexual licence (a failed attempt to separate the drivers from the sex-workers by providing alternative stops; the girls simply followed), no effort was made to intervene in gender relations or to link strategies for protection to an understanding of modes of masculinity. The project did not confront the truckers' high level of sexual activity, their responsibilities to wives, children or long-term partners, the gender inequality of men's greater mobility and sexual freedom or the economic basis of women's sex work.

MEN AND THE MILITARY

There is another arena in which more effort has been made: the military. Militarization is bound up with definitions and redefinitions of masculinity (Enloe 1993; Foreman 1999), while male sexuality is often purveyed through the imagery of war. The military in Africa, as in other conflict zones, has done much to spread the HIV virus. Unlike many ordinary men, soldiers have money to pay for sex, with separation from wives and girlfriends feeding the demand, while rape has been considered a weapon of war in many conflicts throughout the world. There is also the possibility that in a setting where men are brought together without women, homosexual liaisons may flourish.[9] High levels of HIV infection are common among army personnel (Foreman 1999; Falobi: af-aids@hivnet.ch, 4 January 2000).

Two common approaches to male sexuality in an army setting suggest contrasting perceptions of masculinity. In one, masculinity represents itself as tough and authoritative uniformity: hard men facing danger in a regimented way; in the other as glorified machismo.

The first approach is exemplified by a reliance on army discipline to limit the risk of soldiers becoming infected and spreading HIV. In several African countries, military policy may require compulsory HIV testing for new recruits or for specific personnel such as pilots (e.g. Malawi and Kenya). The prostitutes who follow armies may be dealt with in a similarly military manner, with testing and treatment for STDs a precondition for their presence near army camps. The army also provides a context in which authoritative education in AIDS awareness can be delivered. As one source put it: 'Soldiers are in effect a captive audience, easily accessible in their barracks, well-defined as a group, under military authority, with a well-established chain of communication and command' (AIDS Analysis Africa 1992b: 4).

As institutions, armies are particularly well placed and may have better facilities to care for troops who fall ill or to provide for their families after death (e.g. in Zambia, Tanzania or Uganda). Some militaries, such as the Ugandan army, have imposed heavy sentences through military courts on soldiers who rape. If one version of military masculinity is unquestioning obedience to authority and cohesive discipline, then this range of solutions rests on that discourse.

Another way is to play up to the bravado and fighting spirit that draw men into the army. In Ghana, the military produced posters which declaimed 'Combat ready, condom ready!' and used military terminology and brutal metaphors to sell the message about fighting AIDS: 'Put the boot on AIDS!' and 'Take the firing squad to AIDS!' (AIDS Analysis Africa 1992b: 4). Condoms were heavily promoted for the troops, their cost subsidized. The message got through. Sales leapt from 500 per month in 1991 to 7,000 per month in 1992.

None of these strategies challenges soldiers' marauding perceptions of sexual activity, expressed here by a Malawian in tellingly martial language: 'soldiers like to conquer. The more women you take to bed the more you feel like a real man' (quoted by Nkosi 1999: 167).

Active service offered these Malawian soldiers an opportunity to 'enjoy life – though their licentiousness set them in competition with other men, their Mozambican allies, who were paid less and were consequently less "popular" with the women. The same phenomenon has been seen in Liberia, where ECOMOG soldiers' monopolisation of women fed bitter jealousy and a sense of humiliation among local men' (Bennett et al. 1995). In their sexual pursuits, men are in competition rather than collusion.

If attention is paid to the kinds of messages that might motivate soldiers to rethink their behaviour, it is usually in terms of restating a masculinity which implicitly values sexual aggression and which is often equated to war. Campaigns rest on the masculine authority and discipline of army life. While this may seem limited, it is foolish to undervalue the extension of condom use or even STD control among camp followers – undoubtedly this has had benefits for both men and women, halting the spread of infection. It compares favourably with denial of the problem of soldiers' sexuality, which is the case in Kenya: 'Condom distribution ... in the military has not been seriously proposed or discussed' (Kiama 1999: 125). In Malawi, despite a high rate of HIV infection among soldiers, fanned by their participation in the Mozambican conflict, it has taken more than a decade for the military to address it (Nkosi 1999).

MEN, WOMEN AND SEX

Where AIDS initiatives attempt to confront entrenched versions of masculinity, they may meet entrenched resistance. Commentary on family planning programmes is instructive here. Omuodo, of the International Planned Parenthood Foundation (*AIDS Analysis Africa* 1996: 7), reports that men are often hostile. Family planning programmes 'contain words or slogans which threaten men ... endow[ing] women with too much freedom and so reducing a husband's span of control over a wife's sexuality'.

An account of the introduction of female condoms in Africa echoes this response: 'In Senegal it was found that marketing [the female condom] as a device for women's empowerment led to men opposing it. Men would only concur if it were presented in terms of "family welfare" and *they* made the decision to employ it' (*AIDS Analysis Africa* 1997: 10).

An even more thought-provoking example comes from South Africa. A project to work with footballers[10] was based on impeccable gender criteria: 'It envisaged ... men using their control and gender roles to provide training and support for other men as well as their sexual partners. The decision to target men was based on ... the evident failure of programmes which expect women to negotiate AIDS prevention. Women lack the power to make decisions' (Makhaye 1998: 93). The project had a telling slogan, 'Play it safe', but some aspects of the practice raise doubts:

the facilitator asked the participants to pair up and sit really close because

they were going to discuss something they all enjoyed. Then they were
asked to explain in detail their last exciting sexual encounter to their
partners/friends. They had to start from when they were both naked
until the sex act was complete. None of the workshop participants could
start[!]. They complained that this was a bedroom story and that it was
better to communicate with the real partners – the women. The next
exercise began with envisaging a scene where the wife wants to ask for
a change in the sexual position since she is tired of the traditional one
where the man is on top. The participants became very aggressive as: 'it
is not for the women to say how it (sex) should be done'. (Makhaye
1998: 95)

Makhaye does not explain whether the intervention aimed to be
deliberately confrontational, shocking men out of their self-definitions
as hard and unemotional and in control of women. Is this the way to
'empower men to disempower themselves' (Redman 1996), or would it
simply have strengthened their hold on power and their threatened
identities? Makhaye claims that the intervention was successful but
without offering any critical reflection on the process. More thought
needs to be expended on how 'masculine' views can be challenged
without alienating men.

CONCLUSION

This chapter explores a new avenue opening up in AIDS work and
links it with theoretical accounts of men and masculinities. It makes no
claims to be definitive, but is intended to provoke discussion about both
theory and practice and lead to more searching and critical research
into AIDS interventions.

It is important to listen to what men say about sex and about their
relations with women; but this needs to be done in such a way that
those social definitions that threaten women's health are challenged
rather than confirmed or celebrated. Representations and discourses of
masculinity are underwritten by men's power in social life, so men will
generally resist attempts to challenge them; and strategies that offer
them something in return need to be devised (as custodians of family
welfare, as fathers secure in the birth of healthy offspring).

The literature on masculinities yields more than the acknowledgement that men can change; it also alerts us to the possibility of a range of alternative masculine discourses and masculine positions. We need to find creative ways of exploiting such variation: for example, the assumptions around 'fatherhood' or 'maturity' may have more resonance for AIDS work than those around the 'conquering hero' or the 'playboy'.

Interrogating empirical data has illustrated masculine diversity and also reminded us that men are divided among themselves in many ways. Power differences may be expressed through the control and limitation of sexual activity – by field commanders over their troops, or elders over the young. This is not always to women's disadvantage. Competitiveness among men (often noted as a mark of masculinity) may inhibit men uniting on gender lines against women. It can be advantageous to some men to take women's side.

If most campaigns focus on men's interactions with commercial sex-workers, the 'hidden' women to whom they return as husbands and boyfriends are at greater risk. When women are more economically independent (even as sex-workers), they have choices and it is harder to coerce them into submission (being beaten up or denied a livelihood). They have more scope to refuse sex or demand condoms. Displays of hegemonic masculinity expressed in interpersonal relations within the domestic context cannot be resolved with a condom. Ways need to be found of targeting both men and women for greater mutuality in sexual relations.

NOTES

This chapter was previously published as an article in *Agenda*, 44 (2000), Durban, South Africa.

1. The research project, 'Gender Relations as a Key Factor in the Fight Against Aids in Tanzania and Zambia', was funded by the Economic and Social Research Council of Great Britain, and directed jointly by Janet Bujra and Carolyn Baylies. It involved team-working at six sites. For further details see Baylies and Bujra (2000). Acknowledgement is due to Gill Seidel for her support and critical assessment in the writing of this article.

2. In describing AIDS as gendered, it is acknowledged that patterns of blaming and stigma also build on other pre-existing forms of social denigration framed by class, ethnicity, religion and so on.

3. See for example Phillips (1994); Ampofu (1993); *Sauti ya Siti* (1993); Maitse (1997).

4. See Kiama (1999); Porter (1995). In some places, such as the East African

coast, homosexuality has been culturally tolerated from the pre-colonial period. In the South African gold-mines, Moodie tells us that it was institutionalized as an expression of power exerted by older men over younger recruits. Young men accepted it because they were recompensed with gifts or cash at a time when they needed to accumulate savings to build up rural holdings. Given the rarity of penetration – release was through friction between the thighs, permitted only to the older partner, Moodie compares homosexuality favourably with resort to prostitutes – it was safer sex; and its abandonment more recently (with the divorce of the labour force from rural means of production) is seen as a dangerous development.

5. Cited in *Guardian Weekly* (24–30 January 1999; 7 October 1999). President Mugabe is reported to have described homosexuals as lower than dogs and pigs.

6. Research extended for eight months over two years (1995–96). In the second phase of the research, the workshop facilitators were Tanzanian AIDS activists who were members of our project team, together with the AIDS coordinating officer and AIDS counsellor from Lushoto district hospital. These workshops were not occasions for didactic posturing but successfully engaged the audience in confronting the problems raised by AIDS. Women and men met separately in open meetings of from twenty to seventy people. I am indebted to Haji Ayoub, Helena Anthony, Naomi Kaihula, Sister Lightness Kusaga, Julius Mwabuki and Marik Msuya for their contributions and for the skilful and sensitive way in which they handled charged issues.

7. Following one man's death from AIDS, his wife was not inherited and was forced to return to her natal kin. Such returnees are rarely welcome (Bujra and Baylies 1999).

8. No claim is made that the material in this section is representative of prevention work targeting men in Africa. It is based on materials and ephemera collected as the opportunity arose and from which I have selected thought-provoking examples.

9. In the military and in prisons, homosexual activity, including rape, is often denied. In South Africa condoms are available in prisons – elsewhere this move is resisted despite a rising tide of HIV infection among prisoners (*AIDS Analysis Africa* 1998). A recent survey of more than 2,000 prisoners by the Nigerian Institute of Medical Research found 69 per cent of them to be HIV-positive. Prison authorities refused to distribute condoms even though sexual relations between male inmates were common; it would encourage immoral behaviour (*The Voice*, 24 January 2000).

10. In many countries sport is an arena where men congregate and masculinity in the form of physical strength, prowess and toughness is displayed. Again, AIDS campaigns may simply confirm the terms of this rather than challenging its assumptions.

REFERENCES

Abdool Karim, Q. (1998) 'Women and AIDS – the Imperative for a Gendered Prognosis and Prevention Policy', *Agenda*, 39.

Agenda (1998) 'AIDS: Counting the Cost', *Agenda*, 39.

AIDS Analysis Africa (1992a) 'Tanzania Targets its Long-distance Truckers', *AIDS Analysis Africa*, 2(1).

— (1992b) 'AIDS and the Military', *AIDS Analysis Africa*, 2(5).

— (1996) 'Africa takes a more male-friendly approach to family planning', *AIDS Analysis Africa*, 6(10).

— 1997) 'The Female Condom: Questions of Price, Re-use and Image', *AIDS Analysis Africa*, 7(5).

— (1998) 'AIDS in Prisons – Good Intentions, Harsh Realities in Africa's Penitentiaries', AIDS Analysis Africa, 8(3).

Altman, D. (1994) *Power and Community: Organisational and Cultural Responses to AIDS* (London: Taylor and Francis).

Amadiume, I. (1987) *Male Daughters, Female Husbands* (London: Zed Books).

Ampofu, A. (1993) 'Controlling and Punishing Women: Violence Against Ghanaian Women', *Review of African Political Economy*, 56.

Anane, M. (1999) 'Religion, Men and HIV/AIDS in Ghana', in M. Foreman (ed.), *AIDS and Men* (London: Panos Publications/Zed Books).

Ankrah, M. (1991) 'AIDS and the Social Side of Health', *Social Science and Medicine*, 32(9).

Bassett, M. and M. Mhloyi (1991) 'Women and AIDS in Zimbabwe: the Making of an Epidemic', *International Journal of Health Services*, 21(1).

Baylies, C. and J. Bujra (1995) 'Discourses of Power and Empowerment in the Fight Against HIV/AIDS in Africa', in P. Aggleton, P. Davies and G. Hart (eds), *AIDS, Safety, Sexuality and Risk* (London: Taylor and Francis).

— (2000) *AIDS, Sexuality and Gender in Africa: Collective Strategies and Struggles in Tanzania and Zambia* (London: Routledge).

Bennett, O., J. Bexley and K. Warnock (1995) *Arms to Fight, Arms to Protect* (London: Panos Publications).

Bujra, J. (1982) 'Women Entrepreneurs of Early Nairobi', in C. Sumner (ed.), *Crime, Justice and Underdevelopment* (London: Heinemann).

— (2000a) *Serving Class: Masculinity and the Feminisation of Domestic Service in Tanzania* (Edinburgh: Edinburgh University Press/International African Institute).

— (2000b) 'Risk and Trust: Unsafe Sex, Gender and AIDS in Tanzania', in P. Caplan (ed.), *Risk Revisited* (London: Pluto Press).

Bujra, J. and C. Baylies (1999) 'Solidarity and Stress: Gender and Local Mobilisation in Tanzania and Zambia', in P. Aggleton, G. Hart and P. Davies (eds), *Families and Communities Responding to AIDS* (London: UCL Press).

Campbell, C. (1995) 'Male Gender Roles and Sexuality: Implications of Women's AIDS Risk and Prevention', *Social Science and Medicine* 41(2).

Carovano, K. (1995) *HIV and the Challenges Facing Men*, Issues paper 15 (New York: UNDP HIV Development Programme).

Cleland, J. and B. Ferry (1995) *Sexual Behaviour and AIDS in the Developing World* (London: Taylor and Francis).

Connell, R. W. (1987) *Gender and Power* (Oxford: Polity Press).

— (1995) *Masculinities* (Cambridge: Polity Press).

Cornwall, A. (1997) 'Men, Masculinity and "Gender in Development"', *Gender and Development*, 5(2).

Cornwall, A. and N. Lindisfarne (1994) *Dislocating Masculinity: Comparative Ethnographies* (London: Routledge).

Davies, P. M., F. C. I. Hickson, P. Weatherburn and A. J. Hunt (1993) *Sex, Gay Men and AIDS* (London: Falmer Press).

de Bruyn, M. (1992) 'Women and AIDS in Developing Countries', *Social Science and Medicine*, 34(3).

Enloe, C. (1993) *The Morning After: Sexual Politics at the End of the Cold War* (Berkeley: University of California Press).

Foreman, M. (ed.) (1999) *AIDS and Men* (London: Panos Publications/Zed Books).

Hearn, J. (1996) 'Is Masculinity Dead? A Critique of the Concept of Masculinity/Masculinities', in M. Mac an Ghaill (ed.), *Understanding Masculinities* (Buckingham: Open University Press).

Jackson, C. (1998) 'Men's Work, Masculinities and Gender Divisions of Labour', ESRC seminar on Men, Masculinities and Gender Relations in Development, Bradford, September.

Kaleeba, N. (1992) *We Miss You All: AIDS in the Family* (Harare: Women and AIDS Support Network).

Kiama, W. (1999) 'Men Who Have Sex with Men in Kenya', in M. Foreman (ed.), *AIDS and Men* (London: Panos Publications/Zed Books).

Mac an Ghail, M. (ed.) (1996) *Understanding Masculinities* (Buckingham: Open University Press).

McFadden, P. (1992) 'Sex, Sexuality and the Problems of AIDS in Africa', in R. Meena (ed.), *Gender in Southern Africa: Conceptual and Theoretical Issues* (Harare: Sapes Books).

Maitse, T. (1998) 'Political Change, Rape and Pornography in Post-apartheid South Africa', *Gender and Development*, 6(3).

Makhaye, G. (1998) 'Shosholoza's Goal: Educate Men in Soccer', *Agenda*, 39.

Meena, R. (ed.) (1992) *Gender in Southern Africa: Conceptual and Theoretical Issues* (Harare: Sapes Books).

Moodie, T. D. and V. Ndatshe (1994) *Going for Gold: Men, Mines and Migration* (Berkeley and Los Angeles: University of California Press).

Nkosi, K. (1999) 'Men, the Military and HIV/AIDS in Malawi', in M. Foreman (ed.), *AIDS and Men* (London: Panos Publications/Zed Books).

Obbo, C. (1993) 'HIV Transmission: Men are the Solution', in S. James and A. Busia (eds), *Theorizing Black Feminisms* (London: Routledge).

— (1995) 'What Women Can Do: AIDS Crisis Management in Uganda', in D. Bryceson, *Women Wielding the Hoe* (Oxford: Berg).

Phillips, O. (1994) 'Censuring Sexuality and Gender in Zimbabwe', British Sociological Association conference paper, Preston.

Porter, M. (1995) 'Talking at the Margins: Kenyan Discourse on Homosexuality', in W. Leap (ed.), *Beyond the Lavender Lexicon: Authenticity, Imagination and Appropriation in Lesbian and Gay Languages* (Amsterdam: Gordon and Breach).

Reddy, V. (1998) 'Negotiating Gay Masculinities', *Agenda*, 37.

Redman, P. (1996) '"Empowering Men to Disempower Themselves": Heterosexual Masculinities, HIV and the Contradictions of Anti-oppressive Education', in M. Mac an Ghail (ed.), *Understanding Masculinities* (Buckingham: Open University Press).

Rweyemamu, C. (1999) 'Sexual Behaviour in Tanzania', in M. Foreman (ed.), *AIDS and Men* (London: Panos Publications/Zed Books).

SAFAIDS/KIT/WHO (1995) *Facing the Challenges of HIV, AIDS, STDS: A Gender-based Response* (Royal Tropical Institute, Netherlands–KIT; Southern Africa AIDS Information Dissemination Service, Zimbabwe; World Health Organisation).

Sauti ya Siti (1993) 'Violence Against Women in Tanzania', *Review of African Political Economy*, 56.

Seidel, G. (1993) 'The Competing Discourses of AIDS in Africa', *Social Science and Medicine*, 26(3).

Shire, C. (1994) 'Men Don't Go to the Moon: Language, Space and Masculinities in Zimbabwe', in A. Cornwall and N. Lindisfarne (eds), *Dislocating Masculinity: Comparative Ethnographies* (London: Routledge).

Sweetman, C. (1998) '"Sitting on a Rock": Integrating Men And Masculinities into Gender and Development', ESRC seminar on Men, Masculinities and Gender Relations in Development, Bradford, September.

Turshen, M. (1999) 'West African Workshop on Women in the Aftermath of Civil War', *Review of African Political Economy*, 79.

Turshen, M. and C. Twagiramariya (1998) *What Women Do in Wartime: Gender and Conflict in Africa* (London: Zed Books).

Ulin, P. (1992) 'African Women and AIDS: Negotiating Behavioural Change', *Social Science and Medicine*, 34(1).

Van de Ven, P.J., J. French, J. Crawford and S. Kippax (1999) 'Sydney Gay Men's Agreements about Sex', in P. Aggleton, G. Hart and P. Davies (eds) *Families and Communities Responding to AIDS* (London: UCL Press).

Wellings, K., F. Field, A. M. Johnson and J. Wadsworth (1994) *Sexual Behaviour in Britain* (London: Penguin Books).

White, L. (1990) *The Comforts of Home: Prostitution in Colonial Nairobi* (Chicago: University of Chicago Press).

White, S. (1997) 'Men, Masculinities and the Politics of Development', *Gender and Development*, 5(2).

— (1998) 'Masculinities in Development: the Danger of a New Hegemony', ESRC seminar on Men, Masculinities and Gender Relations in Development, Bradford, September.

Index